ARMS AND DISARMAMENT IN DIPLOMACY

Arms and Disarmament in Diplomacy

Editors

Keith Hamilton
Edward Johnson

VALLENTINE MITCHELL
LONDON • PORTLAND, OR

First published in 2008 by Vallentine Mitchell

Suite 314, Premier House,   920 NE 58th Avenue, Suite 300
112–114 Station Road,   Portland, Oregon,
Edgware, Middlesex HA8 7BJ   97213-3786

www.vmbooks.com

Copyright © 2008
Keith Hamilton and Edward Johnson

British Library Cataloguing in Publication Data

Arms and disarmament in diplomacy
 1. Arms control – History – 20th century 2. Disarmament –
 History – 20th century 3. Diplomacy – History – 20th
 century 4. Military history, Modern – 20th century
 I. Hamilton, Keith, 1942– III. Johnson, Edward
 327.1'74'0904

ISBN 978 0 85303 756 9 (cloth)
ISBN 978 0 85303 757 6 (paper)

Library of Congress Cataloging-in-Publication Data:

A catalog record for this book is available
from the Library of Congress

All rights reserved. No part of this publication may be reproduced, stored in or introduced into a retrieval system, or transmitted, in any form or by any means, electronic, mechanical, photocopying, recording or otherwise, without the prior written permission of the publisher of this book.

Printed by Biddles Ltd, King's Lynn, Norfolk

Contents

Dick Richardson – A Dedication — vii

Notes on Contributors — ix

Introduction   Keith Hamilton and Edward Johnson — 1

1. Britain and The Hague Peace Conference of 1899   Keith Hamilton — 9

2. 'What we desire is confidence':
The Search for an Anglo-German Naval Agreement, 1909–1912   T.G. Otte — 33

3. French Assistance to Russian Armament Production, 1914–1917   David Watson — 53

4. Mission Accomplished?
Britain and the Disarmament of Germany, 1918–1923   Alan Sharp — 73

5. Sunk Before We Started? Anglo-American Rivalry at the Coolidge Naval Conference, 1927   Carolyn Kitching — 91

6. Arms Control and the Anglo-Soviet Naval Agreement of 1937   Keith Neilson — 112

7. Disarmament and Peace Movements in British and US Feature Films of the Inter-War Period   David Dunn — 129

8. Britain and the Provision of Arms to Finland, 1936–1940   Glyn Stone — 151

9. Britain and an International Force:
The Experience of the League of Nations and the United Nations Military Staff Committee   Edward Johnson — 173

Index — 194

In Memory of Dick Richardson (1946–1997)

Dr Dick Richardson, to whose memory this volume is dedicated, was a founder member of the British International History Group (BIHG). After the Group's establishment in 1988 he served on its executive committee and he was appointed its first Treasurer. Tragically, while returning from the Group's annual conference in 1997 he was killed in a road accident. His colleagues within the BIHG have assembled this collection of essays in recognition of his life and his contribution to the study of disarmament and international history.

Educated at the London School of Economics and the University of British Columbia, Dick received his PhD from the former for a thesis entitled *The Conservative Government of 1924–29 and the Problem of Disarmament*. Throughout his academic career, first as a lecturer, and then as a reader, in politics at the University of Teesside, Dick continued to focus upon disarmament as an issue in diplomacy. He wrote extensively on the subject, and his publications include *The Evolution of British Disarmament Policy in the 1920s* (London: Pinter, 1989), and a volume, which he edited with Glyn Stone, *Decisions and Diplomacy: Essays in Twentieth-Century International History* (London: Routledge, 1995). Dick also had a passionate interest in Green Politics: he founded the Green Politics Standing Group of the European Consortium for Political Research (ECPR); he directed a number of ECPR workshops; he stood as a Green Party candidate for the European Parliament; and he jointly edited, with Susan Baker, Maria Rousis and Stephen Young, *The Politics of Sustainable Development* (London: Routledge, 1997). Just prior to his death, he had negotiated a contract with Routledge to publish the *International Encyclopaedia of Environmental Politics*. This later appeared in June 2001 under the editorship of Gene Frankland and John Barry.

Dick's concern for the environment was matched by his devotion to friends and associates. But for those who came to know him in the BIHG he is probably best remembered as an active committee member, a diligent scholar, and an engaging colleague and companion.

Notes on the Contributors

David Dunn is Senior Lecturer in Film at Southampton University. He completed a PhD on Bernard Shaw, and has published on US and Soviet foreign policies, and history and computing. He writes poetry and plays. He is the Treasurer of the British International History Group.

Keith Hamilton works part-time as an Historian in the Foreign and Commonwealth Office. He co-edits *Documents on British Policy Overseas*, and was primarily responsible for the last two volumes in the series, *The Year of Europe: America, Europe and the Energy Crisis, 1972–1974* and *The Southern Flank in Crisis, 1973–1976* (2006).

Edward Johnson teaches History and Politics at the University of Central England where he is Reader in Public Policy. He has written widely on British policy in the United Nations, over Suez, Cyprus, Spain and Greece and on the role of the UN Secretary-General. He is the Vice-Chairman of the British International History Group.

Carolyn Kitching is Reader in British International History at the University of Teesside where she was a colleague of Dick Richardson. She has written widely on disarmament, including *Britain and the Problem of International Disarmament, 1919–34* (1999) and *Britain and the Geneva Disarmament Conference, 1932–34* (2003).

Keith Neilson is Professor of History at the Royal Military College of Canada. He has written several books dealing with Anglo-Russian/Soviet relations, the most recent of which is *Britain, Soviet Russia and the Collapse of the Versailles Order, 1919–1939* (2006). At present, he is writing a book on Anglo-American relations in the First World War.

T.G. Otte is Senior Lecturer in Diplomatic History at the University of East Anglia, specialising in the history of nineteenth-century Great Power relations. His most recent publications are *Railways and International Politics: Paths of Empire, 1848–1945* (edited with Keith Neilson, 2006) and *The China Question: Great Power Rivalry and British Isolation, 1894–1905* (2007).

Alan Sharp is Professor of International Studies and Provost of the Coleraine campus of the University of Ulster. In 1991 he published *The Versailles Settlement: Peacemaking in Paris 1919*, a second edition of which is about to appear. He was joint editor, with Glyn Stone, of *Anglo-French Relations in the Twentieth Century: Rivalry and Cooperation* (2000), and, with Professor Conan Fischer, of a special edition of *Diplomacy and Statecraft, The Versailles Settlement: Enforcement, Compliance, Contested Identities* (2005).

Glyn Stone is Professor of International History, University of the West of England, Bristol. His publications include *The Oldest Ally: Britain and the Portuguese Connection, 1936–1941* (1994), *Spain, Portugal and the Great Powers, 1931–1941* (2005), *Decisions and Diplomacy: Essays in Twentieth Century International History* (1995) (co-edited with Dick Richardson) and *Anglo-French Relations in the Twentieth Century: Rivalry and Cooperation* (2000) (co-edited with Alan Sharp). He is Secretary of the British International History Group.

David Watson graduated from Oxford University in 1956 and taught history at the University of Dundee from 1961 until his retirement. He is the author of *Georges Clemenceau, a Political Biography* (1974) and of many articles on different aspects of French history from 1870 to the present day.

Introduction

War remains the *ultima ratio* of diplomacy. Donald Rumsfeld, the former United States Secretary of Defense, was simply stating the obvious when he recalled Al Capone's aphorism: 'You get more with a kind word and a gun than you do with a kind word alone.'[1] Success in negotiation has not infrequently been predicated upon the knowledge that the alternative may be a resort to force. But armaments, their deployment, manufacture, sale and supply have, often in conjunction with initiatives aimed at avoiding and regulating conflict, also long been the subject matter of diplomacy. In the aftermath of the Napoleonic wars, the Russian Emperor, Alexander I, added proposals for the reduction of armed forces in Europe to his scheme for establishing universal peace, and since the mid-nineteenth century governments have increasingly sought through multilateral dialogue to secure general acceptance of rules governing warfare. The Paris declaration of 1856 dealt with the divisive issue of naval blockade, and international conferences at Geneva (1864), St Petersburg (1868), Brussels (1874) and The Hague (1899 and 1907) achieved broad agreement on measures aimed at curbing some of the worst excesses of modern warfare, at defining the status of combatants and non-combatants, and at easing the plight of the wounded and the dispossessed. The European powers and the United States likewise endeavoured, largely with a view to stabilising the frontiers of empire and suppressing the slave trade, to impede arms trafficking in Africa, and the resulting Brussels Convention of 1890 prefigured later action by the League of Nations aimed at controlling the international commerce in armaments. Meanwhile, technological advances in weapons production, a growing public awareness of the cost and destructive capacity of the latest armaments, and a desire to contain and mitigate the international rivalries to which they were perceived as having contributed, placed arms limitation and control firmly on the diplomatic agenda. When in the midst of the Great War the American President, Woodrow Wilson, appealed for a peace which would permit a reduction in armaments 'to the lowest point consistent with domestic safety', he evoked a sentiment already shared by many sickened by the horrors of over three years of conflict in Europe.[2]

International disarmament was an enduring interest of Dick Richardson. While in his monograph, *The Evolution of British Disarmament Policy in the 1920s* (London: Pinter, 1989), he focused upon one particular aspect of the subject, in subsequent papers and an unpublished typescript, *A History of*

Arms Control and Disarmament, he expanded upon his original researches to develop a broader interpretation of the problems faced by diplomats engaged in disarmament negotiations and the conditions essential for their success. He was well aware of the obstacles, practical and theoretical, on which attempts to achieve agreement could founder. Not the least of these is the feasibility of defining and relating the security interests and requirements of individual states. In 1816 the British Foreign Secretary, Lord Castlereagh, rejected the Emperor Alexander's disarmament proposal in terms which, in 1975, one senior Whitehall official, Crispin Tickell, still thought relevant to the Vienna-based talks on Mutual and Balanced Force Reductions (MBFR) in central Europe. Castlereagh observed:

> It is impossible not to perceive that the settlement of a scale of force for so many Powers – under such different circumstances as to their relative means, frontiers, positions and faculties for re-arming – presents a very complicated question for negotiation: that the means of preserving a system if once created are not without their difficulties, liable as States are to partial necessities for an increase of force: and it is further to be considered that on this, as on many subjects of a jealous character, in attempting to do much, difficulties are rather brought into view than made to disappear.[3]

Much the same point was made in June 1899 by Colonel Gross von Schwarzhoff, the German military delegate to the first Hague Peace Conference, when he contended that the size of a country's armed forces could not be discussed without reference to military training and length of service, its geographical location, railway network and fortified places. And so conspicuous was the failure of the delegates to make any progress on the disarmament issue that, in 1907, the subject was specifically excluded from the agenda of the second Peace Conference at The Hague.

The first of the two Hague Conferences was, however, about far more than arms limitation and reduction. It was also concerned with achieving agreement on measures which would make the recourse to war less likely and with outlawing weapons whose employment could result in what was deemed unnecessary human suffering. The establishment of the Permanent Court of International Arbitration was its most memorable achievement. Yet, as the first chapter in this book makes clear, the major powers were reluctant to concede that either arbitration or mediation should be made obligatory, and conceived of their application only to essentially minor matters of international contention. Lord Salisbury, the British Prime Minister, distrusted the possible prejudices of third-party arbitrators and had earlier insisted that nations could not afford to run the risk of leaving 'to the vote of one man, and that man a foreigner', decisions 'by which their national position may be affected, or a number of their fellow-subjects transferred to foreign rule'.[4] Others had qualms about restricting the development of armaments whose very capacity to maim and devastate could serve as a deterrent to future wars. None of the great powers was in any case prepared to sacrifice perceived military or naval advantage for the sake of world peace or humanitarian principles. Cecil Fisher, the son of Vice-Admiral Sir John Fisher, probably came as close to summing up the British Admiralty's general view of the conference, when on the eve of its assembly he asked his father, 'as we are able to boss the seas why should we do any thing to debar ourselves from holding that excellent position?'[5]

Within the next decade that 'excellent position' seemed to be increasingly threatened by German naval expansion. The resulting Anglo-German naval rivalry was one of the defining features of international relations in the years preceding the outbreak of the First World War. So also were the diplomatic efforts made to mitigate the antagonism it generated, and in his contribution to this collection, T.G. Otte explores the pursuit by the British and German Governments of an understanding embracing naval and political issues. He focuses particularly upon the endeavours of the Liberal Foreign Secretary, Sir Edward Grey, to promote the idea of a technical accord governing the mutual exchange of information on their warship specifications and naval construction programmes. The notion of what in the late twentieth century would be referred to as confidence-building measures was not new. Castlereagh, in his message to the Tsar, had suggested that each state should on its own responsibility reduce its armaments to the minimum it considered necessary and then 'explain to the Allied and Neighbouring States the extent and nature of its arrangements as a means of dispelling alarm and of rendering moderate establishments mutually convenient'.[6] Grey evidently hoped that if the British and German Governments were better informed of each other's intentions, they could at least avoid some of the public alarm and misapprehension caused by the surprise announcement of the laying down of additional keels. Since, however, Berlin judged insufficient the political assurances offered by Grey, and the British were reluctant to sign up to anything that might impede their freedom to assist the French in the event of war, nothing ultimately came of this initiative. Meanwhile, partly in response to Russia's revived military might, the Germans switched resources to the strengthening of their land forces, and by 1913 an Anglo-German naval agreement was close to becoming a diplomatic irrelevance.

Grey, like Salisbury, was concerned about the economic and social repercussions of escalating military and naval budgets, and especially about the domestic discontent to which they might give rise. Elsewhere, and Germany was an obvious example, increased spending on armaments was sometimes regarded by governments as a means of building a national consensus and of reinforcing existing political structures. Indeed, the war of 1914–18 was to demonstrate the colossal sacrifices that individuals and societies were prepared to make for the sake of patriotic endeavour. However, as David Watson reminds us, a boom in arms manufacturing played a major part in destabilising imperial Russia. In his chapter on French assistance to Russian armament production during the Great War, he argues that the economic success of the expansion of defence-related industries in Russia created social stresses that were to erupt in the revolution of February 1917. French investment in Russia, including the close association of Schneider-Creusot with the Putilov arms works in St Petersburg, had been an important element in the development of the pre-war Franco-Russian alliance. During the war, French ministers, officials and business representatives were to become actively involved in efforts to reorganise and step up the manufacture of artillery and munitions in Russia. Yet the state sequestration of the Putilov group in 1916 and the imposition on it of military control, the result of an ongoing conflict between Duma liberals and the Tsarist Government, arguably contributed to a breakdown in relations between labour and management, and to strikes and demonstrations which would change more than the face of Russia. Armaments and diplomacy were intimately connected with the onset of revolution, outside military intervention in Russia, and the transformation of eastern Europe.

The defeat of Germany and its allies in 1918 appeared to offer exponents of international disarmament an opportunity to put principles into practice. Grey was firmly of the opinion that the enormous growth of armaments in pre-1914 Europe had made war inevitable, and in 1919 the Treaty of Versailles linked the disarmament of Germany to the initiation of a general limitation of armaments of all nations. Nonetheless, the terms imposed on Germany owed less to the aspirations of international disarmers than to the desire of the British to rid themselves of a dangerous naval rival, and the hopes of the French that they might thereby permanently reduce the military prowess of a potentially stronger neighbour. Alan Sharp, in his contribution on Britain and Germany's disarmament, examines in detail the measures undertaken by the victorious allies in order to apply and monitor the stipulations of the treaty. Those charged with this task had to face up to many problems, including those related to deciding what constituted armed forces and what were the military needs of a Germany threatened by internal dissent and exposed to Polish land-grabbing in the east. They had naturally to reckon with German evasion and resistance, and in the process the British and French found plenty of scope for quarrelling between themselves. Yet, given that this was the first occasion on which a major industrial power had been subjected to enforced disarmament, the achievements of the control commissions were, at least in so far as weaponry was concerned, substantial. As Alan Sharp maintains, by 1925 the allies could console themselves with the knowledge that any future German rearmament could not be carried out in secret.

Despite the reference in the Versailles treaty to further measures aimed at achieving international disarmament, only limited progress was made in this direction during the succeeding years. Anxious to avoid a new naval arms race, five powers, Britain, France, Italy, Japan and the United States, agreed at the Washington Conference of 1921–22 to a ratio restricting their capital ships and aircraft carriers. But neither the preparatory commission established by the League of Nations in 1925 with a view to drafting a disarmament treaty, nor the disarmament conference of 1932–34, could be judged successes. In her chapter on Anglo-American rivalry at the Coolidge Naval Conference of 1927, Carolyn Kitching reaffirms her view that during the years between the two world wars there was no belief amongst the British policy-making élite in the idea of disarmament. The same, however, could equally be said of other countries. Those with armaments insisted that they needed them for their security, and those forcibly disarmed demanded recognition of their equality of rights. Even at the Coolidge Conference, where participation was limited to three powers, America, Britain and Japan, and where their prime concern was with restricting cruiser strengths, agreement proved impossible. As Kitching demonstrates, the conference lacked those diplomatic, political and technical criteria which Dick Richardson considered essential for success in disarmament negotiations. Also lacking, she argues, was the political necessity, the political imperative, which was present at the Washington Conference and which, in 1930, made possible the London naval agreement by which the British conceded parity to the Americans in cruisers.

After Germany's departure from the League of Nations in October 1933, British arms negotiators seemed less concerned with the pursuit of disarmament than with the management of German rearmament. Indeed, the Anglo-German naval agreement of 1935, which permitted Germany a fleet 35 per cent the scale of that of Britain, was perceived by its critics as an example of the British Government condoning treaty-breaking. It also had broader international ramifications. The implementation of the accord was dependent on the conclusion in 1937 of a parallel Anglo-Soviet agreement and, as Keith Neilson argues in his chapter, those engaged in negotiating the latter could not neglect its likely influence upon naval construction elsewhere. Moreover, as in the case of Britain's previous negotiations with the United States, there remained the problem of reconciling the naval requirements of a maritime empire with those of a continental power with only limited overseas interests and commitments. Two of the conditions set by Richardson for success in disarmament negotiations were, however, in Neilson's view present in those the British undertook with the Russians. Both sides wanted the talks to succeed, though both had rather different assumptions about the purposes of the agreement they were seeking; and the British, even if their evaluation of Soviet naval needs was not that of the Russians, were able to persuade Moscow of the advantages of what was on offer. That said, the resulting understanding was of little or no significance, given Japan's resort to force in China and Hitler's increasingly aggressive stance in Europe. The Anglo-Soviet negotiations served not so much to demonstrate the virtues of disarmament as to re-emphasise the limits of what, in time of crisis and conflict, diplomats could achieve in the way of bilateral arms control.

During the inter-war years the diplomacy of disarmament attracted considerable media attention. Yet the public debate on the issue was often superficial, and the opinions expressed fickle and contradictory. Arms reductions were viewed as a laudable objective; and so also was armed resistance to aggression. While, however, the press continued to reflect and shape public opinion, popular perceptions of world politics, war and diplomacy were also influenced by the growth of the cinema industry. Motion pictures such as *All Quiet on the Western Front* may have entertained, but they also reinforced images of the futility of war. The storylines of others may have encouraged audiences to draw parallels between their own politically troubled times and the historical or futuristic events depicted on the screen. Meanwhile, newsreels offered information and selective judgement upon current developments. David Dunn, in his essay on disarmament and peace movements in British and American feature films, surveys the diplomatic and political content of a range of B-movies and animations from the 1920s and 1930s, including Old Mother Riley's posturing as Minister for Strange Affairs and Krazy Kat's efforts to bring peace to a war-weary jungle. He concludes that the cinema 'embellished and made crude versions of the reality that increasingly framed other media's commentaries and hence the popular consensus'. The messages delivered on the silver screen may, nonetheless, have been more sophisticated than audiences appreciated. Walt Disney's *Ferdinand the Bull*, the tale of a bull who preferred flower-sniffing to fighting, emerges, according to one interpretation, as an allegory of America's reluctance to assist beleaguered Republicans in the Spanish Civil War. Many must surely have accepted Ferdinand as no more than a cartoon character, loveable, though socially disorientated, in his unmetaphorical bovinity.

One of the most divisive diplomatic questions raised by the war in Spain concerned the supply or non-supply of arms to the belligerent parties.

INTRODUCTION   7

Indeed, during the late 1930s the export of armaments was increasingly linked to the attainment of foreign policy objectives. As Glyn Stone reveals in his chapter on the provision of arms to Finland preceding and during the Winter War of 1939–40, the British Foreign Office assumed a crucial role in helping to define the political priorities governing the export of arms and munitions. Finland had not previously figured large in Whitehall's assessments of British strategic interests. But the Soviet invasion of Finland, three months after the outbreak of war with Germany, compelled officials in London to consider whether military assistance to the Finns would serve to deny resources to Germany, or simply strengthen the bonds between Moscow and Berlin. In the end their meagre response to Finnish appeals for arms was conditioned by their own continuing concerns over the rearmament and re-equipment of British forces. By 1940 arms in diplomacy took second place to the diplomacy of war.

Diplomats and statesmen of the anti-Axis coalition were, nevertheless, soon engaged in planning for the establishment of a new world organisation to manage and maintain their anticipated victory. In London and Washington, if not in Moscow, there was an expectation that the United Nations had to set right the errors of the League of Nations in ensuring international peace and security. To that end, the UN Charter required, amongst other things, that member states take steps towards the creation of an international force enabling the UN to intervene to maintain the post-war settlement: something which the League had never enjoyed. The League was, from its beginning, caught in a dilemma over the link between maintaining security and encouraging disarmament. States in the inter-war period were reluctant to disarm until their security was assured, and yet the League lacked the political will and the military capabilities to deliver that security. In 1899, on the eve of the first Hague Peace Conference, the British War Office had accepted that there could be no restraint on military expenditure in the absence of any tribunal with the power to enforce its judgements. Yet, as the final chapter in this book reveals, in the aftermath of the Great War, British Governments were, despite domestic pressure and in contrast to the French, distinctly unenthusiastic about the idea of endowing the League with its own military force. They had concerns not only about the feasibility of an international force but also, had it come about, the powers it might have devolved upon the League. Even in the early days of the United Nations, before the onset of the Cold War, the idea of creating an international force fell victim to the political and diplomatic wrangling of Britain and the nascent superpowers. The organisation was thus left free to offer many kind, and unkind, words, but it was not provided with a gun.

Sir John Fisher boasted in 1899 that 'the supremacy of the British Navy [was] the best security for the peace of the world'.[7] But war had not been avoided during a hundred years of Britain's almost complete maritime hegemony. Nor were the best efforts of diplomats and international lawyers to promote arms control and disarmament to spare the world from armed conflict in the succeeding century. Indeed, one underlying theme of this book is the failure of diplomacy to achieve its stated ends. The first Hague Peace Conference made little progress towards restraining weapons development; the pre-1914 Anglo-German naval talks did not result in an understanding; the efforts of Britain and France to disarm Germany in the 1920s were only partially, and then temporarily, successful; the Coolidge Conference achieved nothing notable in the way of naval disarmament; and the Anglo-Soviet naval agreement of 1937 was, within two years of its conclusion, almost an anachronism. Only a fictional and very unbullish Ferdinand could remain true to his inclinations. That said, however, the essays in this volume also suggest that success in negotiation cannot be judged solely in terms of agreements achieved, or the latter be divorced from the contexts in which they are pursued. In 1989, after more than fifteen years of apparently fruitless negotiation in Vienna, the head of the British delegation to the MBFR talks claimed that they had succeeded as an 'exercise in damage limitation'. Undertaken to satisfy opinion in Britain and the United States, they had not led to the withdrawal of any American forces from Europe or a weakening of the Atlantic alliance, but 'the burden of unreduced military expenditure [had] made its contribution to the crippling of the Soviet economy'.[8] As this exercise demonstrates, the role of arms in diplomacy is not always restricted to disarmament.

NOTES

1. *US Congressional Record*, Senate (14 October 1998), p. S12568.
2. Pierre Renouvin, *L'Armistice de Rethondes* (Paris: Éditions Gallimard, 1968), p. 357.
3. Charles Webster, *The Foreign Policy of Castlereagh, 1815–1822: Britain and the European Alliance* (2nd edn, London: G. Bell and Sons, 1963), pp. 97–98. G. Bennett and K.A. Hamilton (eds), *Documents on British Policy Overseas*, series iii, vol. iii, *Détente in Europe, 1973—76* (London: Frank Cass/Whitehall History Publishing, 2001), p. 136.
4. Salisbury to Pauncefote, letter, 7 February 1896, and despt. no. 65, 5 March 1896, Hatfield House, Salisbury MSS, 3M/A140.
5. C. Fisher to J. Fisher, letter, 16 May 1899, Churchill Archive Centre (Cambridge), Fisher MSS, FISR 2/1.
6. Webster, *The Foreign Policy of Castlereagh*, p. 98.
7. R.H. Bacon, *The Life of Lord Fisher of Kilverstone, Admiral of the Fleet*, 2 vols. (London: Hodder and Stoughton, 1929), vol. i, p. 121.
8. *Documents on British Policy Overseas*, series iii, vol. iii, p. 475.

1

Britain and The Hague Peace Conference of 1899

KEITH HAMILTON

The third Marquess of Salisbury possessed firmly held moral and religious convictions. He believed the avoidance of war to be one of the principal objects of diplomacy.[1] Yet, in his dual role as British Prime Minister and Foreign Secretary during the last five years of the nineteenth century, he understood fully that success in negotiation and the security of Britain's interests, its trade and overseas possessions, must ultimately depend on the country's capacity to resort to the use of force. Reluctant to enter into formal ties of alliance with other major powers, he was fortunate in generally being able to assume that differences amongst Britain's imperial rivals would impede the formation of hostile coalitions. Nevertheless, during 1898 and 1899 he had to reckon with the expansion of Russian influence in the Far East, confrontations with France on the Niger and the Nile, the threat of armed conflict with Spain over the future security of Gibraltar, and the outbreak of war in southern Africa. In addition, officials in Whitehall could not neglect the fact that Russia, France's ally in Europe and Britain's antagonist in Asia, had recently embarked on a massive programme of naval construction. They were therefore, to say the least, bemused when on the eve of the Fashoda crisis with France, they received news of the proposal of the Russian Emperor, Nicholas II, for an international conference to consider the 'maintenance of universal peace and a possible reduction of the excessive armaments which weigh upon all nations'.[2] Salisbury applauded the initiative. The burden imposed on the populations affected by the cost of modern armaments must, he feared, whatever their deterrent value, eventually 'produce a feeling of unrest and discontent menacing both to internal and external tranquility'.[3] Not, however, for the last time in modern European history, it fell to British diplomats to draw practical advantage from the rhetoric of Russia's rulers.

The proposal for a conference, which Nicholas II's Foreign Minister, Count Michael Nikolaevich Muraviev, delivered to foreign representatives in St Petersburg on 24 August 1898,[4] gave rise to a good deal of speculation in London and elsewhere with regard to Russian motives and intentions. In truth, the imperial rescript owed more to the strained state of Russia's finances and the potentially ruinous costs of keeping up with military developments in neighbouring countries, than to the idealism of the young Emperor. A multilateral accord limiting spending on land armaments would, as the British suspected, permit Russia to concentrate on building up its naval strength and consolidating its position in east Asia.[5] But the Foreign Office was also uncertain as to what might be the likely agenda of the projected gathering, and whether or not delegates would be invited to examine current and potential sources of international friction.[6] Some satisfaction could be drawn from the evident discomfort of the French, whose ally had proposed a conference which might underscore a European territorial status quo which France so obviously wished to change. Yet of more immediate concern to the British was the way in which a conference might impinge on developments in southern Africa if the Transvaal, whose sovereignty Britain contested, were invited to participate. This seemed like a distinct possibility when in January 1899 they learned that The Hague was to be the conference venue. Conscious of public sympathy in the Netherlands for the Boer cause, Sir Charles Scott, the British Ambassador in St Petersburg, discreetly indicated to his Dutch colleague the difficulties which such an invitation might raise.[7] The issue was a source of considerable embarrassment for Dutch diplomacy. But, as in the case of the Pope, to whose participation the Italians objected, the Netherlands Government ultimately complied with the wishes of the great powers.[8]

The proposed conference meanwhile attracted considerable popular support in Britain. True, the Conservative press suspected the Russians of wishing to win time in order to consolidate recent gains. In combination with other countries, Russia, it was suggested, might seek to secure agreement on principles which would inhibit Britain's ability to exploit fully the size and technological superiority of its navy.[9] There was also the problem of how a limitation on armaments might affect relations with those who lived beyond the pale of 'civilised' states: the 'savages' and fanatics who refused to play by rules devised by European diplomacy. Sidney Low, a leader writer of the *Daily Telegraph*, argued that the 'Aryan race' should not disarm in the face of the black and yellow menace, and that it would be a crime against humanity to leave civilisation 'at the mercy or the forbearance of Slavonic and Asiatic hordes'.[10] Others were firmly of the opinion that the only real deterrent to armed conflict was the destructive capacity of weapons available. 'War', wrote Rudyard Kipling, 'will last until some inventive genius furnishes a machine which will annihilate fifty per cent of the combatants as soon as they face one another.'[11] But none of this seemed to dampen the ardour of those for whom the Russian rescript represented the most significant development in over half a century of their propagating the cause of universal peace. The radical journalist and editor of the *Review of Reviews*, William T. Stead, took the lead in Britain in rallying public opinion in favour of the conference: he founded a weekly newspaper, *War Against War!*, to campaign in its favour, and helped organise public meetings and petitions culminating, on 21 March 1899, in the assembly in central London of the National Convention of the British Crusade for Peace.[12] 'If', Stead declared, 'we contrast the unanimous sentiment of our public meetings with the half-hearted, cynical, grudging, carping comments that abound in our newspapers, we have at least some reason for feeling glad that the Crusade has rendered articulate the better sentiment of the nation.'[13]

The Russians had by then further refined their ideas. After discussions with other ministers and with the eminent jurisconsult, Feodor de Martens, who probably introduced him to his own ideas on the peaceful settlement of disputes, Muraviev circulated a second note on 11 January 1899. In this he put forward eight points which might serve as a programme for the conference. These proposals fell into four broad categories: the non-augmentation of armed forces (point 1); the restriction of improvements in weapons development (points 2–4); the regulation of the conduct of war (points 5–7); and the use of good offices, mediation and arbitration (point 8).[14] An invitation on this basis was gladly accepted by Salisbury. Indeed, he considered the British Government's commitment to the cause of arbitration and mediation for the avoidance of war to be such as to require no fresh declaration on its part.[15] Yet at the same time he had doubts about the exact meaning of some of Muraviev's points. He questioned, for instance, whether the term 'armed forces' would cover civilians who had received military training: if not, any limitation on force numbers would be unlikely to impede the mobilisation of a vast army. And he queried whether a prohibition on increased naval forces would apply to unarmed vessels designed for conversion to warships at short notice. He was also unclear as to how conference decisions were to be put into effect. Prohibitions, Salisbury reasoned, could only be of value if some organisation were established to assure they were respected. And consideration of the plan by which such 'inspecting and restraining power' should be organised must, he thought, precede an enumeration of the 'prohibitions' it was to enforce. For the moment, however, Salisbury felt that Muraviev's proposals must be submitted to 'careful expert examination', and this meant seeking the advice of the Admiralty and the War Office.[16]

Both departments had serious reservations about what the conference might hope to achieve. The Admiralty's response was brief almost to the point of brusqueness. In a one-page letter of 16 May, Evan Macgregor, its

Permanent Secretary, explained to the Foreign Office that he thought it 'quite impracticable to come to any agreement on the meaning of the term "effectifs actuels"', or to ensure that it would be carried out; that since any agreed limit on naval budgets would require safeguards as to the inspection of accounts, it could not fail to break down; and that any restraints on weapons improvement would be a 'retrograde' step favouring the interests of 'savage nations' over the 'more highly civilized'. The Admiralty also considered that new weapons had neither added to the suffering caused by war nor to the percentage killed and wounded: that was dependent on the 'courage, discipline, and experience of war of the contending forces'. The same naval experts were equally of the opinion that binding Britain to regulations on the conduct of war would be certain to lead to mutual recrimination, and they rejected any extension of the laws and customs of war on land to cover naval operations. Where arbitration and mediation were concerned, the Admiralty note simply recommended that attention be paid to 'conditions as to naval and military movements ... permissible and prohibited during the period of mediation'.[17]

The War Office assumed a broadly similar stance. But the twenty-seven page memorandum which the army's Director of Military Intelligence, Major-General Sir John Ardagh,[18] transmitted to the Foreign Office on 17 May made up for the brevity of the senior service. Indeed, Ardagh's paper incorporated what amounted to a summary history of warfare, a comparative review of government spending on armies in Europe and the United States, and statistical tables listing casualties in every major military engagement between the battles of Blenheim (1704) and Tel-el-Kebir (1882). These Ardagh deployed in support of his opposition to (1) restrictions on the size of Britain's military forces, and (2) what he termed the 'restraint of the employment of new developments of destructive agencies'. The British Empire, he argued, employed, in terms of the armed forces bearing on the population, the extent of territories to be defended, and the value of interests at stake, 'relatively a smaller number of soldiers than any considerable nation in the world except the United States'. Unlike its continental neighbours, Britain did not maintain a large conscript army and, if its military budget was high in comparison to its armed strength, this was due to the government having to compete in the labour market and the consequent size of the emoluments paid to those who voluntarily enlisted. Ardagh, in any case, doubted the motives of those advocating a general reduction of armies in Europe. Evidently with Russia in mind, he argued that some governments were simply seeking to switch resources to the expansion of naval forces 'with the intention of forming a coalition for the purpose of overthrowing the maritime supremacy of the United Kingdom'. He likewise sought to demonstrate that the introduction of improved armaments had historically been accompanied by a curtailing of the duration and frequency of wars, a diminution of the percentage of losses in battle, and an amelioration of the treatment of non-combatants. The fourteenth century had seen the Hundred Years War, the seventeenth the Thirty Years War, the eighteenth the Seven Years War and the nineteenth the Seven Weeks War. Modern military organisation and refined weaponry had, he continued, rendered a small force capable of both controlling a large unorganised civil population and easily suppressing riot or rebellion, and in consequence popular resistance to invasion had been rendered useless and futile. The imperious necessities of self-preservation which had once justified in some degree the complete subjection or extermination of a population had, he concluded, ceased to exist.[19]

Such arguments seemed to take little account of either the Revolutionary and Napoleonic Wars or the four-year-long American Civil War. The former Ardagh chose to regard as a series of separate conflicts in which 'popular excitement and personal ambition played a greater part than military considerations', and the latter's duration he attributed to the need of both sides to recruit and train armies of a size they had not previously possessed. Guerrilla warfare, which had been such a significant feature of the Peninsular and Cuban Wars and which was soon to tie down the British army in South Africa, did not merit even a mention. Ardagh was, however, at one with many of his contemporaries in believing that the costs of modern war, as well as the losses and sufferings involved, would tend to restrain governments and peoples from resorting to, or prolonging, armed conflict. He also feared that such restrictions as Muraviev had in mind might deprive Britain of the advantages it derived from its scientific and industrial achievements in weapons development. This, he held, would be to the benefit of the more populous nations, and in 'warfare with uncivilised races, in which we are so frequently engaged, the latter would, under such a regime, gradually approximate in quality and in weapons, to the fixed stand beyond which we had engaged ourselves not to advance'. Moreover, the War Office had yet to take full account of recent advances in artillery and, Ardagh queried, of what use would be the restraints proposed in the absence of any tribunal with the power to enforce its judgements?[20]

Ardagh was similarly unsympathetic towards Muraviev's proposal that participating states should seek to revise the as yet unratified declaration emanating from the Brussels Conference of 1874 on the laws and customs of war. This document, elaborated by the representatives of twelve European powers, covered the rights of belligerents towards each other and towards private individuals, and inter-belligerent relations. But in

January 1875 the British Government had declined a Russian invitation to transform it into an international act on the grounds that its text dealt inadequately with the administration of hostile territory in military occupation, and that in the last resort such rules of war could only be enforced by neutral intervention in the conflict. 'Above all', noted Lord Derby, the then Foreign Secretary, 'the rules defining the term "belligerent", tended to deprive a patriotic *levée en masse* of the rights of belligerents, the effects of which would be to facilitate aggressive wars and paralyse the patriotic resistance of an invaded people'. Ardagh's main concern was not, however, with the substance of what had been agreed at Brussels, but with the principle of 'whether a codification of any of the laws and customs of war ... would serve any useful purpose'. He admitted that, with the exception of a few sections of the Army Act, there appeared to be no authorised exposition of the laws and customs of war officially recognised in the British Empire. A British commanding officer in wartime was very much a law unto himself and this imposed a 'grave responsibility', and often compelled him 'to act promptly upon such conceptions of propriety, expediency, or equity as may evolve at the moment from his inner consciousness'. Ardagh nevertheless endorsed the view expressed by a large body of American and British jurists that the essence of codification was the 'imposition of restrictions', and that if the latter were to influence the duration of war, 'the tendency must be rather to lengthen than shorten it'; and since it was in the interests of humanity to shorten wars, belligerents should be able to use any means at their disposal for reaching a 'prompt and energetic solution of the conflict'. Furthermore, he argued, on the basis of evidence derived from the Franco-Prussian War of 1870–71, codification seemed likely to lead only to bitter recrimination amongst belligerents over real and supposed violations of agreed rules of war. It was, he thought, 'to the last degree utopian' to suppose that powers would constitute themselves into a tribunal in order to enquire into, and pass judgement upon, alleged breaches of the code in wartime. Yet, he concluded, without such a tribunal 'positive law, whether written or unwritten [was] worthless'. All he could therefore recommend was that the government should indicate its readiness to cause articles of war for the instruction and guidance of its armed forces to be compiled and promulgated, and to embody in these such portions of the Brussels declaration as appeared to conform to the principles on which Britain had hitherto acted.[21]

A far less negative note was struck by Ardagh in his commentary on Muraviev's proposals regarding arbitration and mediation. Indeed, several of the points he had made with regard to arms limitation and the conduct of war were, he admitted, 'necessarily speculative and inconclusive' because of the absence of any prescribed method of resolving differences over the interpretation of internationally agreed rules and declarations. If the conference should lead to the inception of an 'International Court of Appeal' then, he thought, many of the risks and dangers against which military authorities had to provide would be diminished in intensity. Likewise, he believed that the fear of a sudden outbreak of hostilities such as accompanied international crises would be mitigated and probably removed by the 'mere delay and procrastination' which would accompany resort to arbitration or neutral mediation.[22] It was a view towards which Salisbury had seemed recently to incline. When in 1895 the United States President, Grover Cleveland, intervened in a longstanding dispute between Britain and Venezuela over the frontiers of British Guiana, Salisbury had at first resisted American pressure to refer the matter to impartial arbitration. Only after discussion with Cabinet colleagues, some of whom were alarmed by the concurrent deterioration in Britain's relations with its European neighbours, did Salisbury give way. He also, with a view to defusing the transatlantic controversy, took up an earlier American proposal for the establishment of a 'system of international arbitration of disputes between the two [British and United States] Governments'. In a despatch of 5 March 1896 to Sir Julian Pauncefote, the British Ambassador in Washington, he put forward a very modest proposal for an Anglo-American arbitration agreement.[23]

Salisbury had been sceptical about this method of settling international disputes. And distrustful of the possible prejudices of third-party arbitrators, he ruled out unrestricted arbitration. Instead, in a draft treaty which he appended to his despatch to Pauncefote, he proposed the appointment by the British and US Governments of judicial officers who, along with an umpire, would act as arbitrators, and, where territorial differences were concerned, review by a court of appeal composed of judges from their respective supreme courts. Any differences which in the judgement of either power materially affected 'its honour or the integrity of its territory' were not to be subject to arbitration 'except by special agreement'.[24] Richard Olney, Cleveland's Secretary of State, considered the project too limited in scope.[25] Salisbury protested that obligatory arbitration on territorial claims was 'in more than one respect, an untried plan, of which the working [was] consequently a matter of conjecture'.[26] As he had previously argued, apprehension regarding the workings of arbitration would 'only be overcome, if at all, by tentative treatment'.[27] There nonetheless emerged from the subsequent deliberations between Olney and Pauncefote a draft general treaty of arbitration. This committed both countries to submit all differences between them that could not otherwise be adjusted by diplomacy to joint arbitral tribunals. It also made special provision for territorial disputes, specifying that resulting awards could be rejected by governments when unsupported by fewer than five of the six tribunal members.[28]

In one respect the Olney–Pauncefote Treaty set a poor precedent for the peace conference at The Hague: opposition to it in the Senate's foreign relations committee meant that the treaty failed to secure the two-thirds majority necessary for ratification. The treaty had in any case been essentially a manifestation of transatlantic *Realpolitik*, designed in part, as Pauncefote admitted, to 'take the wind out of the sails of the Jingoes as regards Great Britain'. But Pauncefote's role in the preceding negotiations and his handling of the submission of Venezuela's claims to arbitration appear to have made him an obvious choice for the leadership of the British delegation to The Hague.[29] His credentials were sound, some might say, impeccable. A former Attorney General of Hong Kong and Chief Justice of the Leeward Islands, he had served in the Foreign Office, first as Legal Under-Secretary, and then as Permanent Under-Secretary, before his appointment to Washington in 1889. Moreover, Salisbury seems to have come to accept that the notion of an independent judicial tribunal, as provided for in the draft treaty with America, might have the potential for universal application. Any system of arbitration adopted by Britain and the United States ought, he had informed Pauncefote in 1896, 'to be such as [could] in principle be applied, if necessary, to their relations with other civilised countries'.[30] He, in any event, considered Pauncefote in no need of further instructions on arbitration since during his negotiations in Washington he had been 'placed in full possession of the views of Her Majesty's Government on the subject'. The Prime Minister felt sanguine that at The Hague Pauncefote's efforts might 'equally be productive of good result'.[31] Indeed, few envoys in modern times could have embarked on so major a negotiation with so little briefing or so broad a mandate.

Pauncefote arrived in The Hague on 17 May accompanied by Ardagh and Vice-Admiral Sir John Fisher,[32] both of whom Salisbury had personally selected as technical delegates. The British team was a strong one. Pauncefote's deputy, Sir Henry Howard, the British Minister at The Hague, was a career diplomat well versed in the political wrangling that had preceded the opening of the conference; Fisher was an outspoken and innovative navalist who, Salisbury hoped, would put up a stout resistance to any attempt to cripple Britain's power at sea; and Ardagh was a wiry Irishman with a formidable intellect and a thorough grasp of contemporary strategic issues. But Fisher, whose robust performance in committee had so impressed ministers in Whitehall and whose equally versatile performances on the dance floor were so much admired by other conference participants, was no linguist and in need of assistance with his French.[33] It was partly to remedy this deficiency that soon after the conference proceedings began the delegation sought and acquired the services of Lieutenant-Colonel Charles à Court, the British Military Attaché at Brussels and The Hague.[34] Accommodated in the Hotel des Indes, rooms in which Howard had reserved early for reasons of economy, the labours of the British representatives were divided amongst the conference's three commissions. The first dealt with projected limitations upon armaments, the second with the rules and conduct of war, and the third with arbitration and mediation. It was in the last that Pauncefote made what was probably the most significant British contribution to the work of the conference.

During the second meeting of the third commission on 26 May, Pauncefote took the initiative and moved that delegates consider the creation of a permanent tribunal of international arbitration. He argued that if the conference were to confine itself to framing rules of procedure for the use of international tribunals it would not materially advance the cause of arbitration. A permanent tribunal would, he thought, give great encouragement to the pacific settlement of international differences and considerably accelerate the development of a systematic code of international law. The idea was, as Salisbury subsequently confirmed, 'entirely in accordance with the general views [the British Government] held on the subject'.[35] But it was hardly new. Three years earlier the Chevalier Édouard Descamps, a Belgian member of the third commission, had published a seminal essay on the subject.[36] Ardagh had referred in his memorandum to the advantages to be derived from establishing such a tribunal; and in his opening address the president of the commission, the former French Premier, Léon Bourgeois, had mentioned the possibility of setting up a 'permanent *international institution* to act ... in the form of an international tribunal'. The Americans also had in draft a scheme not dissimilar to that proposed by Pauncefote; and the Russians, who had already tabled the outlines of a draft convention covering good offices and mediation, international arbitration and commissions of enquiry, and a draft arbitral code, were contemplating the introduction into the latter of provision for some kind of permanent institution. Both, however, were ready to proceed on the basis of the proposition which on 31 May Pauncefote submitted to the *comité d'examen*, the expert legal committee charged specifically with handling the issue. Added to the final chapter to the Russian project as a basis for further consideration, it foresaw the establishment at Berne, Brussels or The Hague of a permanent office with appropriate staff; the nomination by each of the participants of two eminent jurists, who would be ex officio members of the tribunal and from whom litigants might select arbiters for their particular case; and the formation of a council of administration. The tribunal was to be governed by rules and practices contained in a convention, and the costs of the office and the council would be borne equally by all the signatories.[37]

Unlike the American proposal, Pauncefote's scheme was unhampered by procedural detail. It was also somewhat more specific than the formula submitted by the Russians for possible inclusion in their project. But while it commanded broad support within the third commission, other major powers had doubts about what the establishment of a permanent tribunal might imply. France's Foreign Minister, Théophile Delcassé, was concerned lest a permanent organ come to exercise 'une sorte de contrainte morale' on French foreign policy. Less civilised countries might, he feared, one day have recourse to an international institution dispensing justice according to 'des conditions ou des précédents d'ordre purement européen'.[38] The Germans were even more alarmed by Pauncefote's project. No mention of a permanent tribunal had featured in Muraviev's previous proposals, and the Foreign Ministry in Berlin already had serious misgivings about Germany adhering to fresh arrangements on international arbitration. Indeed, Friedrich von Holstein, the head of the Ministry's Political Department, had seemed to share Salisbury's earlier expressed doubts on the subject when, in a memorandum of 9 May, he argued that it would be practicably impossible for the powers represented on an arbitral tribunal to separate their own interests from any case under consideration and to judge the matter impartially.[39] Count Georg zu Münster, the veteran Hanoverian diplomat who headed the German delegation, was of much the same opinion. He thought that a tribunal could menace Germany's independence and deny its armed forces the advantages they derived from their ability to mobilise rapidly in time of international crisis.[40] And on 9 June, Professor Philipp Zorn, Germany's representative on the third commission, despite offering his personal assurances that he would 'render all the assistance in his power to complete the work in view', insisted in the *comité d'examen* on the need for more experience with arbitration before his Government could agree to the organisation of a permanent tribunal.[41]

The Germans were, however, alone in their opposition to the project. Delcassé was ready to waive his objections and allow Bourgeois a free hand, and even Germany's allies, Italy and Austria-Hungary, were reluctant to obstruct progress. Count Constantino Nigra, the Italian head of delegation, urged Zorn to abandon his opposition, and Professor Heinrich Lammasch, Austria-Hungary's representative on the third commission, announced his willingness to participate in debating plans for an international court.[42] Eventually, following hurried visits by Zorn and

George Holls, a member of the American delegation to Berlin, and frenzied discussions there amongst ministers and diplomats, the Germans gave way. Münster could see little point in jeopardising Germany's otherwise favourable diplomatic position, and the German Ambassador at St Petersburg warned the Wilhelmstrasse of the serious harm that obstruction of the arbitration project might do to Russo-German relations, especially as the Russians now regarded the permanent court 'as the only possible result of any value' likely to emerge from the conference.[43] On 1 July Zorn announced in the *comité d'examen* that Germany was ready to set aside its objections to a permanent tribunal, and he asked in return that there should be no question of arbitration being made obligatory, and that the arbitrary body be called a court rather than a tribunal. Two days later, he also succeeded in persuading the committee that each country should appoint four, rather than two, judges to the court, a move generally interpreted as being intended to dilute its international authority. Nevertheless, the only substantial change to the British scheme was that made to take account of Russian objections to the articles relating to the Permanent Council of Administration. The Russians preferred that the authority to control the International Office, which the Conference decided to establish at The Hague, should be vested in the Netherlands Government. But they were prepared to compromise, and it was finally settled that the Council should consist of the representatives of the signatory powers at The Hague under the presidency of the Dutch Foreign Minister.[44]

So irritated was Pauncefote by German conduct that when, on 16 June, Münster sought to postpone consideration of the British project in the *comité d'examen*, he contemplated pressing for a continuation of the proceedings without a German presence.[45] Yet other delegates had been far from enthusiastic about aspects of the outline Russian draft convention on arbitration which appeared to threaten their particular national or service interests. True, much to Delcassé's relief, article viii of Muraviev's draft specifically excluded from arbitration issues 'including vital interests and national honour'.[46] However, even the Americans, who had once posed as champions of compulsory arbitration, were alarmed when they discovered that the relatively minor matters on which Muraviev proposed to make arbitration obligatory included differences over transoceanic waterways, such as that planned to link the Atlantic to the Pacific.[47] Fisher too had similar concerns to those of his German colleagues. He was thus wary of any arrangement which might, by delaying the outbreak of hostilities, deprive Britain of the immense advantage which it derived from its naval readiness for war – an advantage which had been only recently demonstrated during the Fashoda crisis.[48] And while Salisbury was ready to accept obligatory arbitration in a number of specified cases, he assured the German Ambassador in London that he 'considered it absolutely out of the question' for the tribunal to deal with any important political issue.[49] He was in any case perturbed by the prospect of an international convention requiring Britain to refer disputes with other powers to mediation before resorting to arms. When, during the early stages of the conference, the text of the original Russian draft was amended to make mediation obligatory in all but 'exceptional circumstances', he vigorously protested. He feared that in disputes where weaker powers had no good case, they would always use mediation for delay. 'Great Britain', he minuted, 'has for so many years been so profoundly unpopular with all Powers, that she would be much embarrassed if she was asked to what Power she would be disposed to entrust mediation for she would either have to confess to her want of friends, or to accept a rival. It is a provision which will not make for peace & can do us nothing but harm.'[50] The Prime Minister need not have worried. Other powers were equally reluctant to accept any open-ended commitment to mediation, and the final text of the convention on the pacific settlement of international disputes obliged recourse to friendly mediation, as also to commissions of enquiry, only as far as 'circumstances allow[ed]'. Meanwhile, article xix left open the possibility of signatories concluding accords to extend obligatory arbitration to all cases for which they considered it appropriate.[51]

A greater and more immediate threat to British interests was perceived by Pauncefote and his colleagues in the work of the first commission, whose agenda covered points 1 to 4 of Muraviev's January circular. Its first (land warfare) and second (naval) subcommissions were very much concerned with matters relating to the proposed limitation of technological improvements in ammunition and weaponry; and both were therefore likely to envisage ends contrary to the needs of a country which believed its imperial security to be in large part dependent on the innovative capacity of its scientists and its armaments industries. Fortunately, from the British point of view, Russian efforts to secure agreement on restricting the development of army ordnance were opposed by the representatives of the other great powers at the conference.[52] British delegates were, nonetheless, forced on to the defensive when the first subcommission, began to consider the prohibition of 'expanding' bullets, that is, bullets whose core was almost wholly, though not completely, covered by a hard case or envelope. The British army already employed such a projectile, the Mark IV bullet, and British forces in India were equipped with another, the Dum-Dum bullet.[53] But members of the first commission's military subcommission and of the subcommission of the second commission, set up to consider revision of the Brussels declaration, appear to have been much influenced by recent experiments conducted at Tübingen University which indicated that excessively severe wounds resulted from the way in which such bullets flattened and expanded on entering the body. This was also an issue on which the Russians could unite with others in opposition to their rivals, and on 31 May members of the military subcommission accepted an article proscribing their use in wartime. The British protested. In their experience, the expanding bullet had a much greater capacity to shock and halt an enemy advance than completely mantled ammunition, and was of particular value in the kind of colonial conflicts in which British forces were most frequently engaged. Ardagh explained in graphic detail to the subcommission that in 'savage warfare' the Dum-Dum bullet had proved indispensable since it had been demonstrated that men who had several times been penetrated by the latest pattern of small-calibre projectile, which made a 'small clean hole', were still able to 'rush on and come to close quarters'. He further observed:

> Your civilized soldier, ... when he has a bullet through him, recognizes the fact that he is wounded, and knows that the sooner he is attended to the sooner will he recover. He mounts his cacolet, or lies down on his stretcher, and is taken off the field to his ambulance, where he is dressed and bandaged by his doctor or his Red Cross Society, according to the prescribed rules of the game, as laid down in the Geneva Convention.
>
> But your fanatical barbarian, when he receives wounds of a like nature, which are insufficient to stop or disable him, continues to dash on, spear or sword in hand, and before you have had time or opportunity to represent to him that his conduct is in flagrant violation of the understanding relative to the proper course for a wounded man to follow, he may have cut off your head ...[54]

Ardagh subsequently denied the relevance of the Tübingen experiments, which had been conducted with a bullet whose core was more fully exposed than the Dum-Dum, and suggested that the wounds inflicted by the latter were unlikely to be worse than those resulting from the use of the larger, smooth-bore spherical bullets of the past. In any case, he argued, it was 'hardly necessary to affirm that public opinion in England would never tolerate or sanction the employment of a projectile calculated to occasion unnecessary suffering'. The American delegate, Captain William Crozier, after initially assuming a contrary stance in the subcommission, eventually came to Ardagh's support in opposing the inclusion in any interdiction of details of the technical construction of bullets such as would specifically prohibit the Dum-Dum and the Mark IV.

Nevertheless, at a meeting of the first commission on 22 June, the Dum-Dum bullet was condemned by a vote of twenty to two (Britain and the United States).[55] A fortnight later, at an informal meeting on 8 July, the Dutch reporter of the first commission, Jonkheer van Karnebeek, tried unsuccessfully to overcome British opposition by suggesting that the prohibition be put in the form of an additional article to the St Petersburg Declaration of 1868 prohibiting the use of exploding bullets, which, since it was only binding on signatory and acceding powers, would not apply to 'savage warfare'. He added that Dutch experts thought that what the expanding bullet offered in stopping power was lost in its powers of penetration. Dutch troops attached more importance to the latter, 'as it enabled fully mantled bullets to reach their foes behind the shelter of jungle and stockade'. But, as Ardagh explained, although the British were continuing experiments with a view to producing a bullet which would 'comply with the military as well as the humanitarian requirements', there could be no question of their accepting a formula which explicitly forbade designs currently in use.[56]

The British were equally reluctant to accept restrictions on naval armaments and explosives. Fisher employed much the same argument as Ardagh, insisting that their imposition must work to the disadvantage of civilised nations in war against less civilised peoples and savage tribes, and that, without the establishment of an international control committee, it would be impossible to limit the invention of new weapons.[57] He was in any case personally convinced that peace depended on the maintenance of a powerful deterrent, and that, in the case of Britain, meant a strong and efficient navy. 'If', he told Stead, 'you rub it in both at home and abroad that you are ready for instant war with every unit of your strength in the first line, and intend to be first in and hit your enemy in the belly and kick him when he is down, and boil your prisoners in oil (if you take any!), and torture his women and children, then people will keep clear of you.'[58] This was, of course, hyperbole, as was his claim that diplomacy at The Hague was 'a case of *Britannia contra mundum*'.[59] In committee, though not in private, Fisher's comments were rather more restrained and his arguments very much more refined.[60] His initial opposition to Russian proposals to restrict the calibre of naval guns was thus expressed in terms calculated to appeal to other delegates. He did not see how agreement could be achieved 'without at the same time fixing the limits of armour, and it did not appear to him practicable to state a formula which would prove satisfactory in this sense, even if the fundamental difficulty of control could be got over'.[61] As Captain Alfred Mahan, the American historian and naval delegate, pointed out, Russia's proposals would have probably occupied an ordnance committee for about six months.[62] But Fisher was prepared to accept the prohibition of submarines and naval rams so long as agreement was unanimous – a significant qualification since it was from the first apparent that neither the Americans nor the French would agree to forego submarine development, and Austria-Hungary declined to commit itself on rams. Indeed, even the prohibition of the use of asphyxiating gases, which fourteen countries supported, was rejected by Mahan on the grounds that the 'objection that a war-like device is barbarous has always been made against all new weapons, which were nevertheless eventually adopted'.[63] Every country, Fisher remarked, wished 'to use the best weapon it [could] procure', and in his opinion military inventions served 'rather to hinder and retard war'.[64]

By 17 June it was already clear that no real progress was likely to be made in the naval subcommission towards an understanding on points 2 to 4 of Muraviev's memorandum.[65] Even more remote was the prospect of agreement on the proposals the Russians put to the first commission on 23 June for limiting the size of armed forces. These, which included provision for a five-year limit on troop numbers, the maintenance of existing military budgets, and a three-year freeze on naval expenditure, were wholly incompatible with the views previously expressed by the Admiralty and the War Office. But in this instance the British delegates were able to assume a relatively low profile. None of the great powers was enthusiastic about what the Russians had in mind, and on 26 June, Colonel Gross von Schwarzhoff, the German military delegate, explained, in what Pauncefote termed a 'speech of great force and ability', his Government's objections.[66] He stated that the question of 'effectives' could not be discussed by itself as there were many others to which it was in some measure subordinated, such as the length of service, the number of cadres, the amount of training received by reserves, the situation of the country itself, its railway system and the position of its fortresses. On Pauncefote's prompting the matter was referred to special committees of military and naval experts, and in the latter of these Fisher was able to render a further service to Russian *amour propre*. He voted against an immediate and adverse report on the Russian proposals and persuaded other delegates to support their submission to participating governments. 'It may be added', he subsequently noted, 'that it is fully understood by all the Delegates that no hope is entertained of any of the Russian proposals being accepted.'[67] And when on 30 June, the first commission met to consider the reports of the expert committees, it was agreed that the conference should simply limit itself to recommending that further consideration of the matter by the powers would prove of great benefit to humanity.[68]

Fisher was able to play an altogether more constructive role in the second commission, which dealt with the rules of war. The first of its two subcommissions was charged with reviewing the adaptation to naval warfare of the stipulations of the Geneva Convention of 1864 on the basis of articles agreed, but not ratified, in 1868. The British delegates, though opposed to all diminution of the rights of belligerents in a naval war, were nonetheless prepared to agree to the revised rules which emerged from the subcommission's deliberations. Fisher's particular concern was with the rules governing hospital ships during naval engagements. He believed that the presence of neutral vessels in any form could give rise to great difficulties and therefore sought, successfully, to redraft the 1868 articles in such a way as to permit belligerent admirals to order all such vessels to leave the scene of operations. But the Admiralty was doubtful about giving conventional force to the additional articles. It also objected to the terms of article x which required neutral governments to guard and disbar from further participation in the war shipwrecked and wounded officers and men who might be disembarked upon their territory.[69] Mahan too questioned an article, which appeared to make it too easy for enemy seamen to escape capture.[70] Pauncefote was, nonetheless, able to persuade Salisbury that it would be unfortunate if Britain alone were to stand out against the wishes of others to include the revised humanitarian provisions in this extension of the Geneva Convention. The insertion, in article x, of a clause allowing for the conclusion of contrary arrangements between belligerents and neutrals, temporarily overcame the Admiralty's objections.[71] Pauncefote's triumph was short-lived. The Solicitor General pronounced that enforcement of the provision would require the passage of enabling legislation, and this and continuing Admiralty misgivings, led finally to the decision that Britain, while subscribing to the convention, should enter a reservation on the offending article.[72]

Meanwhile, Ardagh seemed ready to set aside his earlier doubts regarding the revision and status of the Brussels declaration on the laws and customs of war on land. He shared the concern of the representatives of some of the smaller powers lest their already limited powers of defence be diminished further by the enactment of restrictions on the rights of their citizens to resist foreign occupation. But in the discussions of the subcommission of the second commission to which the declaration was referred, he displayed little sympathy for Belgian demands for the wholesale suppression of six of the articles of the 1874 declaration. He personally thought it preferable to attempt to define the respective rights and duties, both of occupying belligerents and of populations under enemy occupation, rather than leave occupants free to exercise unlimited power over populations who could appeal to no authority other than the vague and indeterminate conceptions of undefined international law. He nevertheless continued for some time to argue against transforming the declaration into an international convention. Given the diversity of opinions expressed and of interests engaged, he believed the pursuit of such a course would end in failure, and he persisted in urging that delegates confine themselves to revising articles which their governments might adopt in whole or in part and incorporate in their army instruction manuals.[73] Progress within the subcommission towards the revision of the declaration in a sense largely in accord with his own thinking on the subject appears, however, to have weakened Ardagh's opposition to its inclusion in an international convention. He thus drew particular satisfaction from the fact that on 20 June the subcommision, partly in response to his own intervention, unanimously agreed to a preambular statement formulated by its president, de Martens. This stated that, until a more complete code of the laws of war had been issued, the parties deemed it expedient to declare that 'in cases not included in the regulations adopted by them, the inhabitants and belligerents remain under the protection and the rule of the principles of the law of nations, as they result from the usages established among civilised peoples, from the laws of humanity, and from the dictates of the public conscience'.[74]

The general effect of discussion within the subcommission had, Ardagh concluded, been to demonstrate that the British Government earnestly supported the cause of the weaker powers and the right and duty to put up a patriotic resistance to an invader. Moreover, he considered the revised articles, when taken in connexion with the preamble, formed a 'most valuable exposition' of the laws and customs of war by which the British Government had hitherto been guided. It was therefore hardly surprising that in a memorandum of 5 July he should have questioned the continuing validity of the arguments set forth in his paper of 17 May. Conditions, he reasoned, had so very much altered that the matter should be reconsidered by the high military and legal authorities. He was, he confessed, now of the opinion that the arguments against entering a convention of the nature framed at the conference were far weaker, and those in favour of doing so far stronger, than before. 'The extreme pretensions of the weaker States, and the claims of the stronger ones to exercise an arbitrary control over the vanquished populations, have', he noted, 'been mollified and moderated, and both are now more ready to recognize that the restrictions of a reasonable code are preferable to the vague uncertainty in which the entire absence of rules left the conflicting interests of the parties concerned.' The rules agreed did not aim at legalising the supremacy of the conqueror and the subjection of the vanquished, but, while recognising the inevitable consequences of war, admitted them as a fact, and not as a right.[75]

Pauncefote nonetheless found it necessary to oppose the pretensions of one weaker state. The Danes sought to have included in the article of the revised declaration dealing with an enemy occupants' rights over means of transport and communication a reference to the shore ends of submarine telegraph cables. This, as the Admiralty were well aware, could set a precedent for the future extension of international law to cover belligerent rights and submarine cables which might work to Britain's disadvantage. No great maritime war had occurred since submarine cables had come into use, and it was in the Admiralty's opinion better that there should be no attempt to introduce regulations since control of cables in wartime would 'really rest with the Power which [held] the command of the sea'.[76] The Danish delegate was not inclined to resist British objections on this point and at a conference plenary on 25 July he agreed to the withdrawal of the reference to shore ends.[77] The Admiralty's concern over the future of weapons development also led the British delegates to change their stance on the interdiction of asphyxiating shells. Fisher had originally voted in the first commission's naval subcommission for the prohibition of such shells, but on the understanding that the vote was unanimous. When, however, during a plenary session of the first commission on 20 July, Mahan maintained his opposition to the interdiction on the grounds that he was averse to placing any restriction on the 'inventive genius' of American citizens, Pauncefote voted with him.[78] Mahan explained that although no such weapon yet existed, it would be less inhumane than submarine warfare and asphyxiation by water and, he added, a shell would doubtless be devised so as to permit the ultimate recovery of its victims. 'No doubt', Fisher commented, 'an American invention will shortly appear on these lines, and chloroform has already been suggested as the base.'[79] Anglo-American controversy was in the meantime avoided when the second commission agreed that consideration of a proposal from Andrew White, the US head of delegation, for the exemption of private property from capture at sea should be postponed to a further conference.[80]

By 26 July the work of the conference was virtually complete. Its final act was ready for signature and to it were attached the three conventions: (1) for the pacific settlement of international disputes; (2) for the adaptation to maritime warfare of the principles of the Geneva Convention; and (3) respecting the laws and customs of war on land. There were, in addition, three declarations relative to the prohibition of: (1) the discharge of explosives and projectiles from balloons; (2) the employment of asphyxiating projectiles; and (3) expanding bullets. Salisbury still had one condition to add to the convention on the pacific settlement of disputes: he required that it contain no words implying Britain's consent to the subsequent adherence of other parties without the general agreement of signatories. The danger was that the Transvaal might wish to adhere. The matter was, however, settled on 28 July when, after an acrimonious debate in the drafting committee, the convention was so amended as to make conditions relating to the accession of non-participants dependent on later agreement,[81] and the next day the final act was signed. During the subsequent consideration of the conventions and declarations in London, only the War Office offered serious objections. Thus, on the basis of a paper which recited many of the arguments originally put forward by Ardagh in his memorandum of 17 May, Lord Wolseley, the army's Commander-in-Chief, advised Lord Lansdowne, the Secretary of State for War, against Britain adhering to the convention on the rules of war on land. He also opposed Britain's acceding to any of the three declarations, including that prohibiting for five years the discharge of explosives and projectiles from balloons. British delegates had only withheld from opposing the latter proposal in order to win American support on the issue of expanding bullets. But any restriction on the use of balloons could be to Britain's disadvantage since the relatively small size of its army made it to some extent dependent on the exploitation of scientific inventions. Aerial bombardment of fortified places would, the War Office claimed, shorten sieges and thereby reduce the privations suffered by their inhabitants. Moreover, as the Russians evidently appreciated, in 1899 Britain still led the world in the military development of captive balloons and man-lifting kites. Lansdowne did not question the 'soundness, from a purely military point of view', of Wolseley's judgement: he, nevertheless, recognised that diplomatic considerations might have to be taken into account. Given the strength of international support for the convention on the laws and customs of land warfare, he thought it might be difficult for Britain to withhold its consent. He was equally uncertain as to whether Britain could retreat from its previous concurrence in the declaration on the employment of balloons.[82]

Wolseley's doubts about codifying the rules of war were set aside; his advice on aerial bombardment prevailed. On 25 October Salisbury authorised Pauncefote and Howard to sign all three of the conventions, but with a reservation on article x of that covering naval warfare. They were also instructed not to sign any of the three declarations.[83] Dutch insistence that other signatories must first assent to the British reservation on the maritime convention delayed Britain's accession until 29 December.[84] By then Britain was already at war in southern Africa. The conflict was, admittedly, an intra-imperial one between the British crown and two Boer republics over whom it claimed to exercise suzerainty. Yet in this context, as also in the horrors to which it gave rise, the Second Boer War foreshadowed later twentieth-century conflicts which straddled the fine line between the civil and the international. The course of the war and the strains which it placed upon Britain's relations with its continental neighbours seemed to belie the optimism exhibited by Pauncefote and Howard in their final conference despatch. 'Thus', they asserted, 'the new century will open with brighter prospects of international peace, and all nations must hail with satisfaction the admirable work of the Conference in humanizing the laws of war both on land and at sea.'[85] By contrast, Fisher's verdict on his times appears all the more poignant. 'The humanizing of War!' he protested, 'You might as well talk of humanizing Hell!'[86]

Such verbal broadsides reveal more about Fisher's temperament than his achievements. In July 1899 his reporting on the conference was rather less jaundiced, and he viewed with some satisfaction the protection which the extension of the Geneva convention to naval warfare would henceforth afford for shipwrecked and wounded seamen. The ten maritime articles were, he wrote, 'considered to be in favour of England, as being the strongest belligerent'.[87] The failure of the conference to make much progress towards an agreement on arms limitation was also regarded as being to Britain's advantage. As à Court pointed out in an analysis of this aspect of the conference's work, Germany, the 'military centre of gravity of Europe', had stood out against any restrictions on the size of its army, and continuing competition amongst the great military powers of the continent would 'not allow any great or very sudden increase of naval expenditure at the expense of army budgets'. Neither France nor Russia would therefore be able to afford to mount a serious challenge to Britain's maritime supremacy, and Germany must meanwhile shoulder the moral burden for its role of spoiler in the negotiations.[88] Yet, in practice, the British were no less ruthless than the Germans in opposing measures deemed likely to conflict with their freedom of manoeuvre in times of crisis and of war. Unattached to either of the continental alliance blocs and increasingly exposed to pressure from their foreign rivals, the British perceived their security as depending in large part upon their ability to make the fullest use of latest weapons technologies and, alone amongst the conference participants, refused to subscribe to all three declarations. Nonetheless, as Foreign Secretary of the most globally extended of the great powers, Salisbury also came to see in the promotion of international arbitration a means of reducing those sources of friction which could so easily lead to costly confrontation. 'Presumably', Fisher aptly noted, 'the greater or less readiness for war of the nations in question will have an important influence on the progress of the arbitration.'[89] In this respect as in others British diplomacy at The Hague responded as much to the strategic requirements of empire as to the humanitarian aspirations of the British Crusade for Peace.

NOTES

An earlier, shorter version of this chapter was included on a CD-Rom attached to the book, edited by Frits Kalshoven, *The Centennial of the First International Peace Conference. Reports and Conclusions* (The Hague: Kluwer Law International, 2000). The author is grateful to Koninklijke Brill NV for permission to reproduce unrevised sections of this text here.

1. J.A.S. Grenville, *Lord Salisbury and Foreign Policy: The Close of the Nineteenth Century* (London: Athlone Press, 1964), pp. 6, 22; D. Gillard, 'Salisbury', in Keith Wilson (ed.), *British Foreign Secretaries and Foreign Policy: From Crimean War to First World War* (London: Croom Helm, 1987), pp. 119-37.
2. The National Archives [hereafter TNA], FO 881/7473, paper by Muraviev in Scott to Salisbury, despt. no. 293, 25 August 1898.
3. G.P. Gooch and H.V. Temperley (eds), *British Documents on the Origins of the War, 1898-1914*, 11 vols. (London: HMSO, 1926-38), vol. i [hereafter cited as *BD*, i], no. 270.
4. Scott to Salisbury, tel. no. 116 P(araphrase), 24 August 1898, TNA, FO 881/7473.
5. Jost Dülffer, *Regeln gegen den Krieg? Die Haager Friedenskonferenzen von 1899 und 1907 in der internationalen Politik* (Frankfurt a. M.: Ullstein, 1981), pp. 19-38; Arthur Eyffinger, *The 1899 Hague Peace Conference: 'The Parliament of Man, the Federation of the World'* (The Hague: Kluwer Law International, 1999), pp. 16-34.
6. Balfour to Scott, tel. private, 30 August 1898, TNA, FO 65/1558.
7. Scott to Salisbury, despt. no. 61, 2 March 1899, TNA, FO 881/7473.
8. Eyffinger, *The 1899 Hague Peace Conference*, pp. 77-96.
9. A.J. Marder, *The Anatomy of British Sea Power: A History of British Naval Policy in the Pre-Dreadnought Era* (London: Frank Cass, 1964), pp. 341-44.
10. Cited in Merze Tate, *The Disarmament Illusion: The Movement for a Limitation of Armaments to 1907* (New York: Macmillan, 1942), p. 221.
11. Cited in Eyffinger, *The 1899 Hague Peace Conference*, p. 63.
12. TNA, FO 83/1738, *passim*.
13. *War Against War!*, 24 March 1899.
14. Enclosure in Scott to Salisbury, despt. no. 13, 12 January 1899, TNA, FO 881/7473; Eyffinger, *The 1899 Hague Peace Conference*, pp. 37-38.
15. Salisbury to Scott, despt. no. 36, 14 February, 1899, TNA, FO 881/7473.
16. Salisbury to Scott, despt. no. 37, 14 February, 1899, ibid.
17. Macgregor to Sanderson, letter, 16 May 1899, TNA, FO 83/1702 (cf. expurgated text in *BD*, i, no. 274).
18. See T.G. Fergusson, *British Military Intelligence, 1870-1914: The Development of a Modern Intelligence Organization* (London: Arms and Armour Press, 1984), pp. 104-6.
19. Memo. by Ardagh in War Office to Foreign Office, letter, 17 May 1899, TNA, FO 83/1702.
20. Ibid.
21. Ibid.
22. Ibid.
23. The original US proposal for an arbitration treaty had been put to Pauncefote by Cleveland's first Secretary of State, Walter Q. Gresham, during the spring of 1895. C.D. Davis, *The United States and the First Hague Peace Conference* (Ithaca, NY: Cornell UP, 1962), pp. 24-25; David Steele, *Lord Salisbury: A Political Biography* (London: UCL Press, 1999), pp. 330-32. Hatfield House, Salisbury MSS, 3M/A140, Salisbury to Pauncefote, letter, 7 February 1896, and despt. no. 65, 5 March 1896.
24. Ibid.; Andrew Roberts, *Salisbury: Victorian Titan* (London: Phoenix, 1999), pp. 632-33.
25. Olney to Pauncefote, letter, 11 April 1896, TNA, FO 5/2290.
26. Salisbury to Pauncefote, despt. no. 128, 18 May 1896, TNA, FO 5/2288.
27. Salisbury to Pauncefote, letter, 21 February 1896, Salisbury MSS, 3M/A140.
28. Final Draft Treaty of General Arbitration, 12 January 1897, TNA, FO 5/2330.
29. Charles S. Campbell Jr., *Anglo-American Understanding, 1898-1903* (Baltimore: Johns

Hopkins Press, 1957), p. 6; R.B. Mowat, *The Life of Lord Pauncefote: First Ambassador to the United States* (London: Constable, 1929), pp. 160–202.
30. Salisbury to Pauncefote, despt. no. 128, 18 May 1896, TNA, FO 5/2288.
31. *BD*, i, no. 275.
32. Pauncefote to Salisbury, despt. no. 1, 17 May 1899, TNA, FO 83/1695.
33. R.H. Bacon, *The Life of Lord Fisher of Kilverstone, Admiral of the Fleet*, 2 vols. (London: Hodder and Stoughton, 1929), vol. i, pp. 120–21.
34. Maxwell to Hopwood, letter, 18 May 1899; Pauncefote to Salisbury, despt. no. 2, 19 May 1899, TNA, FO 83/1695; A.J. Marder (ed.), *Fear God and Dread Nought: The Correspondence of Admiral of the Fleet Lord Fisher of Kilverstone*, 3 vols. (London: Jonathan Cape, 1952–59), vol. ii, pp. 131–33, 147 and 167.
35. Salisbury to Pauncefote, despt. no. 6, 31 May 1899, TNA, FO 83/1702.
36. Édouard Descamps, *Essai sur l'organisation de l'arbitrage international; mémoire aux puissances. Projet d'institution d'une Cour permanente d'Arbitrage international adopté par la conférence internationale de Bruxelles* (Brussels, 1896).
37. Pauncefote to Salisbury, letter, 31 May 1899, Salisbury MSS, 3M/A140; Eyffinger, *The 1899 Hague Peace Conference*, pp. 382–83.
38. Ministère des Affaires Étrangères, Commission de Publication des Documents relatifs aux origines de la Guerre de 1914, *Documents Diplomatiques Français*, 3 series (Paris, 1929–57), 1ère série, vol. xv [hereafter cited as *DDF*, i/xv], no. 204.
39. Norman Rich, *Friedrich von Holstein: Politics and Diplomacy in the Era of Bismarck and Wilhelm II*, 2 vols. (Cambridge: Cambridge University Press, 1965), vol. 2, pp. 603–4.
40. J. Lepsius, A. Mendelsohn Bartholdy and F. Thimme (eds), *Die Grosse Politik der Europäischen Kabinette, 1871–1914* (Berlin: Deutsche Verlagsgesellschaft für Politik und Geschichte, 1922–27), vol. xv [hereafter cited as *GP*, xv], no. 4276.
41. Eyffinger, *The 1899 Hague Peace Conference*, pp. 387–88; Pauncefote to Salisbury, letter, 10 June 1899, Salisbury MSS, 3M/A140.
42. Davis, *The United States*, pp.149–50.
43. Rich, *Friedrich von Holstein*, vol. 2, pp. 605–7; Christopher Eick, 'The German Reich at the Hague Peace Conference', on CD-ROM accompanying Frits Kalshoven (ed.) *The Centennial of the First International Peace Conference: Reports and Conclusions* (The Hague: Kluwer Law International, 2000), pp. 10–12.
44. Pauncefote to Salisbury, despt. no. 28, 15 June 1899, TNA, FO 83/1695; Pauncefote to Salisbury, despt. no. 45, 27 June 1899, FO 83/1696; Pauncefote to Salisbury, tel. no. 4, 21 June 1899, FO 83/1698.
45. Davis, *The United States*, p. 155; Pauncefote to Salisbury, letter, 19 June 1899, Salisbury MSS, 3M/A140.
46. *DDF*, i/xv, no. 204.
47. Davis, *The United States*, pp. 146–47.
48. Memo. by Fisher, in Pauncefote to Salisbury, despt. no. 67, 26 July 1899, TNA, FO 881/7473; *GP*, xv, no. 4274.
49. Campbell, *Anglo-American Understanding*, p. 158.
50. Sanderson to Pauncefote, private, 5 June 1899, TNA, FO 83/1702; minute by Salisbury on Pauncefote to Salisbury, despt. no. 19, 8 June 1899, FO 83/1695.
51. J.B. Scott, (ed.), *The Proceedings of the Hague Peace Conferences: The Conference of 1899* (Oxford: OUP, 1920), pp. 235–46.
52. Davis, *The United States*, pp. 111–13.
53. The bullets were so known after the military arsenal at Dum-Dum, near Calcutta, where they were first manufactured. The Dum-Dum bullet consisted of a solid core which, except just at the extreme point of the projectile, was covered by cupro-nickel. The Mark IV had a similar cupro-nickel envelope, but at the point of the bullet was a cylindrical cavity, 0.3 inches deep, over the edge of which the cupro-nickel was turned down. Both were designed to flatten easily in the human body. Knox to Sanderson, letter, 22 June 1899, TNA, FO 83/1702.
54. Memo. by Ardagh enclosed in Pauncefote to Salisbury, despt. no. 27, 15 June 1899, TNA, FO 83/1695.

55. Memo. by Ardagh enclosed in Pauncefote to Salisbury, despt. no. 43, 25 June 1899, TNA, FO 83/1696; Scott, *Proceedings*, pp. 276–80; Davis, *The United States*, pp. 114–15 and 121.
56. Memo. by Ardagh enclosed in Pauncefote to Salisbury, despt. no. 56, 10 July 1899, TNA, FO 83/1696.
57. Davis, *The United States*, p. 117.
58. Cited in R.F. Mackay, *Fisher of Kilverstone* (Oxford: Clarendon Press, 1973), p. 223.
59. Marder, *Fear God and Dread Nought*, vol. i, p. 141.
60. R. Hough, *First Sea Lord: An Authorized Biography of Admiral Lord Fisher* (London: Severn House, 1969), pp. 114–18.
61. Memo. by Fisher and Ardagh in Pauncefote to Salisbury, despt. no. 11, 30 May 1899, FO 83/1702.
62. Memo. by Fisher in Pauncefote to Salisbury, despt. no. 16, 9 June 1899, TNA, FO 83/1702.
63. Davis, *The United States*, pp. 119–21; Scott, *Proceedings*, p. 296.
64. Scott, *Proceedings*, p. 293.
65. Memo. by Fisher in Pauncefote to Salisbury, despt. no. 32, 20 June 1899, TNA, FO 83/1702.
66. Pauncefote to Salisbury, despt. no. 44, 27 June 1899, TNA, FO 881/7473.
67. Ibid., enclosed memos by à Court and Fisher.
68. Pauncefote to Salisbury, despt. no. 48, 30 June 1899, TNA, FO 881/7473.
69. Letter from Admiralty enclosed in Salisbury to Pauncefote, despt. no. 28, 21 June 1899, TNA, FO 83/1702.
70. Davis, *The United States*, p. 131.
71. Pauncefote to Salisbury, despt. no. 35, 22 June 1899, TNA, FO 83/1696.
72. Letter from Admiralty in Salisbury to Pauncefote, despt. no. 52, 28 July 1899, TNA, FO 83/1702.
73. Memo. by Ardagh in Pauncefote to Salisbury, despt. no. 24, 12 June 1899, TNA, FO 881/7473.
74. This provision, usually referred to as the Martens Clause, is currently regarded as applicable to all fields of the laws of war. Prior to its drafting, Ardagh had sought acceptance of an article which asserted that nothing in the chapter relating to belligerents should 'be considered as tending to diminish or suppress the right which belongs to the population of an invaded country to patriotically oppose [sic] the most energetic resistance to their invaders by every means'; enclosures in Pauncefote to Salisbury, despt. no. 52, 6 July 1899, TNA, FO 83/1696.
75. Ibid.
76. Macgregor to Sanderson, letter, 6 July 1899, TNA, FO 83/1702.
77. Scott, *Proceedings*, pp. 100–1; Pauncefote to Salisbury, despt. no. 72, 31 July 1899, TNA, FO 83/1697.
78. Memo. by Fisher in Pauncefote to Salisbury, despt. no. 60, 20 July 1899, TNA, FO 83/1696.
79. Memo. by Fisher in Pauncefote to Salisbury, despt. no. 67, 26 July 1899, TNA, FO 881/7473.
80. Davis, *The United States*, pp. 133–37.
81. Pauncefote to Sanderson, tels., 25 and 26 July 1899, TNA, FO 83/1698; Salisbury to Pauncefote, tel. no. 7P, 27 July 1899; Pauncefote to Salisbury, despt. no. 76, 31 July 1899, FO 881/7473.
82. War Office to FO, 11 October 1899, with enclosures. TNA, FO 881/7473; memo. by Fisher enclosed in Pauncefote to Salisbury, despt. no. 67, 26 July 1899, FO 83/1697; Davis, *The United States*, p. 121. See also K.A. Hamilton, 'The Air in Entente Diplomacy: Great Britain and the International Aerial Navigation Conference of 1910', *International History Review*, iii, 2, (1981), pp.169–200.
83. Salisbury to Pauncefote, despt. no. 55, 25 October 1899, TNA, FO 881/7473.
84. Howard to Salisbury, despt. no. 147, 29 December 1899, TNA, FO 881/7473.

85. *BD*, i, no. 283.
86. Marder, *Anatomy*, p. 347.
87. Memo. by Fisher in Pauncefote to Salisbury, despt. no. 67, 26 July 1899, TNA, FO 83/7473.
88. *BD* i, no. 282.
89. Memo. by Fisher in Pauncefote to Salisbury, despt. no. 67, 26 July 1899, TNA, FO 83/7473.

2

'What we desire is confidence': The Search for an Anglo-German Naval Agreement, 1909–1912

T. G. OTTE

Naval arms races feature prominently in scholarly accounts of Great Power politics before 1914. It is widely accepted that the latter part of the long nineteenth century was intensely navalist. A combination of factors accounted for this. The strategic significance attributed to naval power in an increasingly global international environment was one factor; another was the revolutionary changes in naval technology and battleship design. The rise of new naval powers – Japan, the United States and Germany – alone would have ensured the navalist character of this period.

The Anglo-German naval race, more especially, has occupied a prominent place in studies of the origins of the Great War. The strategic significance of the German challenge has been analysed extensively.[1] Examinations of the attempts, between 1909 and 1912, to arrive at a negotiated settlement of the naval question, meanwhile, have tended to focus on the political aspects of these exchanges. No doubt the perceived political and strategic ramifications of a naval agreement were at the root of its demise. An important sub-theme of the Anglo-German discussions, however, has been neglected – the pursuit of a technical naval agreement. Ultimately, the notion of such an agreement fell stillborn. Nevertheless, it contained forward-looking elements of international competition management that would be developed more fully in the later twentieth century in the shape of confidence-building measures.

Naval arms races were nothing new for the Royal Navy. British diplomats were also well used to dealing with the political consequences of the competitive building of battleships. Naval rivalry with France and Russia was a source of constant friction from the 1880s, and even caused invasion scares in Whitehall. Until 1904–05, Britain was locked in a naval race with the Franco-Russian combination that was more intense, and potentially entailed graver strategic risks, than the later competition with her German cousin.

One key difference between the strategic landscape of the 1890s and that of the last decade before 1914, however, was the extent to which the powers were prepared to commit resources to armaments.[2] The intensity of armaments competition and the rapid pace of technological developments gave the period its own distinctive flavour. Indeed, Britain's pre-war Foreign Secretary, Sir Edward Grey, later reflected that 'the sense of insecurity and fear' caused by the 'enormous growth of armaments' was the underlying cause of the conflict.[3]

Most powers in this period undertook substantial naval construction schemes.[4] For Britain, the efforts of the other powers entailed increased naval expenditure of her own. Already, the expansion and acceleration of the French and Russian programmes of the 1890s had been met by substantial British counter-measures under the 1889 Naval Defence Act and the Spencer programme of 1893–94. Technological changes in battleship design and metallurgical advances caused further expenditure hikes. The introduction of larger calibre guns, increased displacement of capital ships, and the concomitant need for more extensive armour-plating drove up costs. Between 1889 and 1904, production costs per battleship alone doubled, those per armoured cruiser increased fivefold.[5]

This is not to argue that Britain suffered from a degree of financial overstretch. If anything, the nation's finances were in rude health. Even the extraordinary additional expenditure caused by the Boer War had not affected Britain's underlying financial robustness.[6] The real problem was not financial capacity. The real problem, under Conservative and Liberal administrations alike, was the reluctance of Britain's political élite to commit a growing portion of the budget to arms expenditure.[7]

This is not the place to reopen the historiographical controversy surrounding the origins and nature of the so-called 'Dreadnought revolution', but concerns about the perceived need to economise informed naval policy making around 1904–05. The introduction of the new, 'all-big-guns' battleship held out the promise of a sizeable reduction in naval expenditure, especially since it was accompanied by the decommissioning of older types of vessels. Ironically, the launch of this new class of warship raised international naval competition to a new level.

Much attention has been given to the 'Anglo-German' aspect of the 'Dreadnought revolution'. But it is worth recalling that the development of this new warship was not caused by concerns about Germany. Nor was the scheme of the First Sea Lord, Admiral Sir John Fisher, for the redistribution of the fleet a reflection of Germany's rise as a naval power. Both were the result of technological changes; and they were informed by 'global [strategic] thinking'. They were intended to meet the contingencies arising out of the antagonism with the Franco-Russian combination.[8] But the disruption of the European equilibrium by Russia's defeat at the hands of Japan in 1905 magnified the emergence of Germany as a naval power.[9]

It was against this backdrop that British policy-makers had to devise the means for dealing with Berlin's naval armaments programme. There were also competing financial demands on the Liberal Government. These reflected, and in turn reinforced, ideological fissures within the ruling party. At least initially, Radical 'economists' and Liberal Imperialists were agreed on the desirability of reducing naval spending.[10] Grey, too, was inclined to accept this in principle, but insisted on reciprocity. Any British reduction should be contingent upon similar statements of intent by the other powers, more especially by Germany.[11] This was the nub of the problem. The new government had committed itself to some form of armaments reduction. The 'Two-Power-Standard', as the measurement of Britain's naval superiority, however, was not negotiable, even if there was no longer a clear understanding as to what precisely constituted that standard.[12]

The internal struggle between 'economists' and 'navalists' became wound up in the Russian initiative of April 1906 for a second peace conference at The Hague. The Admiralty resisted Radical pressure for a reduction of the Cawdor programme, inherited from the Conservatives, from four capital ships to three.[13] For the Chancellor of the Exchequer, Herbert Henry Asquith, himself instinctively on the imperialist side of the divide, there was 'a prima facie case for a considerably larger reduction' still. The impasse was eventually broken by R.B. Haldane, the Secretary of State for War, who proposed a reduction of the construction programme from four to three in 1906–07 and to two-plus-one ships in the following year. This meant that two vessels were to be laid down, and the third, though contracted, was to be held in suspense. Its construction was contingent upon the success or failure of arms limitation talks at The Hague Conference.[14]

In this fashion, the requirements of party management were reconciled with the imperatives of naval defence. Radical sensibilities were appeased, but the Admiralty had not been forced to make unpalatable sacrifices. In fact, the reduction envisaged under Haldane's compromise formula was easily affordable. If anything, the elimination of the Russian navy at Tsushima, the improved relations with France, the technological advance represented by the Dreadnought class and, finally, the numerical superiority in pre-Dreadnought capital ships, had enhanced Britain's naval position. This was readily acknowledged by the Admiralty. As Fisher declared with characteristic exuberance, Britain's 'present margin of superiority over Germany (*our only possible foe for years*), is so great as to render it absurd in the extreme to talk of anything endangering our naval supremacy, *even if we stopped all shipbuilding altogether!!!*'[15]

Britain's strong naval position notwithstanding, unilateral reductions had little to recommend themselves to Grey as a viable diplomatic strategy. Between mid-1906 and spring 1907 he concentrated his efforts on pressing the question of naval armaments on the other powers. His insistence on a multilateral settlement was sensible enough. In practice, however, it rendered such a settlement impossible. For one thing, the French Government refused even to countenance a reduction in its naval programme, 'not even if we offered her a defensive alliance with ourselves'. Fear of increased dependence on Britain in the face of a militarily superior Germany counselled against such a step. For another, the Roosevelt administration was reluctant to commit itself to a definitive course of action.[16]

The key, however, lay in Berlin. German opposition to naval arms limitation talks at The Hague remained insuperable. Curbing the construction programme was contrary to the logic of *Flottenpolitik*. In so far as the High Seas Battle Fleet had any kind of strategic rationale, it was meant to operate against Britain, either to force Britain into an alliance with Germany or in preparation of a hegemonial conflict.[17] Geopolitical grand designs aside, much political capital was tied up in the naval programme as part of a wider strategy of consolidating the latent fragility of the imperial regime. Concessions to Britain at sea, therefore, entailed not inconsiderable domestic risks.[18] The well-ordered institutional chaos of Wilhelmine Germany further complicated Anglo-German naval talks. Bureaucratic turf wars between the *Reichsmarineamt* (RMA) under its charismatic State Secretary, Grand Admiral Alfred von Tirpitz, and the Chancellor, as the political head of the *Auswärtiges Amt*, thus added a further dimension to the naval question. The balance of internal influence between these competing centres of authority depended largely on Germany's volatile monarch, Emperor Wilhelm II.[19]

Germany's uncompromising stance was further underlined by the publication, in November 1907, of the 1908 *Novelle*. This amendment of the naval legislation reduced the active service period of all capital ships to twenty years, thus increasing the German navy's effective strength as obsolete vessels would be replaced sooner. The *Novelle* also increased the pace of construction from three to four keels per annum. Finally, it presaged further expansion after the *Novelle*'s expiry in 1912. As Eyre Crowe, senior clerk in the Foreign Office's Western Department, commented: 'we must reckon with it as a hard fact that, whatever the cost, the German government will build the big and powerful navy, and construct the naval works, which they have so systematically planned'.[20]

Following the failure to reach an understanding on naval armaments reduction, the British Government had little choice but to lay down the third dreadnought suspended under the Haldane compromise formula. Furthermore, in response to the *Novelle*, the Admiralty successfully agitated for the construction of an additional capital ship.[21] From 1908 onwards, British diplomacy pursued a twin-track strategy towards Germany. It was a mixture of conciliation and compulsion. It held out the prospect of a naval agreement as an inducement, while simultaneously underlining Britain's resolve to maintain the established margin of superiority so as to compel Berlin to moderate its naval programme. This reflected the growing conviction amongst senior diplomats that it was 'a fruitless task to attempt to purchase friendly relations with Germany by repeated concessions'.[22] In the short term, this mixture of conciliation and firmness yielded no results. Neither signals of a willingness to negotiate nor reaffirmations of resolve brought the Germans to the negotiating table.[23]

In the face of Berlin's persistent refusal to enter into bilateral talks, Asquith, by now Prime Minister, steered another increase in Britain's construction programme through Cabinet at the end of 1908. Already in November, he had reiterated his government's commitment to the 'Two-Power-Standard', now redefined as superiority by a margin of 10 per cent.[24] Ironically, German officials interpreted this as a sign of British weakness, since the Royal Navy was weaker than the combined strength of the United States and Germany.[25]

At the beginning of 1909, Anglo-German relations reached their nadir with the so-called 'acceleration crisis', sparked by intelligence that Tirpitz covertly sought to increase construction by hoarding materials in advance of the official laying down of ships. In breach of the law, he also placed contracts for the battleship *Oldenburg* and the battle-cruiser *Goeben* in advance of parliamentary approval.[26] The acceleration led to sharp exchanges between Downing Street and the Wilhelmstrasse. It also plunged the Cabinet into another crisis over the 1909–10 estimates. Caught between Admiralty demands for six additional dreadnoughts and Radical resistance to any expenditure increases, the Government eventually settled for a compromise. Four ships were to be laid down immediately, with provisions for a further four, contingent upon German progress. It was an ingeniously Asquithian solution. It accommodated Radical demands. But, in practice, it meant the building of eight ships.[27]

The 'acceleration crisis' was significant for the future course of Anglo-German naval relations on a number of counts. At home, the Asquith Government came under pressure from a well-organised 'We-want-eight, and-we-won't-wait' navalist agitation. This, and the concurrent naval scare, forced Grey and Asquith into making further emphatic declarations of the Government's determination to defend Britain's naval superiority.

Radical criticism, meanwhile, was contained by the revelation of the abortive arms limitation initiative.[28]

In terms of the diplomatic dynamics of Anglo-German relations, this revelation placed Berlin at a disadvantage. The latter was forced to acknowledge that Britain had indeed offered naval talks. Crucially, evidence now emerged of growing financial strains on Germany as a result of her naval build-up and the formation of a shipbuilders' cartel.[29] At last, the Germans seemed prepared to move. Alfred von Kiderlen-Wächter, the Under-Secretary at the *Auswärtiges Amt*, hinted informally at 'the desirability of a Naval Convention between the two countries'. Apparently officially-inspired articles in major German newspapers argued along similar lines. Britain's new ambassador at Berlin, Sir Edward Goschen, seized on this as evidence that Berlin was seeking a way out of its present predicament. Naval pressure should be kept up, he urged: 'I think that as soon as the Germans are absolutely convinced, *and they have nearly reached that point*, that we have made up our minds to maintain our superiority at sea ..., they will calm down and ... be glad ... to ease the strain on their finances by dropping a ship or two.'[30]

Goschen's analysis was shrewd. Wilhelmstrasse planning had, indeed, come to focus on an Anglo-German agreement. In June, an interdepartmental conference at the Reich chancellery paved the way for a diplomatic initiative in that direction.[31] In Britain, meanwhile, Goschen's advice reinforced the thinking of senior Cabinet ministers. At the end of July 1909, the First Lord of the Admiralty, Reginald McKenna, announced the release of the four reserve dreadnoughts. It was a clear signal of the Government's determination to maintain Britain's preponderance in capital ships.[32]

By the summer of 1909, Grey's diplomacy appeared to have manoeuvred Germany into the position which he had designated for her since 1906. Less than a month after McKenna's announcement, Theobald von Bethmann Hollweg, the new German Chancellor, proposed a 'scheme for a general good understanding'. This would be based on a naval arrangement, enshrining a 4:3 ratio in capital ships in Britain's favour. In return, Bethmann was prepared to drop the 1912 *Novelle*.[33] The Chancellor's démarche not only seemed to vindicate Grey's policy of compellance tempered by conciliation; it also met practical concerns on the part of Britain. Since the summer of 1908, Eyre Crowe had been pressing for Whitehall-internal discussions to determine 'at least the outlines of a workable scheme [of arms limitation]'. The practical difficulties involved were substantial. Determining 'a certain proportionality' between the British and German programmes was one problem. Providing for the maintenance of that ratio within the overall framework of the 'Two-Power-Standard' in the eventuality of a third naval Power emerging, was another.[34] Unsurprisingly, in light of such practical difficulties, no such outline ever emerged.

The positions of the two governments were far apart from the beginning. Both, moreover, projected onto the other their own difficulties. In London, the Radicals' clamour for urgent retrenchment notwithstanding, Grey and his advisers concluded that Germany had reached the end of her financial tether.[35] In Berlin, the prevailing impression was that London's tough language scarcely concealed the acute financial pressures on the Liberal Government.[36] Both sides concluded that they had a decisive degree of leverage over the other. And both were wrong.

The core problem was Bethmann's notion of a bilateral, political agreement to accompany a naval convention. At Grey's suggestion the Cabinet decided against entering into arrangements with Germany that might be construed as incompatible with 'the [existing] relations and friendships' with France and Russia.[37] Moreover, the German Chancellor had not reckoned with Tirpitz's resistance. A technocrat himself, Bethmann was reluctant to go against expert advice; and the Navy Secretary, sensing the Chancellor's weakness, excelled at technical obfuscation and bureaucratic obstruction.[38] In consequence, Bethmann's more detailed proposal in October 1909 was substantially diluted. The Chancellor outlined a colonial agreement and a general political agreement with reference to Europe. On the naval question, his scheme was now less conciliatory. A limitation of the German programme was no longer on offer. Instead, he suggested merely 'a relaxation of the tempo' of construction, within the limits of the *Novelle*.[39]

Bethmann's subsequent effort, in November 1909, to sketch out the proposed political agreement, pushed the whole notion of an Anglo-German understanding beyond practical politics. Naval and political talks had to proceed *pari passu*, and the agreement was to contain a reciprocal neutrality pledge by both parties. Given Russia's continued weakness and Germany's military superiority over France, such an agreement was tantamount to giving Germany a free hand on the continent:

> [N]o naval agreement can be of any permanent usefulness to restore friendly relations between Germany and England unless it contains some provisions for the modification of the present German naval programme. No political agreement between the two Powers would be acceptable on the lines suggested by [Bethmann], which are so far-reaching as to be likely to disturb the political equilibrium of Europe.[40]

After the high hopes of the summer, by the turn of 1909–10, senior diplomats conceded that efforts to compel Germany into meaningful naval talks had failed. Britain's chargé d'affaires at Berlin, Count John de Salis, observed that the gap between Berlin's obvious financial embarrassments and 'a genuine desire to limit naval armaments, is a long step'.[41] An official German communiqué affirmed that there could be no reduction in the naval construction programme. It was, as Crowe noted, 'the funeral ceremony of the whole negotiation'.[42] The main attraction of naval talks with Berlin had always lain in the prospect of a curtailment of the German programme. In turn, this would have made further large-scale British expenditure unnecessary: 'It is now abundantly clear that this hope must be definitely abandoned', Crowe commented.[43] Goschen offered a more nuanced assessment. There was, he observed, a genuine desire in official German circles for an understanding with Britain. But he warned that Berlin was 'not keen on a naval understanding on its merits', but regarded it 'as a means for squeezing us on other things'.[44]

Grey and Asquith were not prepared to abandon all hope of coming to an arrangement with the Germans. Nevertheless, further discussions were suspended pending the forthcoming general election. Britain's naval build-up continued. The Navy estimates for 1910–11 envisaged another large construction programme, with provisions for a further five dreadnoughts.[45] The Asquith Government, however, was no longer fully committed to the strategy of compulsion. Britain's own naval expenditure was 'at the very top of the wave', the Prime Minister suggested in the House of Commons in July 1910.[46]

In part, Asquith's conciliatory language reflected the increased influence of the Radicals within the government following the Liberals' loss of their parliamentary majority in the February elections. But it was also a conscious attempt to resurrect the naval talks. And in this, he succeeded. Following a hint by Bethmann that Germany was not opposed to renewed negotiations, the Cabinet forced a somewhat reluctant Grey to reopen talks. A memorandum, drafted by the Foreign Office, but amended by a Cabinet committee, indicated the principal points of an understanding. The British Government would no longer insist on an actual reduction in the German naval programme. Instead, a German pledge not to increase the existing programme would suffice. Linked to this should be a separate agreement on the reciprocal and confidential exchange of technical information between the two Admiralties at regular intervals.[47]

Grey's scheme was significantly more modest than earlier proposals of a comprehensive Anglo-German naval agreement. To some extent this took account of the political hurdles on both sides. It was also an acknowledgement of the complexities of the naval arms race. Grey's initiative opened a new phase in the Anglo-German naval talks. In conceptual terms, the proposed technical agreement marked a significant deviation from previous international practice. The exchange of information concerning the specifications of the ships under construction and the actual progress of construction in the respective yards amounted to a form of confidence-building measure. Not the least benefit of such data exchanges lay in the prevention of further naval scares such as had complicated relations between the two countries in recent years. In essence, the projected agreement aimed at removing the most pressing elements of friction without addressing the underlying causes of that friction. It was a form of competition management. The agreement was to furnish both governments with a new political tool for the containment of the Anglo-German antagonism.

The Wilhelmstrasse reacted cautiously to the latest British initative. In conversation with the German Chancellor, Goschen emphasised that more precise knowledge of the German programme might, in time, lead to a reduction in British naval construction 'as far as we safely could having due regard to our position as a Power to whom strength at sea meant everything'.[48]

Lack of proper policy coordination on the British side complicated the talks. Apparently on his own private initiative, the new Naval Attaché at Berlin, Captain Hugh R. Watson, urged Tirpitz to accept a reciprocal exchange and inspection regime. This would '[p]romote good feelings between the navies of the two countries, and would assist towards a good understanding ... generally.' That phrase, of course, was politically highly charged; and, on receipt of Watson's report, the Foreign Office erupted in fury. The captain's 'independent diplomatizing' was highly irregular and liable to do harm, especially given the Kaiser's 'well-known idiosyncrasies' and his penchant for personal diplomacy through informal channels.[49]

The Admiralty eventually disowned Watson's proceedings. By then, the damage had been done. The chief of the Kaiser's Navy Cabinet, Admiral Georg von Müller, indicated support for the proposed scheme. Watson's German opposite number in London, Captain Wilhelm Widenmann, meanwhile, suggested direct, high-level talks between the naval authorities of the two countries.[50] Watson's initiative threatened to decouple the technical aspects of the proposed exchange arrangement from its wider purpose of managing the naval competition. The restoration of political control over the negotiations was therefore essential.[51] The Naval Attaché's suggestion of frequent meetings between middle-ranking naval officers caused further embarrassment, especially in light of recent German practice which accompanied 'ostentatious fraternization' with a vigorous press campaign designed to impress France and Russia with a sense of British unreliability.[52]

Bethmann's official response to Grey's August memorandum underscored the political nature of the naval question. The Chancellor had no objection to the reciprocal exchange of information and inspections by the naval attachés. Berlin, he indicated, was ready to modify the rate of shipbuilding within the limits of the 1908 *Novelle*. If, however, Britain sought a more comprehensive naval arrangement, 'assured good relations should form a prior indispensable condition'. Having enumerated various instances of alleged British unfriendliness to Germany in various Near Eastern questions, the Chancellor insisted on 'a simultaneous political exchange of views' in order to find a 'political formula'.[53] Bethmann's interview with the Ambassador was 'perfectly friendly' in tone, but did not move matters forward. The Chancellor's exposition was couched in vague language. Finally, whilst it was understood in London that Bethmann regarded a political agreement as a *sine qua non* of a naval understanding, it remained unclear whether he was prepared to accept the interchange proposal on its own or only as part of a general understanding.[54]

In a detailed examination of Bethmann's memorandum, Eyre Crowe averred that the naval talks were 'one of those cases where the whole essence and principle of an agreement consists in the detailed particulars and that without the particulars there is really nothing to agree upon'. Entering into a pledge to reduce armaments, and to leave the details for further discussions was a recipe for failure. At any rate, since the German Chancellor insisted on a political understanding as a precondition of a naval agreement, the matter had lost all practical importance.[55] Crowe's suggestion that a draft outline of a naval agreement be prepared before any further official talks with the German Government reflected the strained relations between Foreign Office and Admiralty more than it helped to clarify official thinking on the subject.[56]

Bethmann's apparent insistence on a linkage was unwelcome news to senior officials in London. Crowe had consistently argued that the German Government had 'merely held out the bait of their possibly consenting to such agreement [on naval armaments limitation], for the purpose of getting their political agreement'. There was the added complication of Bethmann's fraught relations with Tirpitz. The Chancellor's own sincerity was never questioned. What was in doubt was his ability to prevail over the Grand Admiral.[57]

For his part, Goschen shared the Foreign Office's misgivings. Germany's ultimate objective was hegemony over continental Europe. To achieve this, she had to neutralise Britain's naval strength: 'They want to have an understanding which would have that effect.' The ambassador conceded that a political understanding would allow for a degree of naval retrenchment. But the price would be a '[w]edge between G[rea]t B[ritai]n and France and Russia and our possible isolation'.⁵⁸ There was the risk of relations turning sour were the talks to 'run into the sand'. On the other hand, the talks might help to 'clear the air'. Whether the eventual outcome was an informal Anglo-German détente or a more definite understanding, no progress was possible unless the German Government was forced 'to respect us as a Naval Power whose supremacy they cannot dispute. If we depart from that principle they will not think it worth conciliating [us] and our relations will get worse than ever.'⁵⁹ These were weighty reasons for Grey to proceed with caution. The impending second general election of December 1910 caused further delays. Ultimately, Bethmann broke the impasse by unconditionally accepting the proposal for an exchange arrangement.⁶⁰

At the end of January 1911, Grey moved to initiate final talks on the details of the projected technical agreement. He suggested a four-point arrangement. The two governments were to exchange information on the dimensions of the ships laid down; on their armoured protection, armaments, and speed; and on the construction schedule and completion of individual vessels. Reciprocity was crucial since the specifications of British ships were published in the Navy Estimates, while the German data become public knowledge only some time after the vessels had been launched. Finally, the naval attachés should be allowed periodically to inspect government and private shipyards. Given the rapid advances in naval technology, Grey stipulated that the agreement had to be 'sufficiently elastic' to allow for the inclusion of additional information which might become relevant at a future date.⁶¹

Progress was slow. While Grey gave Count Paul von Wolff-Metternich, the German Ambassador, assurances of Britain's desire for improved relations with Germany, the Kaiser cast doubt on the reciprocal exchange of information.⁶² In March 1911, Grey sought to break the deadlock. The British response to Bethmann's October memorandum was drafted by Grey, but once again scrutinised and amended by a Cabinet committee. It emphasised the 'considerable effect' an exchange agreement would have 'in convincing public opinion in both countries that the two Governments do not cherish any hostile designs against each other'. Assurances were given that Britain's existing agreements were not aimed against Germany and, indeed, were not based on prior political agreements. In the same manner, whatever arrangement might be arrived at, this was not to disrupt the existing ties with France and Russia. Discussions about a 'political formula' were not ruled out, but greater emphasis was placed on agreements on the Baghdad and southern Persian railways questions, the construction of which had long been a source of Anglo-German friction. Crucially, the British Government accepted Bethmann's point 'that some wider agreement is essential to any arrangement about naval expenditure'.[63]

As the ongoing struggle between Tirpitz and the German Chancellor threatened further delays,[64] Grey pressed for the resumption of technical talks in a Commons debate on Radical amendments of the Navy Estimates on 13 March. He prefaced his remarks by stressing the financial burden of the continued 'rivalry of armaments'. This threatened 'in the long run [to] break civilization down.' Grey painted a stark picture of all the powers being plunged into domestic turmoil because they had begun 'to make hunger by taxation'. The greatest danger facing Europe was not war; it was 'the danger ... of bleeding to death in time of peace'.[65]

Grey's speech went some way towards assuring his domestic critics of the Government's commitment, at least in principle, to curbing defence expenditure. But if it was meant to reinvigorate the naval discussions, it failed. At least part of the reason lay in Goschen's decision to delay transmitting the March memorandum until the matter of data exchanges had been settled. This reversed the sequence of Grey's communications addressed to Berlin. His dark prognostications about continued armaments competition now preceded his practical proposals contained in the memorandum. As a result, the Germans attached far greater significance to his public utterances than the Foreign Secretary had intended.[66]

Grey's speech put senior officials in Berlin 'in high good humour'.[67] It confirmed German assumptions that the financial pressures on Britain had become unbearable. There been an appreciable softening of the British position since 1909. Indeed, Widenmann now detected the tacit replacement of the 'Two-Power-Standard' by a '"Two-to-Three-Standard"', the true objective of Tirpitz's strategy. The speeches by Grey and McKenna seemed to signal Britain's surrender in the face of rising defence expenditure. Under Tirpitz's influence, the Emperor arrived at the same conclusion: 'An arrangement can only be political and, broadly conceived, [must] extend across the whole globe.'[68]

The consequences of Goschen's decision were far-reaching. It detached the technical from any wider agreement, and so reduced its potential utility as a means of détente in Anglo-German relations. Bethmann accepted Grey's proposals of February 1911 as the basis of negotiations for a technical agreement. On the wider question, however, the perception of increased German leverage made it practically impossible for the Chancellor, had he wished to do so, to overcome Tirpitz's resistance. Yet even in the matter of the data exchanges, Berlin's attitude hardened. On the reciprocity question, the German reply merely stipulated simultaneous exchanges in the autumn of each year, but gave no assurances of the kind sought by the Admiralty. Even on the question of shipyard inspections, the reply was guarded. This did not augur well for the projected confidence-building measures, as Crowe minuted: 'What we desire is an arrangement that shall inspire confidence. As at present suggested the terms ... are unfortunately calculated ... to give rise to a suspicion that fair and straight dealing will be evaded.'[69]

In a further twist, Kiderlen-Wächter, by now State Secretary, impressed upon Goschen the need for simultaneous exchanges, and hinted that they ought to include a binding statement on the numbers of ships to be laid down. Though seemingly innocuous, this proposal was problematic. Only the simultaneous exchange of the ships' specifications in the spring, after both sides had finalised their naval budgets, could remove the prevailing atmosphere of suspicion, Watson argued. It would also remove the incentive of '"going one better in the dark" ... in bringing out something better than it is probable the other has'. Finally, issuing a binding statement of the numbers to be laid down in advance of the Navy Estimates would still allow Germany to increase her construction programme in a new *Novelle*. The attaché's comments were seized upon by Crowe and Sir Arthur Nicolson, the Permanent Under-Secretary at the Foreign Office, as an attempt by Berlin to include what amounted to an arms limitation clause in the arrangement. If Britain were bound under such an agreement, she would be unable to respond to increases in the programmes of Germany's allies or other powers secretly aided by her.[70]

It was only following Bethmann's communication on the data exchanges that Goschen submitted Grey's memorandum on the wider question. The Chancellor's reaction was not encouraging. The settlement of Near Eastern railway questions was an insufficient return for an agreement on the mutual reduction of naval expenditure. Bethmann once more insisted on 'a good understanding ... before any reduction of naval armaments could be made'.[71]

The German stance hardened appreciably at the end of March when Bethmann used a speech in the *Reichstag* to dismiss notions of international arbitration and arms limitation as Utopian.[72] There was no obvious way out of the impasse. As Goschen observed, the only acceptable agreement was one under which Germany recognised Britain's 'undoubted superiority at sea, against all likely combinations'. The necessary counter-concession, 'a political understanding ... we in our turn could never accept'.[73]

Bethmann had by no means abandoned his plans for an agreement. But faced with strong opposition by the RMA, and convinced that Britain's position was weakening, he raised the stakes.[74] He insisted on a political agreement with a non-aggression clause. A reduction of armaments, however, was no longer possible. In response, Crowe observed that German diplomacy had repeatedly manoeuvred Britain into making vital concessions. Her previous opposition to accepting the post-1908 German construction programme as the basis of talks had been abandoned; and so had her refusal to entertain the idea of a political agreement. Britain had been induced to discuss a 'political formula', but Bethmann had 'throw[n] the naval agreement overboard altogether'. Britain now faced increased German demands and the 'imminent risk of practically breaking up the entente with France and Russia'. Nicolson's analysis ran along similar lines: unless prepared 'to reverse our foreign policy of preserving the equilibrium in Europe, we cannot tie our hands'. Any political formula required prior consultation with France and Russia. The Foreign Secretary also conceded that Bethmann's reply was 'most unsatisfactory'.[75]

German diplomacy kept pressing for a political arrangement between the two countries. A reciprocal undertaking not to join in military operations against each other, Metternich impressed upon Grey, 'would be more effective than anything else'. Britain's current ties with France and Russia were no obstacle to this.[76] This was little more than a revised version of Bethmann's original demand for a neutrality agreement. The implicit inclusion of Britain's *entente* partners was no concession to Britain. It was an extension of that demand.

Under these circumstances, Grey sought to salvage at least the technical agreement. His initiative, in June 1911, envisaged simultaneous exchanges (a concession to the Germans), but in the spring, following the publication of the naval estimates. Detailed information on the vessels' specifications could realistically only be imparted once construction had commenced. As to the suggestion of a binding statement on numbers, Grey called Bethmann's bluff. Such a proviso seemed more suitable to an arms limitation or reduction agreement. Grey laid particular stress on periodic inspections by the naval attachés of naval shipyards.[77]

In the end, on 27 June 1911, Berlin decided to accept Grey's proposals.[78] Much political energy had been expended to establish agreement on the need for such confidence-building measures. That it had taken a whole year to get this far was a reflection of the complexities of the naval arms race. And yet, as a result of the Agadir crisis in July 1911, the technical agreement was not finalised.

Agadir soured Anglo-German relations. In the naval question, the German decision to move the publication of the navy budget to March, to coincide with the British estimates, introduced an element of opacity into the naval race since it no longer allowed the British to base their estimates on the known German building programme. This step thus ran counter to the precepts of the projected technical agreement, which was meant to create greater transparency.[79] British assumptions of deliberate German provocation were strongly influenced by Agadir, but were not an accurate reading of the situation. At the root of the delay was the fierce battle between the RMA and Bethmann, who had, at least temporarily, the upper hand over Tirpitz. The Chancellor continued to work for an arrangement with Britain, and sought to torpedo plans for a further *Novelle*.[80]

Following encouraging hints by Metternich, Grey made a final attempt to revive talks for an exchange arrangement in early 1912.[81] The circumstances seemed propitious. There were no foreign crises, threatening to complicate Anglo-German naval talks; and neither government faced elections. Indeed, in a mirror image of the 1910 elections, the January 1912 *Reichstag* elections had produced a massive swing to the socialists and robbed the pro-government 'bloc' of its majority. Under such circumstances, a naval compromise seemed more likely. Any optimism was short-lived, however. Although Goschen opened discussions with Kiderlen-Wächter, the notion of a more narrowly focused technical agreement that excluded political matters ultimately sank without a trace following the failure of Haldane's mission to Berlin in February.[82]

Neither Haldane nor later Winston Churchill were able to restart the naval talks. Nevertheless, by 1913, the Anglo-German naval race was over. The shift in German defence spending to the army under the 1913 *Wehrvorlage* amounted to a unilateral declaration of naval arms limitation on Berlin's part. By then, British diplomats had concluded that a resumption of naval talks would impede the emerging détente with Germany.[83] It was the combination of Germany's precarious finances and the shift in the military balance of power in Europe following Russia's revival after 1912 that brought the naval race to a close.

Grey's search for common ground through confidence-building measures was a sophisticated attempt to manage antagonistic relations. To an extent it had been forced upon him by the earlier failure of attempts to negotiate a comprehensive naval agreement with Berlin, one that safeguarded British superiority at sea without sacrificing the entente arrangements. Ultimately, this more modest scheme also failed. Mutual misperceptions, German failure to appreciate Britain's defensive strength, and the chaotic ways of Berlin decision-makers ensured that it remained ahead of its time.

NOTES

1. The classic studies remain A.J. Marder, *From Dreadnought to Scapa Flow*, 5 vols. (London: Frank Cass, 1961–70); E.L. Woodward, *Great Britain and the German Navy* (London: Frank Cass, reprint edn, 1964); P.M. Kennedy, *The Rise of the Anglo-German Antagonism, 1860–1914* (London: Ashfield, 1987).
2. See the statistics in D. Stevenson, *Armaments and the Coming of War: Europe, 1904–1914* (Oxford: Clarendon, 1996), pp. 2–9.
3. Viscount Grey of Fallodon, *Twenty-Five Years, 1892–1916*, 2 vols. (New York: Frederick Stokes, 1925), i, p. 90.
4. Memo. McKenna, 'Battleship Building Programmes of Great Britain, Germany, France, United States, Italy and Austria', 14 July 1909, The National Archives, Kew [hereafter TNA], CAB 37/100/97. See J.A. Grant, 'The Arms Trade in Eastern Europe, 1870–1914', in D.J. Stoker Jr. and J.A. Grant (eds), *Girding for Battle: The Arms Trade in a Global Perspective, 1815–1940* (Westport, CT: Praeger, 2003), pp. 34–38.
5. Memo. Spencer, 'Naval Estimates 1893–94', 13 December 1893, TNA, CAB 37/34/59. For details of expenditure see J.T. Sumida, *In Defence of Naval Supremacy: Finance, Technology, and British Naval Policy, 1889–1914* (London: Routledge, reprint ed., 1991), pp.18–20.
6. For the notion of overstretch and incipient decline, see P.M. Kennedy, *The Rise and Fall of the Great Powers: Economic Change and Military Conflict, 1500–2000* (London: Fontana, reprint ed., 1989), pp.290–99; A.L. Friedberg, *The Weary Titan: Britain and the Experience of Relative Decline, 1895–1905* (Princeton, NJ: Princeton University Press, 1988), pp. 99–134. For an effective critique, see K. Neilson, '"Greatly Exaggerated": The Myth of the Decline of Great Britain before 1914', *International History Review*, xiii, 4 (1991), pp. 695–725.
7. Hicks Beach to Salisbury, 13 September 1901, St. Aldwyn MSS, Gloucestershire Record Office, PCC/34; memo. Tweedmouth, 'Navy Estimates, 1908–09', 18 December 1907, TNA, CAB 37/90/112.
8. Neilson, '"Greatly Exaggerated"', p.701. For the technological changes, see Bethell to Fisher, 22 May 1905, McKenna MSS, Churchill College Archive Centre, MCKN 3/4.
9. Memo. Battenberg, 7 January 1905, TNA, ADM 116/900B; R.F. Mackay, 'The Admiralty, the German Navy and the Redistribution of the British Fleet, 1904–05', *Mariner's Mirror*, lvi, 3 (1970), pp. 341–46.
10. See speeches by Campbell-Bannerman and Haldane, *The Times*, 22 December 1905 and 15 September 1906. For a discussion of the background, see the author's 'Problems of Continuity: The 1906 General Election and Foreign Policy', *Journal of Liberal History*, 54 (2007), pp. 6–13, 21.
11. Minute Grey, n.d., on Dumas to Whitehead (NA Report no. 20), 4 July 1906, TNA, FO 371/78/23178.
12. Memo. Clarke, 'Notes on Comparative Naval Strength', 1906, Campbell-Bannerman MSS, British Library, ADD.MSS. 41213; A.T. Sidorowicz, 'The British Government, the Hague Peace Conference of 1907, and the Armaments Question', in B.J.C. McKercher (ed.), *Arms Limitation and Disarmament: Restraints on War, 1899–1939* (Westport, CT: Praeger, 1992), pp. 3–4.
13. Memo. Tweedmouth, 'Naval Estimates, 1907–08', 26 June 1906, TNA, CAB 37/83/60.
14. Memo. Asquith, 'Naval Expenditure', 8 July 1906, and Tweedmouth, 'Memorandum relative to meeting, under presidency of the Prime Minister, on Thursday, 12 July', 17 July 1906, ibid. /63 and 65.
15. Fisher to Tweedmouth, ? September 1906, in A.J. Marder (ed.), *Fear God and Dread Nought: The Correspondence of Admiral of the Fleet, Lord Fisher of Kilverstone*, 3 vols. (London: Jonathan Cape, 1952–59), ii, p. 91 (original emphasis).
16. Bertie to Grey (private), 1 June 1906, G.P. Gooch and H.W.V. Temperley (eds), *British Documents on the Origins of the War, 1898–1914*, 11 vols. (London: HMSO, 1926–38) viii, no. 160 [hereafter *BD*]; Roosevelt to Grey (private), 22 October 1906, Grey MSS, TNA, FO 800/110.

17. 'Denkschrift' Tirpitz, July 1897, in V.R. Berghahn and W. Deist (eds), *Rüstung im Zeichen der wilhelminische Weltpolitik: Grundlegende Dokumente, 1890–1914* (Düsseldorf: Droste, 1988), no. II/10; see also P.M. Kennedy, *Strategy and Diplomacy, 1870–1945: Eight Studies* (London: Fontana, 2nd edn, 1989), pp. 130–35.
18. For a succinct summary of the argument, J. Steinberg, *Yesterday's Deterrent: Tirpitz and the Birth of the German Battle Fleet* (London: Macdonald, 1965), pp. 31-60; V.R. Berghahn, 'Der Tirpitz-Plan und die Krise des preussisch-deutschen Herrschaftssystems', in H. Schottelius and W. Deist (eds), *Marine und Marinepolitik im kaiserlichen Deutschland, 1871–1914* (Düsseldorf: Droste, 2nd ed. 1981), pp. 89–115.
19. J.C.G. Röhl, *The Kaiser and His Court: Wilhelm II and the Government of Germany* (Cambridge: Cambridge University Press, 1996), pp. 107–30; P.M. Kennedy, 'The Kaiser and German *Weltpolitik*: Reflexions on Wilhelm II's Place in the Making of German Foreign Policy', in J.C.G. Röhl and N. Sombart (eds), *Kaiser Wilhelm II – New Interpretations: The Corfu Papers* (Cambridge: Cambridge University Press, 1982), pp. 143–68.
20. Minute Crowe, 13 January 1908, on Lascelles to Grey (no. 9), 9 January 1908, TNA, FO 371/457/1185. For the 1908 amendment, see J. Steinberg, 'The Novelle of 1908: Necessities and Choices in the Anglo-German Naval Arms Race', *Transactions of the Royal Historical Society*, xxi, 5 (1971), pp. 25–44; V.R. Berghahn, *Der Tirpitz-Plan: Genesis und Verfall einer innenpolitischen Krisenstrategie* (Düsseldorf: Droste, 1971), pp. 556–91.
21. Memo. Tweedmouth, 'Naval Estimates, 1908–09', 18 December 1907, TNA, CAB 37/90/112; Fisher to McKenna, 22 December 1908, McKenna MSS, MCKN 3/4/23; also B. Semmel, *Liberalism and Naval Strategy: Ideology, Interest, and Sea Power during the Pax Britannica* (Boston, MA: Allen and Unwin, 1986), pp. 120–33.
22. Cartwright to Hardinge (private), 20 February 1907, TNA, FO 371/257/5980; Hardinge to de Salis (private), 29 December 1908, Hardinge Mss, Cambridge University Library, vol. 13. On 'anti-Germanism', see Z.S. Steiner, *The Foreign Office and Foreign Policy* (Cambridge: Cambridge University Press, 1969), pp. 103–4. For the concept of compellance see A.L. George, *'Forceful Persuasion': Coercive Diplomacy as an Alternative to War* (Washington, DC, 1991), pp. 3–14.
23. Grey to Lascelles (private), 12 November 1907, Grey MSS, TNA, FO 800/61; Campbell-Bannerman speech, March 1908, *Parliamentary Debates*, clxxxv, 4 (1908), cols. 1336–8 [hereafter *PD*].
24. *PD* cxcvi, 4 (1908), col. 560; Asquith to King Edward VII, 19 December 1908, TNA, CAB 41/31/74.
25. Widenmann to Tirpitz (no. 869), 13 November 1908, in J. Lepsius et al. (eds), *Die Grosse Politik der europäischen Kabinette*, 40 vols. (Berlin: Deutsche Verlagsanstalt für Politik und Geschichte, 1924–28), xxviii, no. 10226 [hereafter *GP*]. This was a misreading of British naval policy. The US Navy had been effectively excluded from calculations of the 'Two-Power-Standard' since 1901, see J.A.S. Grenville, 'Great Britain and Isthmian Canal, 1898–1901', *American Historical Review*, lxi, 1 (1955), p. 69.
26. Asquith to McKenna (confidential), 1 January 1909, McKenna Mss, MCKN 3/3; Tirpitz to Bülow, 17 March 1909, *GP* xxviii, no. 10272 . For the crisis, see M.S. Seligmann, *Spies in Uniform: British Military Intelligence on the Eve of the First World War* (Oxford: Clarendon, 2006), pp. 195–203.
27. Lloyd George to Asquith, 2 February 1909, Lloyd George Mss, House of Lords Record Office, C/6/11/2; Grey to Asquith, 4 March 1909, Asquith Mss, Bodleian Library, Asquith 21.
28. *PD* (Commons), (5) iii, cols. 52–70; Metternich to Bülow (no. 286), 17 March 1909, *GP* xxviii, no. 10274; Woodward, *Britain and the German Navy*, pp. 466–67.
29. Goschen to Grey (no. 98), 23 March 1909, TNA, FO 371/670/11373. See M. Epkenhans, 'Grossindustrie und Schlachtflottenbau, 1897–1914', *Militärgeschichtliche Mitteilungen*, 43 (1988), pp. 65–140.
30. Goschen to Grey (private), 9 April 1909, *BD* vi, no. 170 (my emphasis); and (no. 131), 8 April 1909, TNA, FO 371/673/13621.

31. Bülow to Schoen (ganz geheim), 9 April 1909 and draft agreement by Schoen, c. 6 May 1909, *GP*, xxviii, nos. 10295 and 10303; minutes of interdepartmental conference, 3 June 1909, in B. von Bülow, *Denkwürdigkeiten*, 4 vols. (Berlin: Ullstein, s.a. [1930–31]), ii,pp. 429–30.
32. *The Times*, 27 July 1909; memo. McKenna, 'Battleship building programmes of Great Britain, Germany, France, United States, Italy and Austria', 14 July 1909, TNA, CAB 37/100/97.
33. 'Aufzeichnung' Bethmann Hollweg, 13 August 1909, *GP*, xxviii, no. 10325; Goschen to Grey (no. 93), 21 August 1909, *BD*, vi, no. 186; also Zimmermann to Kiderlen-Wächter, 25 August 1909, in E. Jäckh, *Kiderlen-Wächter: Briefwechsel und Nachlass*, 2 vols. (Stuttgart: Deutsche Verlagsanstalt, 1924), ii, pp. 33–37.
34. Minute Crowe, 18 August 1908, on Lascelles to Grey (no. 350), 17 August 1908, TNA, FO 371/461/28482.
35. Minute Campbell, 13 April 1909, on Goschen to Grey (no. 131), 8 April 1909, TNA, FO 371/673/13621; McKenna to Asquith 4 March 1909, McKenna Mss, MCKN 3/17.
36. Wilhelm II to Bülow, ? April 1909, in Bülow, *Denkwürdigkeiten*, ii, pp. 429–30.
37. Asquith to King Edward VII, 1 September 1909, TNA, CAB 41/32/33.
38. Tirpitz to Bethmann, 1 September 1909, in A. von Tirpitz, *Politische Dokumente: der Aufbau der deutschen Weltmacht* (Stuttgart: J.B. Cotta'sche Buchhandlung Nachfolger, 1924), pp. 165–66 [hereafter *TPD*]; vice versa, 16 September 1909, *GP*, xxviii, no. 10340; also E. von Vietsch, *Bethmann Hollweg: Staatsmann zwischen Macht und Ethos* (Boppard: Harald Boldt, 1969), p. 124.
39. Goschen to Grey (no. 356, secret), 15 October 1909, *BD*, vi, no. 200; 'Aufzeichnung' [5 November 1909], *GP*, xxviii, no. 10355; Kennedy, *Antagonism*, pp. 446–47.
40. Minute Hardinge, 10 November 1909, on Goschen to Grey (no. 371, secret), 4 November 1909, *BD* vi, no. 205.
41. De Salis to Grey (no. 385), 19 November 1909, TNA, FO 371/676/42609.
42. Minute Crowe, 3 January 1910, on Goschen to Grey (no. 414, very confidential), 29 December 1909, TNA, FO 371/900/167.
43. Minute Crowe, 3 January 1910, on Goschen to Grey (no. 416), 31 December 1909, *BD*, vi, no. 209.
44. Goschen to Hardinge (private), 18 July 1910, Hardinge MSS, vol. 20.
45. Memo. McKenna, 'Navy Estimates, 1910–11', 14 February 1910, TNA, CAB 37/102/2.
46. *PD* (Commons), xix, 5, cols. 644–45.
47. Memo., 26 July 1910, 29 July, *BD*, vi, no. 387, and *GP* xxviii, no. 10401.
48. Goschen to Grey (private), 19 August 1910 (copy), TNA, FO 371/901/31125.
49. Watson to Goschen (no. 31), 25 August 1910, and minute Crowe, 12 September 1910, TNA, FO 371/901/31333; Seligmann, *Spies in Uniform*, pp.33–34.
50. Watson to de Salis (no. 39), 16 September 1910, TNA, FO 371/901/33817; Greene to Foreign Office, 20 September 1910, TNA, FO 371/901/35553; also W. Widenmann, *Marine-Attaché an der kaiserlich-deutsche Botschaft in London, 1907–1912* (Göttingen: Musterschmidt, 1952), pp. 114–15.
51. Grey to Goschen (no. 289), 7 November 1910, TNA, FO 371/901/37601.
52. Watson to de Salis (no. 40), 17 September 1910, and minute Crowe, 17 October 1910, ibid.
53. Tel. Goschen to Grey (no. 62), 12 October 1910, TNA, FO 371/901/37093; memo. Bethmann, 12 October 1910, *BD*, vi, no. 400, and *GP* xxviii, no. 10416.
54. Minute Crowe, 13 October 1910, on tel. Goschen to Grey (no. 62, secret), 12 October 1910, TNA, FO 371/901/37093; and Goschen to Grey (private), 14 October 1910, *BD* vi, no. 401.
55. Memo. Crowe, 20 October 1910, *BD*, vi, no. 404.
56. Minutes Crowe, 21 November and 5 December 1910, and Ruddock to Tyrrell, 2 December 1910, TNA, FO 371/901/42209.
57. Minutes Crowe, 24 October 1910, and Langley, n.d., on Goschen to Grey (no. 288, secret), 16 October 1910, TNA, FO 371/901/38552. Tirpitz continued to block an agreement, 'Aufzeichnung' Tirpitz, 24 October 1910, *TPD*, pp. 184–85.

58. Goschen to Nicolson (private), 22 October 1910, *BD*, vi, no. 405.
59. Goschen to Nicolson (private), 28 October 1910, TNA, FO 371/901/41807.
60. Metternich to Bethmann (no. 1004), 17 December 1910, *GP*, xxviii, no. 10427.
61. Grey to Goschen (no. 25), 27 January 1911, and Greene to Foreign Office, 3 December 1910, TNA, FO 371/1123/45714; British aide-memoire, 8 February 1911, *GP*, xxviii, no. 10429.
62. Grey to Goschen (no. 45), 16 February 1911, and Watson to Goschen (no. 4), 3 March 1911, TNA, FO 371/1123/5930 and /8053.
63. Memo., 8 March 1911, *BD*, vi, no. 444, and *GP* xxviii, no. 10439. For the role of the Cabinet committee, see Nicolson to Hardinge (private), 2 March 1911, Hardinge MSS, vol. 91.
64. Goschen to Nicolson (private), 3 March 1911, TNA, FO 371/1123/11953.
65. *The Times*, 14 March 1911; see Grey to Goschen (no. 89), 14 March 1911, TNA, FO 371/1123/9827. For the Bethmann-Tirpitz problems, see Goschen to Grey (no. 64, secret), 11 March 1911, *BD*, vi, no. 445.
66. See 'Aufzeichnung' Bethmann, 24 March 1911, *GP*, xxviii, no. 10439. The reasons for the delay are not clear. The memorandum was despatched on 14 March, and arrived at Berlin within 24 hours, see *BD*, vi, p. 598, fn. 1. The decision further to delay transmitting was Goschen's. He had always viewed any kind of 'political agreement' with Germany 'with the utmost nervosity', Goschen to Nicolson (private), 3 March 1911, TNA, FO 371/1123/11853.
67. Goschen to Nicolson (private), 17 March 1911, TNA, FO 371/1123/11855.
68. Widenmann to Tirpitz (no. 190), 14 March 1911, *GP*, xxviii, no. 10434, and marginal comment by Kaiser on Metternich to Bethmann Hollweg (no. 248), 15 March 1911, ibid., no. 10435; see *TPD*, pp. 188–89.
69. Minute Crowe, 27 March 1911, on tel. Goschen to Grey (no. 9, secret), 25 March 1911, *BD*, vi, no. 455; Tirpitz to Bethmann, 17 March 1911, and German aide-memoire, 24 March 1911, *GP*, xxviii, nos. 10436 and 10438.
70. Watson to Goschen (confidential), 30 March 1911, and minutes Crowe, 3 April 1911, and Nicolson, , n.d., *BD*, vi, no. 457.
71. Goschen to Grey (private), 24 March 1911, TNA, FO 371/1123/12050; 'Aufzeichnung' Stumm, 5 April 1911, *GP*, xxviii, no. 10440.
72. *The Times*, 31 March 1911.
73. Goschen to Nicolson (private), 7 April 1911, TNA, FO 371/1123/15331.
74. 'Aufzeichnung' Bethmann, 5 April 1911, *GP*, xxviii, no. 10441; *TPD*, p. 194.
75. Minutes Crowe, 10 April and Nicolson and Grey, n.d., on tel. Goschen to Grey (no. 26, secret), 9 May 1911, *BD*, vi, no. 462; see also Crowe's draft Anglo-German agreement, with amendments by Nicolson, n.d. [1911/12], Crowe MSS, TNA, FO 800/243.
76. Grey to Goschen (no. 116), 18 May 1911, TNA, FO 371/1123/18222; German aide-memoire, 9 May 1911, *GP*, xxviii, no. 10442.
77. Grey to Goschen (no. 121, secret), 1 June 1911, *BD*, vi, no. 469, and *GP*, xxviii, no. 10448.
78. De Salis to Grey (no. 187), 1 July 1911, *BD*, vi, no. 472; German aide-memoire, 27 June 1911, *GP*, xxviii, no. 10452.
79. Minutes Villiers, Crowe and Campbell, 2 and 3 October 1911, on Watson to Goschen (no. 295), 27 September 1911, TNA, FO 371/1123/38377.
80. See Hopman diary, 30 October and 1 December 1911, in M. Epkenhans (ed.), *Albert Hopman: Das ereignisreiche Leben eines "Wilhelminers". Tagebücher, Briefe, Aufzeichnungen, 1901–1920* (Munich: Oldenbourg, 2005), pp. 166–67 and 177. For the background, H. Fernis, *Die Flottennovellen im Reichstag, 1906–1912* (Stuttgart: Kohlhammer, 1934), pp. 94–103; F. Fischer, *Krieg der Illusionen: Die deutsche Politik von 1911 bis 1914* (Düsseldorf: Droste, 1969), pp. 169–89.
81. Grey to Goschen (no. 304), 20 December 1911, TNA, FO 371/1129/51342; and (no. 2), 2 January 1912, TNA, FO 371/1123/51194.
82. Goschen to Grey (nos. 47 and 70), 28 January and 10 February 1912, TNA, FO 371/1372/4980 and /6060; Admiralty memo., [March 1912], Asquith MSS, Asquith 24;

H.H. Herwig, *'Luxury Fleet': The Imperial German Navy, 1888–1918* (London: Ashfield, 1991), pp. 74–81.
83. Minute Crowe, 17 February 1913, on Goschen to Grey (no. 58), 10 February 1913, TNA, FO 371/1647/7482. On the *Wehrvorlage* see Stevenson, *Armaments*, pp. 286–89 and pp. 294–99; S. Förster, *Der doppelte Militarismus: Die deutsche Heeresrüstung zwischen Status-Quo-Sicherung und Aggression, 1890–1913* (Stuttgart: Franz Steiner, 1985), pp. 208–96.

3

French Assistance to Russian Armament Production, 1914–1917

DAVID WATSON

The topic of this chapter is French aid to Russian armaments production during the First World War, from 1914 to the outbreak of the revolution in February 1917, which is here explored from material in French archives. The topic is significant from two points of view. In the first place, French aid, which has scarcely been mentioned in existing published accounts, played an important part in the remarkable expansion of Russian armament production during these two and a half years. In the second place, because of the co-existence in the capital city, St Petersburg, renamed Petrograd in 1914, of the central governmental institutions, and of the vastly expanded industrial workforce required by the armaments firms concentrated there, the very success of the armaments drive became one of the causes of the February revolution. The French were much involved in the largest of the giant Petrograd armament firms, Putilov, whose striking workers were a catalyst for the events of February. Because of this, the French sources used here throw some new light on one of the most important questions of twentieth-century history: the origins of the revolution that brought down the Tsarist regime and opened the way to Soviet Communism. These two aspects will be explored in this chapter.

The reality of the success of Russian rearmament between 1914 and the beginning of 1917 must first be established, in view of the legend of Russian military inadequacy, which used to be a common view. The collapse of the Russian army after the revolution of February 1917 misled several generations of historians into a false appreciation of the Russian military effort before the revolution. They presented a story of continued disasters and defeats from Tannenberg to 1917; the explanation was the incompetence of the high command, and failure to equip the armies with the munitions needed. The canard of whole battalions of infantry being sent into the line without rifles was repeated again and again. Of course, the merest glance at a few maps of the eastern front from 1914 to 1917 would have refuted this version of events. In fact, after the successful advance of the central powers in the summer of 1915, the front was stabilised for two full years, except for the Russian advance in the Brusilov offensive of 1916, the most dramatic allied success of the war up to that time.

In reality, the overall strategic position before February 1917 was much the same on the western and eastern fronts. That is to say, initial German advances were halted well beyond the 1914 frontiers, and years of murderous stalemate followed. For this to be possible, military effectiveness, morale and munitions had to be roughly equivalent everywhere. It was only with the 1917 revolutions that hindsight cast a miasma of defeat and despondency over the Russian efforts in 1915 and 1916. The myth of Russian military failure before February 1917 was enshrined in historiography because all who wrote on the topic were determined to blacken the Tsarist regime. Soviet writing was cast in that mould for obvious reasons, and so also was western historiography, dominated as it was by those associated with the liberal opposition to Nicholas II. The many volumes of the Russian series, *The Economic and Social History of the World War*, under the auspices of the Carnegie Foundation, were written by exiles who had been adherents of the liberal opposition associated with the Progressive Bloc of the Duma. The major British authority, Sir Bernard Pares, himself a friend of the Kadet leader Miliukov and many other liberal Russians, wrote in the same spirit and provided what was for many years the unchallenged account in English.[1]

These critical versions of the Russian effort in the final months of Tsarism specifically charged the regime with a massive failure to equip and supply the armies. In so far as munitions were provided, it was claimed that they were imported from abroad, or produced by the efforts of the War Industry Committees and the voluntary organisations (*Zemgor*), not by the traditional armament factories, state-owned and private, working under normal governmental control. However, the main thrust of this historiography was that armaments were not provided, and that the Russian armies were defeated, however contrary to elementary historical knowledge that might be, as evidenced by the geographical position of the front line in February 1917.

Over the last thirty years, historical writing has provided a very different picture. Since the publication of Norman Stone's *The Eastern Front* in 1975,[2] it has come to be recognised that until February 1917, Russia met the challenge of industrialised warfare as successfully as the other belligerents. None of them had envisaged, before the outbreak of war, the immense scale of munitions required, nor the length of time that war would continue. Initially, just as much as France, Britain and even

Germany, Russia hugely underestimated the needs of its armies in a war that would be neither decisive nor short. In particular, the vast expansion of the use of battlefield artillery had not been anticipated. Russia had its shell crisis in 1915, just as all the other powers did, and a crisis in the production of the guns to fire these millions of shells, just as the other powers did. Russia solved the shell crisis in the course of 1915 and 1916, and by February 1917 had huge stocks of artillery and shells. Roughly speaking, the same was true of other military equipment, Russia being especially strong in aircraft.

Apart from Stone's book, the best account of Russian armaments production at this time is provided by D.R. Jones' chapter in the volumes edited by A.R. Millett and Williamson Murray, *Military Effectiveness*. These results have been utilised in the best recent military histories of the First World War by Huw Strachan and David Stevenson.[3] The latter gives the following summary of Russian armaments production:

> new rifle production rose from 132,844 in 1914 to 733,017 in 1915, and 1,301,433 in 1916; 76mm field guns from 354 to 1,349 to 3,721 in these years; 122mm heavy guns from 78 to 361 to 637; and shell production (of all types) from 104,900 to 9,567,888 to 30,974,678.

Stevenson also states:

> by 1917 Russia was manufacturing all its howitzers and three quarters of its heavy artillery. Not only was the shell shortage a thing of the past, by spring 1917 Russia was acquiring an unprecedented superiority in men and materiel. The price of this Herculean effort, however, was dislocation of the civilian economy and a crisis in urban food supply. The very achievement that moved the balance in the Allies' favour by summer 1916 contained the seeds of later catastrophe.[4]

Strachan's brief account of Russian armaments production, and of the military achievements of the Tsarist army in 1915–16, the retreat from Poland notwithstanding, is similar.

It is to be underlined that these figures are for Russian production. The idea, widespread in 1914 and early 1915, that the Russian armies could only be equipped from Britain, France, the USA and Japan, had to be abandoned. Transport difficulties proved virtually insuperable after the failure of the allies to reopen the route through the Dardanelles. Much of the armaments that got through to the Arctic ports or to Vladivostok stayed there instead of reaching the fronts, as the railways were unable to cope with them.

One important factor in the remarkable achievements just outlined was French technical aid to the Russian munitions factories. This chapter will deal in the first place with this topic, and then with one small but crucial and previously overlooked element in the catastrophe that followed. The catastrophe was the February revolution that overthrew the Tsarist Government, of which the catalyst was a strike at the Putilov munitions factory in Petrograd. The previously overlooked element in the situation, which is well documented in the French sources used here, is the sequestration of the Putilov factory in 1916.

The sources used in this study, being entirely French, offer a new perspective on a topic which touches on questions that previously, if examined at all, have been so only from Russian sources. The French materials are to be found in the military archives at the Château de Vincennes, the Service Historique de l'Armée de Terre (SHAT série 6N and 7N), and the private papers of Albert Thomas (Archives Nationales 94 AP). Eventually, some of these documents will no doubt be published in the new series of *Documents Diplomatiques Français*, covering the gap between the old series on the origins of the First World War and the series beginning in 1920. But at the time of writing, in this new series only volumes covering the period up to 25 May 1915 were available to the author. In the military archives the most useful sources are the reports of the Military Attaché, General Laguiche, and later of General Janin, head of the military mission, and the reports of the special envoy from GHQ, Commandant Langlois, who made several visits to Russia in 1915 and 1916, reporting directly to the French Commander-in-Chief, at that time, General Joffre. Albert Thomas, in his pre-war life a leading figure in the French Socialist party (SFIO), rapidly became one of the most important figures in the wartime Government. He was appointed Under-Secretary for Artillery and Munitions Production and was credited with immense achievements in that post, being seen as the French equivalent of Lloyd George when British munitions minister. He also came to be seen as an expert on Russian affairs as a result of taking part in a mission to Russia in 1916; his most important task in that mission was precisely to help increase Russian munitions production as he had done in France. Having created a sizeable network of contacts in Russia, he was despatched on a second mission in 1917, in the vain hope of inspiring the provisional Government to continue to make an effective contribution to the war. Seen by many as a candidate for the premiership in the autumn of 1917, he was beaten to that post by Clemenceau, and subsequently found himself eclipsed. As a socialist politician fully supporting the war, he fell between two stools when his comrades in the SFIO drifted away from their original pro-war position.

From September 1917 he was first out of office, then out of Parliament and out of France, finding a refuge with the International Labour Organisation at Geneva.[5]

By December 1914, all the belligerents began to realise the scale of their need for munitions, especially for shells. The 'shell crisis' became a vital factor in the political life of Britain, France and Germany, as well as of Russia. In the first instance, the Russian authorities thought that their needs could be met by importing munitions from their allies, and from neutral powers, notably the United States. George Buchanan, the British Ambassador, recorded that on 18 December 1914, together with the French Ambassador, he was called by the Chief of Staff, General Belayev, to an urgent meeting about the depletion of Russian munitions and the need for allied aid.[6] Indeed, this did seem feasible to all parties in early 1915, as at that stage Britain had not put a mass army into the field, and the transportation problems did not appear to be as insuperable as they later proved to be. However, even at this stage, voices were heard suggesting that Russia must be helped to develop her own production, as well as being provided with supplies from abroad. Huge orders for Russia were placed in Britain, France, the United States and Japan, in competition with similar orders for the British and French armies. Much more attention has been paid to the question of Russian ordering of military supplies in allied and neutral countries, although in the French case there has been no definitive study, such as that by Keith Neilson for Britain.[7] That more attention has been paid to the ordering of supplies abroad is not surprising as the Russian orders created enduring problems, which attracted much attention after 1917. In the first place, they had been paid for by advances from Britain and France which added enormously to the Russian debt, whose repudiation by the Communist regime caused endless difficulties. Secondly, the immense stockpiles of war materials still at the Russian ports in 1918, which it was feared could fall into German hands, were a major factor in allied intervention in the Russian civil war. However, these orders and the delay in their delivery are not the topic to be discussed here, but the alternative, already mooted, of helping Russia to revolutionise its own production.

The French role in Russian munitions production can only be understood if the complexities of the system are first outlined. Before the war, armaments were produced in traditional arsenals, owned and managed by the state, and by private contractors, some of which, like Putilov, were among the largest industrial enterprises in Russia. The private firms were predominantly involved in building warships, but did include some working for the army. By early 1915, it was realised that existing stocks were completely inadequate, given the rapid expenditure of munitions in modern war. When importation from abroad proved unsatisfactory, attention was turned to expanding Russian production. This involved ordering from existing large firms, which in many cases had to be converted from naval to land armaments. It also meant bringing into existence a whole kaleidoscope of new, often small-scale, producers not previously involved in armaments work. A similar procedure was organised in France in 1914 and 1915 under the control of Albert Thomas, as Under-Secretary of State for Munitions. When there was talk of bringing his methods to Russia, this was what was meant, for it involved control and supervision of the new subcontracting firms, which often lacked the required technical expertise. One of the leading authorities on Russian economic history has described this industrial expansion in the following terms:

> From early 1915 it became apparent that neither the state arsenals nor the existing armaments firms in the private sector were capable of meeting the insatiable appetite of the military. Accordingly, and in response to generous contracts and prices from the procurement authorities, large and small engineering firms alike converted to the production of armaments. The giant metallurgical firms that belonged to Prodometa switched to the production of high-explosive shell. As in all belligerent countries, the output of shell and other ammunition was revolutionized by the new techniques of mass production. From a managerial point of view, the use of continuous flow methods helped to boost the productivity of the abundant unskilled labour that flooded into the Russian factories.[8]

In addition, from 1915 there came the development of a network of patriotic voluntary organisations aiming at creating new sources of munitions manufacture. These were the War Industries Committees, while the local government bodies, the town councils and *zemstvos* also got involved, so that there appeared a complicated pattern of competing agencies whose conflicts had political overtones.[9]

As early as December 1914, the French Military attaché in Petrograd, General Laguiche, among proposals for equipping the Russian army with imported munitions, suggested that French experts should be sent to advise on methods for increasing Russian production. On 3 January 1915, the French Ambassador in Russia, Maurice Paléologue, after a conversation with Grand Duke Nicholas, the Russian Commander-in-Chief, who had appealed for French munitions to be sent, proposed to telegraph Paris advising rejection: 'We should keep all our offensive resources for ourselves alone.' But after a conversation with Laguiche, he decided that this was too abrupt a refusal, and replaced it with another telegram recommending that the decision be left in the hands of the Commander-in-Chief of the French armies on the western front, Joffre. In fact Joffre did agree to the delivery to Russia of 100,000 shells each month from le Creusot, between January and May, rising to 225,000 a month after May. Whether they were, in fact, delivered is doubtful.

On 13 January 1915, the French Foreign Minister, Delcassé, replied to Paléologue in a telegram informing him that the two French experts, Saint-Sauveur and Darcy, were already engaged in advising Russian firms on increasing their production of munitions. Darcy was a financier and industrialist on the boards of several French-financed Russian companies, including Putilov, while Saint-Sauveur was one of the leading figures in the Schneider-Creusot metallurgical firm. Delcassé wrote: 'Le Creusot will set in train the manufacture of shell in factories which already have the necessary equipment, and will give them its technical support: it will also examine the possibility of equipping one or two other factories in its orbit.'[10]

At this point, Commandant Langlois submitted the report on his first mission to Russia to French GHQ. Among much else, he suggested a French technical mission to help organise Russian shell production. In fact, such a mission had already been planned and it departed in mid-February, under General Pau. It included the artillery expert, Colonel Pyot, who stayed in Russia after Pau's return and played an important part through the rest of 1915 and 1916 in advising the Russians on the production of shells and guns, field artillery and heavy guns. The memoirs of the French President, Raymond Poincaré, refer to Pau's mission. Poincaré asked Pau to obtain information about the state of Russian and Serbian armaments: 'What we know is as vague as it is worrying.' On Pau's return on 13 April 1915, he was somewhat reassured about the state of the Russian army, 'the only dark cloud, but very dark, is that of munitions'.[11] Pyot's role in helping revolutionise Russian munitions production is well documented in the military archives, especially in several reports submitted by Langlois on his frequent visits to Russia during 1915 and 1916. Pyot himself reported back to Paris on 14/27 July 1915:

> We met with three months of hostility from the director of artillery, but General Vankov was more favorable towards us. With his help we have established an office in Moscow where we have been able to draw up plans, meet with industrialists etc. We have been able to organise contacts, discuss prices and so on: our costs have been covered by credits under Vankov's control. The Putilov group has worked alongside us to develop the Russian type of shell.[12]

Pyot's contribution to Vankov's activities is important as one authority has stated that the Vankov organisation was responsible for 44 per cent of total Russian shell production during the war.[13] Armaments production in Russia from 1915 onwards was handled in three ways. One was the Main Artillery Administration of the War Ministry which controlled the state arsenals and issued contracts to the large firms with which it had well established relations from before 1914. The second method was that of the War Industries Committees, seeking to bring new, mainly small, firms into the magic circle of contractors. Although they attracted a lot of attention, they seem not to have produced much armament, but rather to have been important as a forum for the liberal opposition. The third was the Vankov organisation, which, as we have seen, was greatly indebted to French technical assistance. The other area where the French played a role was in the large metallurgical firms of Petrograd, especially the Putilov concern. The French connection here was well established before 1914 as Putilov was financed largely by French capital, and dependent on technical expertise from Schneider-Creusot. There had been a pre-war struggle for links with Putilov that had been won by Creusot and the French over Krupp and the Germans.[14]

A surprising phenomenon of wartime Russia was the growth and institutionalisation of what were called the voluntary organisations. They began with humanitarian efforts, such as bathhouses, canteens, hospital trains, hospitals and convalescent homes, which were paralleled by patriotic organisations in all the belligerent countries. But in Russia the voluntary organisations spread far beyond this type of humanitarian relief work, and became also involved in munitions production. Local authorities, the Union of Municipalities and the Union of Zemstvos (the rural local government bodies) established *Zemgor*, for the supply of the army, to which, in early 1915, was added the War Industries Committees Movement. This began with industrialists from all over Russia volunteering their services to provide for the needs of the army. By the early summer of 1915, a vast network of War Industries Committees existed, with a central committee headed by A.I. Guchkov. Between that date and February 1917, the War Industries Committees were entrusted with huge sums of public money and employed tens of thousands of young men who would otherwise have faced military conscription. The consensus view of historians is that the end result was in no way commensurate with what had been expected. Siegelbaum the historian of the Committees, states that the majority of the 39 million shells produced during the war 'came from the same dozen or so firms on which the state had depended before the war'. The remainder came through the Vankov organisation; very few from the work of the voluntary organisations.[15]

In fact, the War Industries Committees really played a political role. As Siegelbaum explains, they were 'symbiotic' with the Progressive Bloc in the Duma. As a result, questions of armament production became involved with the conflict between the Tsarist authorities and the liberal opposition. This conflict developed from the measures taken to deal with the munitions crises in the early months of 1915, continuing until it produced the stalemate between Tsar and Duma in early 1917, out of which emerged the revolution. From the point of view of this chapter, the political conflict has to be discussed as it explains the sequestration of the Putilov factory in February 1916. Much to the annoyance of the French, the Putilov shareholders became victims of the liberal campaign against Tsarist autocracy.

The activities of Pyot's mission, with regard both to the Vankov organisation and to firms where the French connection antedated 1914, can be followed in detail in the seven reports submitted by Langlois to the French authorities between February 1915 and October 1916. In the April report on his second mission, Langlois noted that Pyot was already working with Vankov to increase production to fill the deficit, estimated at between 100,000 and 150,000 shells. His fourth report, of 16 September 1915, provides much information about Pyot's work. Tests of the French prototype shells had gone well and had persuaded Manikovski, head of the main artillery administration, to adopt them. Another success was the work of a French engineer, Taffenel, in creating a factory in Moscow for filling the shells with explosives. Langlois declared: 'In spite of his innumerable difficulties Commandant Pyot managed to complete the task he had been given, and Russia is now at the point of harvesting the fruits of our mission.' A report of the Military Attaché, Laguiche, praised Pyot's work in Odessa and the south where he had organised shell production in works formerly devoted to building warships, and in networks of small-scale workshops. Laguiche wrote enthusiastically of Pyot's achievements in Odessa: 'The notables of the town rushed to organise munitions manufacture, industrial firms gave their help, transformed their machinery, the smallest brought their lathes, and workers both men and women gave their labour ... cooperatives brought together numerous students who left education to manufacture shells.' He even claimed that Pyot's work at Odessa was the source of the whole War Industries Committee movement, and that in so far as that movement was a success, it was based on its guidance and control by members of Pyot's mission.[16]

As well as Pyot's success in creating new munitions factories, French aid to Russian armament production was evident in old-established factories such as the Putilov factory and its subsidiaries, and subcontractors in

Petrograd. Putilov itself, already large enough in 1914, expanded dramatically in 1915 and 1916, becoming the hub of a complex of munitions producers that accounted for a high proportion of all Russian armaments produced during the First World War. Putilov's achievement rested on links with Schneider-Creusot established before 1914, strongly developed after the outbreak of war. A vital task was to transform the factory from being mainly engaged in naval equipment to the production of artillery and shells for land fighting.[17]

As well as converting the Putilov works itself, a system of subcontracting among smaller factories and workshops around Petrograd, all closely supervised by technicians from Putilov and Schneider, was developed, modelled along the lines of methods introduced by Thomas in France. This meant that the Putilov firm itself became the nucleus of what was called the Putilov group. In spite of the success of this system in organising the production of high explosive and shrapnel shells, and grenades, on a huge scale, the Putilov organisation, seen as a war-profiteering cartel, attracted hostile attention from liberal opponents of Tsarist autocracy. The Putilov group and the Putilov firm itself became victims of the conflict between the governmental bureaucracy and the liberal opposition of the Duma Progressive Bloc and the War Industries Committee movement.

After several investigations and reports from July 1915, this led to the sequestration of the Putilov firm in February 1916, and the eventual dissolution of the Putilov group. These events were of considerable significance. In the first place, they greatly disturbed the French authorities because of their implications for future economic relations between Russia and France. Secondly, sequestration, which meant in practice that the military authorities took over the management of the huge Putilov factory, had serious effects for labour relations there, a factor relevant to the role of the Putilov workers in the February revolution. Sequestration was a legal procedure introduced during the war, supposedly to deal with the problem of enemy-owned property. In the case of a business firm it meant that, although the firm continued as a legal entity, its board of directors and shareholders lost all their powers, both in actually running the factory, and in financial matters, such as drawing up annual accounts and declaring a dividend.

In spite of the crucial importance of the Putilov strikers in February 1917, the essential background of the sequestration and subsequent control of the factory by the military authorities is scarcely mentioned either in Hasegawa's study of the February revolution, or in the immensely detailed and authoritative account of labour relations in Petrograd by R.B. McKean. The latter writes, surprisingly, that 'Petrograd factory owners welcomed military takeover', and that 'factory administrations moreover, proved more than capable of warding off threats to managerial prerogatives'. Hasegawa refers in passing to the sequestration of 1916, and later talks, incorrectly, of Putilov being 'state owned'.[18]

The Putilov affair has left behind it far more documentation in the French archives than any other item within the area of French aid to Russian armaments production. This is justified by the importance of the Putilov organisation as a major supplier of munitions, and by the significance of the role of the Putilov workers as a catalyst of the February revolution. The Putilov affair is also interesting as an illustration of wider aspects of economic relations between France and Russia in 1915–16, and of what the French envisaged for the future.

The sequestration of the Putilov firm in February 1916, and the subsequent dissolution of the Putilov organisation with its implications for contractual agreements with Le Creusot, can only be understood in the light of the conflict between the Tsarist Government, as represented by the Tsar himself and the civil and military bureaucracy, and what was known at the time and in historical writing as 'society', that is, the middle- and upper-class liberal forces which were seeking to turn the limited restrictions on autocratic power granted in 1906 into a fully parliamentary form of government. Both sides were sincerely convinced that their policy alone could produce victory; in the end the conflict between them brought revolution and defeat. The Putilov organisation was at the centre of this battle because it was seen as a major beneficiary of the policy of Russia's War Minister, Vladimir Sukhomlinov, during the first months of hostilities; he had placed huge orders with the traditional suppliers. As soon as 'society' became involved in armaments procurement, Putilov became a target. This happened in May 1915 when the Special Council for Defence appointed a subcommittee under A.I. Guchkov to investigate Putilov's record in delivering munitions.

Guchkov, a leader of the Octobrist party in the Third Duma, regarded himself as a military expert, and had at that time become an enemy of Sukhomlinov. Defeated in the 1912 elections, he was no longer a Duma member, but was able to use the War Industries movement to return to political prominence. The resignation of Sukhomlinov and the appointment of Guchkov's old ally, A.A. Polivanov, as War Minister at the end of July 1915, was a victory for Guchkov. His committee reported to the Special Council for Defence in October 1915, criticising Putilov and recommending sequestration. However, the council voted at this time by fifteen to sixteen to reject sequestration.[19] Over the next five months, although munitions continued to flow from the factories, the underlying problems became much worse. Strikes were frequent, although they were usually rapidly resolved when demands for increased wages were accepted. The military authorities were imbued with the idea that previous contracts had allowed Putilov too much profit, and were determined to renegotiate them. Discussion of both of these questions must bear in mind the rapidly accelerating inflation of this period. Although far less than the runaway inflation that came after February, it was still substantial, and prices rose threefold from 1914 to the end of 1916. This meant that wage rises were continually being eroded, and the usual leap-frogging contest between different groups of workers became endemic. Similarly, what seemed to be large profits were quite illusory when allowance was made for inflation. As the board of directors pointed out, this restriction of profits meant that the firm was losing its working capital, and had to be rescued by a loan from the State. After a year of sequestration, by February 1917 Putilov was on the point of running into a financial impasse.

Five months after the compromise decision of October 1915, sequestration was imposed at the end of February 1916. From that date on, the Putilov factory was managed by the military authorities and from a little later the system of subcontracting in the Putilov organisation was rescinded. One interpretation of the sequestration is that it was designed to ensure that this vital part of Russia's armaments industry did not fall into the hands of the amateurs of the War Industries Committee, but remained under the control of professionals. However, in the eyes of the French, the military professionals were themselves incompetent in managing the factory, and both incompetent and hostile in their attitude towards profits.

The importance of the Putilov affair can be seen from the central place it was given in the Viviani–Thomas mission to Russia in May 1916. By 1916 it was clear that both western and eastern fronts had stabilised, and that a long-drawn-out struggle was in view, the war of attrition. It became more important than ever for the Allies to coordinate their strategy as much as possible, in particular to relieve the pressure on the French at Verdun with counter-attacks on the part of the British and the Russians. Better coordination of the allied efforts was the aim of two high-level missions despatched to Russia, Kitchener's from Britain and the Viviani–Thomas mission from France. The Kitchener mission never arrived, of course, his ship having been sunk off Scotland, but the French mission arrived safely via Sweden and spent two weeks in Russia. The French Cabinet had originally wanted to send Ribot, but he had refused: they fell back on Viviani, who, in spite of his lightweight reputation, was the second most important figure in Briand's Cabinet. The tasks of the mission were to persuade Russia to be more accommodating towards Rumania and on the Polish question, to get 400,000 Russian troops despatched to the western front, and to give more aid with armaments production, essential for continued pressure on Germany from the east. Not much was achieved on the diplomatic front, and eventually only 50,000 Russian troops reached France, but the most important part of the mission was the work of Albert Thomas and his aide, the industrialist Louis Loucheur, towards still further efforts in the production of weaponry. Viviani's role seems to have been mainly ceremonial, making eloquent speeches and listening to Chaliapin sing the 'Marseillaise' at court banquets.[20]

Thomas's papers contain material that provide insight into the French Government's aims for the mission. They include a note from one of the top officials of the French foreign office, de Margerie, accompanying two memoranda, one on the Polish question, and the other by Putilov, describing the sequestration of the Putilov company. Thomas was told to take great care to guard these documents and to keep them secret while in Russia. These memoranda are accompanied by handwritten notes, completed after the mission. They begin:

> Origin of the mission, bad news from Russia since the beginning of April, resignation of Polivanov, sequestration by A.I. Putilov himself, statistics indicating a noticeable fall in production ... Problem of the offensive: when will Russia intervene? It must not be premature (lack of munitions) nor too late. Doubts about the internal situation, especially about the attitude of the working class.

These notes state that the problems of Poland and Rumania had been dealt with by Viviani, while Thomas dealt with the question of the mooted Russian offensive, and the related problem of supply of armaments, and also with the proposed despatch of Russian troops to Salonika and to France. The note also contains an interesting account of Thomas's view of Russian munitions factories, and of attitudes of the Russian military, in shorthand form: 'hatred of foreigners who got involved in their affairs, opposition to Pyot, hatred of private industry seen as profit-hunting, lacking in patriotism and incompetent'. These notes are followed by a twenty-page account of the Putilov sequestration, and by an assessment of the work of the War Industry Committees. One of the conclusions reached was that the French Ambassador should be told to raise the Putilov affair at the highest level.[21] The result was not very satisfactory from the French point of view. Paléologue's telegram to Paris of 6/16 June reports the results of this démarche as follows:

> I demanded, one, that the contracts with Le Creusot should be reestablished, and, two, that the Putilov group should be reinstated.

On the first point I expressed myself so strongly that I hope to get a satisfactory response. On the second, M Sazonov objected with some reason that the suppression of the Putilov group was an internal matter judged necessary by the ministry of war, the director general of Artillery, the Special Commission for Defence. If we overruled the unanimous views of the competent authorities, we would provoke prominent resignations and there would be repercussions in the Duma. He referred confidentially to the unpopularity of Putilov, and the suspicion and hatred for him on all sides in the Duma, and ended by saying that if we insisted on maintaining the Putilov group we would unleash a scandal from which not only Le Creusot, but the whole of the French metallurgical industry would suffer.[22]

Thus the Viviani–Thomas mission failed to alter the decision of the Russian Government about the Putilov affair; sequestration remained in force, and the subcontracting arrangements of the Putilov group were rescinded. However, on other points the mission was more successful. Russian troops, although in small numbers, were sent to the other fronts, where they promptly mutinied. The Russian – Brusilov – offensive began on 4 June, although it had already been decided on by the Russian high command on 14 April, before the mission's arrival. The only authority to discuss the sequestration in any depth is Jonathan A. Grant, who brings out clearly the importance of Guchkov's vendetta against the Minister of War, Sukhomlinov, dating from before 1914. Guchkov, a leader of the Octobrist party, had lost his seat in the Duma in the 1912 elections, and was now seeking to make a political comeback through his role in the War Industries Committee. This resulted in a campaign against the Putilov firm, seen as the beneficiary of Sukhomlinov's policy of placing orders with the big traditional suppliers. Sukhomlinov became the scapegoat for the Russian version of the 1915 shell crisis, eventually being removed from office and accused of treason; the Putilov factory and its mainly French shareholders were ancillary victims of Guchkov's campaign.

Polivanov's action was part of his support for the Moscow element around Guchkov in the War Industries Committee movement against the Petrograd industrialists. Grant argues, convincingly, that sequestration was also designed to ensure that control of this hugely important part of Russia's armaments production did not fall into the hands of the amateurs in the War Industries Committee, but remained under the control of the professionals, experts in the administration. However, another reason for the sequestration was hostility to financiers, to A.I. Putilov personally as one of the leading bankers in Russia, and to the idea of war profiteering. Grant quotes Manikovski's memoirs to show his hostility to bankers and profits, and notes that three of the twenty-eight firms sequestered were financed by Putilov's Russo-Asiatic Bank. He continues: 'Perhaps the most significant advantage Manikovski saw in sequestration was that it restricted company profits and prices.' In the event, the inevitable result of restricting profits on past contracts was that from the time of sequestration the State had to advance huge loans to the firm, 40 per cent of the value of production. The system was running rapidly into a financial impasse by 1917, when all such details were swept away by the inflation let loose after the February revolution. Similarly, problems of labour management and ever-recurring strikes were now the direct responsibility of the Government: 'by taking direct control of the factories, the government could not avoid being identified as the adversary of labour'. This was an important element in the situation that led to the Putilov workers taking to the streets in 1917, one that has not been emphasised enough in accounts of the February revolution. The French authorities were greatly concerned about the sequestration of Putilov, and documentation from the French archives allows insight into the matter from the point of view of the Putilov board and the financiers of the Russo-Asiatic Bank.[23]

Among Albert Thomas's papers is a folder with much documentation about the events of 1915 leading to the sequestration of the Putilov factory in February 1916. It begins with a translation of Guchkov's report and of the discussions in the Special Defence Commission after their visit to the factory on 21 July 1915. This report attacked Putilov's desire to make excessive profits, and required them to satisfy workers' demands for improved wages and other benefits. There is then the reply from the Putilov board of directors, rejecting Guchkov's claims that they were behind with deliveries, and that they had made excessive profits. Contrary to his statements, wages had been increased: if average wages were lower than in 1914, it was because the workforce now had a much higher proportion of unskilled workers, apprentices and women: wages of every category of worker had increased. The response concluded that Putilov had invested twenty-seven million roubles to expand the factory, and that expansion had been achieved while the factory was working to capacity, that the delays in fulfilling orders were due to unavoidable external factors, such as the failure to obtain coal supplies and machine tools, and delays in the inspection process. Every effort had been made to meet the workers' demands.

Among much else, this document was summarised in three reports, a *Note sur les Affaires Poutiloff* of November 1916, and two notes, *Au sujet du séquestre de la société des usines Poutiloff,* of 18–20 April and 1–3 May 1917. The first recounted the enquiries led by Guchkov and Rodzianko in

1915, and the decision of October to impose one civilian and three military officials as members of the board of directors. Far from improving matters, this led to the bigger strikes beginning in January 1916, resulting in the sequestration of 29 February 1916. The note stressed that this taking over of the Putilov firm itself overturned the 'Groupement Poutiloff', the arrangements by which during 1915 production of shells had been vastly increased through use of subcontractors. After some weeks of confrontation between General Drozdhov, the Government's new director of Putilov proper, and the subcontractors, on 26 May 1916, the Government overturned all the previous contractual agreements.[24]

The note concludes that, in view of the importance of this matter for French interests in Russia, General Manikovski's promises should be endorsed by a verbal note submitted by the French Ambassador, and accepted by the Russian Foreign Ministry. However, the dossier includes a copy of the telegram of 17 June 1916 from the French Ambassador to the Quai d'Orsay, informing his superiors there that, although the contracts with Le Creusot would be honoured, the reorganisation involving the dissolution of the Putilov group had to be maintained for reasons of internal politics.

This telegram is significant in bringing out very clearly the political conflicts behind this apparently technical matter, and also the reluctance of the Tsarist Government to confront the liberal opposition in the Duma and the voluntary organisations, that is, the War Industries Committees. Further notes of April/May 1917 provide a broader account of the sequestration, beginning with a history of the affairs of the Putilov firm from before the outbreak of war. Beginning with pre-war plans which were made impossible by the state's failure to provide stable ordering, and continuing with their immense achievement in producing, from new installations, 240,000 shrapnel shells per month by October 1915, while production of field guns had risen from thirty to two hundred and fifty per month by January 1916. These achievements had been made possible by financial backing from the Russo-Asiatic Bank, until the sequestration made it impossible to continue. It was only then that the firm had to request financial advances from the state. The consequence of interference by the Special Defence Commission and the Duma delegation was that management lost authority over the workforce. Duma members and members of the War Industries Committee maintained constant contacts with the factory, which became the scene of disorder accompanied by attacks on foremen and engineers.

At this point, sequestration was pronounced and the military authorities took over the factory. As the strike continued, the director attempted first to subject the strikers to conscription and then rescinded this measure, thus losing control of the situation. Another effect of the sequestration was to prevent a planned merger between Putilov and the Hughes firm in the Ukraine, a merger which was thus carried out by Parvainen. These notes end with an account of further negotiations between Paléologue, Saint-Sauveur, the representative of Schneider, and Baron Nolde for the Russian Foreign Ministry in November and December 1916. The notes conclude with the French hope that the governmental changes of January 1917 would produce a more sympathetic response to their complaints. Nevertheless, by the second half of 1916 Russian munitions production had achieved dramatic results. So that when the allies began to plan for the campaign of 1917 they could hope to be in a position to press the Germans hard from both west and east. Of course that was not to be, because of the February revolution, which itself was sparked off by the strains placed on the economic and social life of the Russian empire by the boom in armaments production. This is not the place for a general analysis of the causes of the February revolution, but one aspect of February is involved with the French role in the armaments campaign, and is well illustrated in the French sources. It has therefore been examined here in some detail.

It is clear that the catalyst for the disastrous events of February, and thus of everything that followed, was the strike at the Putilov factory in Petrograd. The strike turned into a violent demonstration, and the failed attempt to restore order produced the mutiny of the Petrograd garrison which brought down the Tsar. All this is well known but in spite of the detailed studies which have been made of this question, an important element in the situation, the sequestration of the Putilov factory by the military authorities in 1916, has been virtually ignored. The sequestration caused much dismay to the French, and the French archives contain a lot of material on it, material which throws an interesting light on this essential background to the February revolution.

The important part played by French technical assistance in the remarkable achievements of Russian armaments production between 1914 and 1917 is demonstrated in the French archives. French investment before 1914 had laid the foundation on which Russian industrial firms could build during the war. Although wartime financial controls meant private investors could not advance new money after August 1914, the French authorities felt strongly that their previous investment, together with intergovernmental financial arrangements backing Russian currency, entitled them to favourable treatment in the Russian market. They were, therefore, all the more annoyed at what they saw as hostile actions detrimental to France and French shareholders in such cases as the Putilov affair.

This chapter also illustrates through one specific case the general point made in all recent accounts of this wartime industrial expansion. The economic success of the industrial expansion of the defence-related industries created social stresses that were to erupt in February. The giant Putilov factory, representative of a virtual revolution in the defence industry, produced the February strikes and demonstrators in Petrograd. French sources suggest, in a way that has not previously emerged, that the strike wave of February followed earlier ones resulting from management by the military authorities after sequestration in February 1916. Perhaps the Putilov management would have achieved nothing better, given the need to keep munitions flowing, and inflationary processes already developing rapidly.

Perhaps they too would have given in to successive groups of strikers, encouraging the leap-frogging strikes that filled the twelve months of sequestration. But the military authorities, unconcerned about profits and dividends, and hostile to the board of directors as war-profiteering financiers, were unlikely to resist the workers' demands. This, as might be expected, produced further demands and further strikes. It is ironic that the skilled workers at Putilov probably enjoyed, in real terms, their highest-ever wages before or after they brought down the Tsarist regime and then the Russian capitalist system. It would be a very long time before their successors, at what became the Kirov plant in Leningrad, achieved an equivalent wage level.

NOTES

1. Bernard Pares, *The Fall of the Russian Monarchy: A Study of the Evidence* (London: Jonathan Cape, 1939: new edn, London: Cassell, 1988); and Pares, *My Russian Memoirs* (London: Jonathan Cape, 1931). N. Golovin, *The Russian Army in the World War* (New Haven, CT: Yale University Press, 1932). Recent military histories that, in the main, follow the older interpretations are: W. Bruce Lincoln, *Passage through Armageddon: The Russians in War and Revolution 1914–1918* (New York: Simon and Schuster, 1986); Ward Rutherford, *The Ally: The Russian Army in World War I* (London: Gordon and Cremonesi, 1977). Even the introductory section of Allan K. Wildman, *The End of the Russian Imperial Army: I, The Old Army* (Princeton, NJ: Princeton University Press, 1980), pp. 75–115, to some extent follows the older interpretation.
2. Norman Stone, *The Eastern Front 1914–1917* (London: Hodder and Stoughton, 1975); and Stone, 'Organising an Economy for War, the Russian Shell Shortage 1914–1917', in G. Best and A. Wheatcroft (eds), *War Economy and the Military Mind* (London: Croom Helm, 1976), pp. 108–19.
3. D.R. Jones, 'Imperial Russia', in A.R. Millet and Williamson Murray (eds), *Military Effectiveness, I, The First World War* (Boston: Unwin Hyman, 1988) pp. 250–327; Hew Strachan, *The First World War: I, The Call to Arms* (Oxford: Oxford University Press, 2001), pp. 1107–13. David Stevenson, *1914–1918: The History of the First World War* (London: Allen Lane, 2004), pp. 235–37.
4. Stevenson, *1914–1918*, p. 237.
5. B.W. Schaper, *Albert Thomas, Trente ans de Réformisme social* (Assen: Van Gorcum, 1959).

6. George Buchanan, *My Mission to Russia and Other Diplomatic Memories*, 2 vols. (London: Cassell, 1923), I, p. 19.
7. Keith Neilson, *Strategy and Supply: The Anglo-Russian Alliance 1914–1917* (London: Allen and Unwin, 1984). Information on the French side can be gleaned from the memoirs of the Russian purchasing agent in Paris: A. Ignatiev, *Cinquante Ans dans le Rang*, 2 vols. (Moscow: Édition du progrès, 1972, translation of *Pjat'desjat let v stroju*, Moscow, 1955).
8. Peter Gatrell, *The Tsarist Economy 1850–1917* (London: Batsford, 1986), p. 185; and Gatrell, *Government, Industry and Re-armament in Russia 1900–1914* (Cambridge: Cambridge University Press, 1994).
9. Lewis A. Siegelbaum, *The Politics of Industrial Mobilization in Russia 1914–1917: A Study of the War-Industries Committees* (London: Macmillan, 1983).
10. *Documents Diplomatiques Français 1915*, vol. I (Brussels: Peter Lang, 2002), p. 15. Paléologue à Delcassé 4 January 1915, and p. 75. Delcassé à Paléologue, 13 January 1915. Letter from Laguiche, 15 November 1914 is in *Service Historique de l'Armée de Terre* [SHAT], Vincennes 6N 33. Note on Schneider in the private papers of Albert Thomas in *Archives Nationales*, 94 AP 175. Darcy was a member of the board of directors of the Putilov company, P.V. 'Ol, *Foreign Capital in Russia* (London: Garland, 1983), translation of *Inostrannye Kapitaly v Rossii* (Petrograd, 1922), pp. 35 and 37.
11. Raymond Poincaré, *Au service de la France*, vol. VI (Paris: Plon, 1926–33), pp. 44 and 158.
12. Thomas papers, *Archives Nationales*, 94 AP 175.
13. Siegelbaum, *The Politics of Industrial Mobilization*, p. 35.
14. On the pre-1914 background of Putilov: R. Girault, *Emprunts Russes et Investissements Français en Russie 1887–1914* (Paris: A. Colin, 1973); Girault, 'Finances internationales et relations internationales à propos des usines Poutiloff', *Revue d'Histoire Moderne et Contemporaine*, 3 (1966); Jonathan A. Grant, *Big Business in Russia: The Putilov Company in Late Imperial Russia 1868–1917* (Pittsburgh: University of Pittsburgh Press, 1999).
15. Siegelbaum, *The Politics of Industrial Mobilization*, pp. 117–18.
16. SHAT, Langlois 6N 33; Laguiche's reports in 7N 757.
17. On Putilov, see the important works by Girault, *Emprunts Russes*, and Grant, *Big Business*.
18. T. Hasegawa, *The February Revolution, Petrograd 1917* (Seattle, WA: University of Washington, 1981); R.B. MacKean, *St Petersburg between the Revolutions, Workers and Revolutionaries, June 1907–February 1917* (New Haven, CT: Yale University Press, 1990). The sequestration is mentioned in passing in E.N. Burdzhalov, *Russia's Second Revolution: The February 1917 Uprising in Petrograd* (Bloomington, IN: Indiana University Press, 1987), translation of *Vtoraia russkaia revoliutsiia: Vosstanie v Petrograde* (Moscow: Nauka, 1967). Another example of Soviet historiography on these issues is T.D. Krupina, 'La Russie, la France et les rapports économico-militaires entre les alliés au cours de la première guerre mondiale', *La Russie et l'Europe XVIe-XXe siècles* (Paris and Moscow: École pratique des Hautes Études, 1970).
19. G. Katkov, *Russia 1917: The February Revolution* (London: Longmans, 1967; pbk Fontana, 1969), pp. 196–217 and 253–61. L. Menache, 'A Liberal with Spurs: Alexander Guchkov', *Russian Review*, XXVI, I, pp. 38–53.
20. Schaper, *Trente Ans*, pp. 128–29; Louis Loucheur, *Carnets Secrets, 1908–1932* (Brussels: Brépols, 1962), pp. 19–21; Thomas papers, *Archives Nationales*, 94AP, 174 and 183. Interesting light on the Viviani–Thomas mission, as seen from the Russian side, is in *Un Livre Noir: Diplomatie de l'avant guerre et de guerre d'après les documents des archives russes (1910–1917)* (Paris: Librairie du Travail, n.d.), iii, pp. 12–18 and 28: Bazily to Sazonov, 28 April 1916; Izvolsky to Petrograd, 30 April 1916; also included is Poincaré to the Tsar, 30 April 1916.
21. Thomas papers, *Archives Nationales*, 94 AP 174 and 183.
22. Paléologue to Paris, tel., 16 June 1916, a copy is in Thomas papers, *Archives Nationales*,

94 AP 174. It should be noted that although the leading figure in the management of the Putilov firm at this time was A. I. Putilov, this is a simple coincidence of names. The original Putilov, who had established the firm in the 1860s, had lost control twenty years later. A. I. Putilov, formerly an official, was a a financier, director of the Russo-Asiatic Bank; he was involved through that bank's investment in the Putilov firm after 1912.
23. Grant, *Big Business*, pp. 121–29. On the role of the Russo-Asiatic Bank, D.R. Watson, 'The Rise and Fall of the Russo-Asiatic Bank: Problems of a Russian Enterprise with French Shareholders 1910–1926', *European History Quarterly*, 23, 1 (1993), pp. 39–49.
24. Thomas papers, *Archives Nationales*, 94 AP 174 and 183.

4

Mission Accomplished? Britain and the Disarmament of Germany, 1918–1923

ALAN SHARP

The disarmament of Germany under the terms of the Treaty of Versailles added to the contentious problems of the execution of the settlement. It was one of several key areas of disagreement between Britain and France, upon whom the responsibility for enforcing the treaty largely fell, after the United States failed to ratify a settlement in whose creation President Wilson and his advisors had played a vital role. The problem was technically, legally and politically complex but it was also part of a larger picture. It revealed much about the divergent interpretations that Britain and France had of their national interest and their wider view of what might constitute a sound basis for a peaceful and stable Europe. It also highlighted the different interpretations each had of the concept of security and the future role of Germany.[1]

The treaty reduced Germany's army to 100,000 men, of whom only 4,000 could be officers. Conscription was banned, all must be long-term volunteers. Other ranks had to enlist for at least twelve years and officers for twenty-five. To prevent Germany using other state organisations like the police, coastguards and customs officials for clandestine army recruitment, the treaty specified their numbers could not exceed those employed in 1913, except where an increase was justified by a commensurate rise in the local population. Such officials must not undergo military training. Germany was allowed only seven infantry divisions and three cavalry divisions, no military aircraft, no tanks, no heavy guns and no poison gas or chemical weapons. Numbers of other weapons were strictly limited. Arms and munitions could be manufactured only in designated plants and the import or export of weapons was prohibited. Germany was allowed no military presence of any kind in the demilitarised zone which covered all German territory on the west bank of the Rhine and the strip of land 50 kilometres to the east of the river. It must not improve the existing frontier fortifications on its eastern and southern boundaries, nor its coastal fortifications. To deprive the military of a central planning mechanism, the general staff was disbanded and its reconstitution prohibited.

Germany's navy, a major source of pre-war Anglo-German antagonism, was reduced to a coastal defence force consisting of only six pre-Dreadnought type battleships, six light cruisers, twelve destroyers and twelve torpedo boats. Germany was permitted no submarines or naval aircraft. Except in the case of accident, none of the larger vessels could be replaced before they were twenty years old (fifteen in the case of the destroyers and torpedo boats) and then there were strict limitations on the displacements for each category. Germany was allowed 15,000 naval personnel, to meet all the requirements of the service. All must be volunteers, only 1,500 could be officers or warrant officers who would serve for twenty-five years, with other ranks engaging for twelve years.

These reductions were indeed dramatic – Germany had committed seventy-eight infantry divisions and five cavalry divisions, or 1.7 million men, to the attack on France and Belgium alone in 1914, whilst Germany's pre-war navy had fifteen post-Dreadnought battleships, five battlecruisers, twenty-two older battleships, forty cruisers and ninety destroyers. At the start of the war Germany had some 4,000,000 men under arms, the treaty now reduced its total armed forces to 115,000.[2] Germany had to implement these reductions and comply with the other military and naval requirements normally within three months. The treaty established three Inter-Allied Commissions of Control to oversee the execution of the military, naval and air clauses. Germany's armed forces were limited to the treaty levels until Germany joined the League of Nations, after which the Council of the League could modify them. Article 213 also required Germany to facilitate any investigation of its armed forces instigated by the Council whilst the treaty remained in force.[3]

Germany's former allies, Bulgaria, Austria, Hungary and Turkey, were also disarmed. There were some precedents for such treatment of defeated powers but this was a relatively unusual aspect of the settlement at the end of the First World War.[4] The experience which clearly most exercised the peacemakers was Prussia's circumvention of Napoleon's attempt to curtail its army after Jena. Several of the military clauses were obviously written to prevent Germany repeating Prussia's deviousness. These included limiting the number of training facilities, prohibiting the expansion of Germany's existing police or other potentially paramilitary organisations, the requirement that service in the armed forces be for continuous and lengthy periods, and the exclusion from any form of military service or training of personnel demobilised in order to meet the treaty reductions. Only 5 per cent of officers (two hundred) could be discharged in any one year before the end of their term of service. University societies, veterans' organisations and sporting clubs were to have no military connection or objectives and Germans were forbidden to enrol in the armed forces of another state (apart from the French Foreign Legion) or to undertake any military training abroad.[5]

Sir Edward Grey, British Foreign Secretary in 1914, was clear why the conflict had occurred: 'The moral is obvious: it is that great armaments lead inevitably to war ... The enormous growth of armaments in Europe, the sense of insecurity and fear caused by them – it was these that made war inevitable.'[6] Yet post-war military disarmament was not high on the allied agenda in 1918. The destruction of Germany as a naval power, on the other hand, was an almost unspoken given amongst British war aims and, whilst there were some lesser naval issues about which Britain and the United States disagreed, their fundamental aims were similar. The final terms reflected this consensus.[7] Lloyd George was delighted, he told Lord Riddell on 30 March 1919, 'The truth is that we have got our way. We have got most of the things we set out to get ... The German Navy has been handed over; the German mercantile shipping has been handed over and the German colonies have been given up.'[8]

Such thinking did not extend to Germany's army. Lorna Jaffe's study concluded that 'Not only was the military disarmament of Germany not a British war aim, but, ... Britain's wartime governments had not seriously contemplated a significant permanent diminution of Germany's military power.'[9] A recent article by David Stevenson has reinforced Jaffe's findings, pointing out that, 'The victors' adoption of the Versailles disarmament programme was ... late and sudden.'[10] It built upon, and was facilitated by, the crippling terms that Marshal Foch, the French Allied Commander-in-Chief, had demanded as the military price of the armistice requested by Germany. Although Sir Eric Geddes, the British First Lord of the Admiralty, might lament, 'Had we known how bad things were in Germany, we might have got stiffer terms', the reality was that, militarily, the armistice amounted to an unconditional surrender which destroyed Germany's capacity to continue the war.[11]

There were three main aspects to British thinking on the question of Germany's land forces, two of which were closely linked, and all of which can be discerned in the important statement of British objectives drafted by Philip Kerr, David Lloyd George's private secretary, after the Prime Minister had summoned his key policy advisers to a conference at Fontainebleau between 22 and 23 March 1919, at a time of deep crisis in the Paris negotiations. The first element entirely conformed to Lloyd George's radical philosophy and reflected his wish for an all-round reduction in armaments and military expenditure. The Fontainebleau memorandum accepted that, in the first instance, the disarmament of the Central Powers must be unilateral, but, it added, 'it is idle to endeavour to impose a permanent limitation of armaments on Germany unless we are prepared similarly to impose a limitation upon ourselves'.[12] The idea of the enforced disarmament of the Central Powers as a precursor to general disarmament was incorporated into the Allied reply of 16 June 1919 to the German observations on the draft treaty terms and became the preamble to the disarmament section of the treaty itself: 'In order to render possible the initiation of a general limitation of the armaments of all nations, Germany undertakes strictly to observe the military, naval and air clauses which follow.'[13] Article 8 of the Covenant of the League of Nations looked forward to 'the reduction of national armaments to the lowest point consistent with national safety'.[14] Carolyn Kitching has concluded, however, 'that Britain had no positive strategy towards international disarmament' in the period between 1919 and 1934, and 'that with one or two notable exceptions, the members of the British policy-making elite did not understand the very concept of international disarmament', confusing the idea with Britain's unilateral arms reductions undertaken mainly for economic reasons.[15] German disarmament rather than the more ambitious universal goal would dominate the early post-war period.

The second and third elements rested upon the resilience of the balance of power as the determining concept in the minds of many British decision-makers, despite the seductive charms of Wilson's notion of collective security. For Britain, Germany had a vital role to play in any continental balance. This could be openly expressed in terms of Germany being a bulwark against both Russia and Bolshevism, but underlying British thinking was also the less easily articulated wish to see Germany as a barrier to any French ambition to become a continental hegemon. Britain thus perceived that it had a strong interest in maintaining Germany as a significant land power, an idea perhaps based on the false premises that the war had destroyed Prussian militarism but revived Napoleonic dreams in France.[16] There were thus two key reasons why it was important to not weaken Germany too much. On the one hand, this might lead to revolutionary despair: 'The greatest danger that I see in the present situation,' wrote Lloyd George, 'is that Germany may throw in her lot with Bolshevism ... If we are wise, we shall offer to Germany a peace, which, while just, will still be preferable for all sensible men to Bolshevism.'[17] On the other, it was crucial not to remove Germany as a factor in the continental military balance, particularly since it would be the French against whom British politicians and defence chiefs anticipated measuring their capabilities in the early post-war years.[18]

The French had a different perspective, dominated by their need for security. The military disarmament debates centred particularly on Anglo-French differences as to the size and method of recruitment of the post-treaty German army. The French wanted a German army of 100,000 men, with long-term volunteer officers and non-commissioned officers and with other ranks conscripted for one year. Foch would allow Germany no frontier defences, but Field Marshal Douglas Haig, the British commander, believed that a larger army of 200,000 or 250,000 was required, not least to maintain internal order, and that Germany had the right to defend its eastern and southern, though not its western, frontiers. The American, General Tasker Bliss, proposed 400,000 men. The Allied military commanders' eventual report suggested a German army of 200,000 men with volunteer officers and conscripted other ranks. On 7 March 1919, Lloyd George suggested a volunteer army and air force of 200,000 men, with a minimum enlistment of twelve years. He was vehemently opposed to conscription, arguing that this would allow Germany to build reserves of trained men. Georges Clemenceau, the French Premier, pointed out that, for at least the next ten years, the war veterans would already constitute a massive trained reserve. He emphasised the dangers of the smaller, professional, army acting as a cadre for a much larger force. He conceded the voluntary principle but insisted that 100,000 men was the limit. Although the Americans supported a larger army of at least 140,000, Lloyd George agreed to 100,000. On 12 March 1919, the Council of Ten prohibited any German air force. The interplay between the Allied negotiators increased the severity of the terms, but left the British, in this, as in many other aspects, sympathetic to Germany's objections and subsequent requests for mitigation.[19]

Three Commissions of Control were established: Military, under the French General Charles Nollet; Naval, under the British Vice-Admiral Sir E.F.B. Charlton; and Air, under the British Air Commodore E.A. Masterman. Each commission had appropriate subdivisions; the Military Commission, for example, had three sub-commissions: munitions, armaments and material; establishments, recruiting and military training; and for fortifications.[20] The Commissions had absolute freedom of movement and right of inspection within Germany and the German Government had to supply qualified liaison officers to provide the Commissions with any necessary documentation or information.[21] As with other difficult areas of execution, disarmament required the cooperation of the German Government and its various agencies, none of which had a vested interest in its success. Obstruction and obfuscation were, unsurprisingly, a common source of complaint from the Commissions and there were, inevitably, some unfortunate incidents generated either by overzealous or insensitive allied inspectors or by resentful and deliberately difficult German officials and industrialists.

Germany's air power was rapidly destroyed, even after the delay caused by its unsuccessful attempt to persuade the Commission to allow some military aircraft for internal policing purposes.[22] There were questions about the effectiveness of the German Government in preventing the illegal export of equipment, amounting to over 1,000 aeroplanes and 1,000 engines.[23] There were also uncertainties about the 'supposed existence of unknown quantities of hidden aeronautical material'. As Masterman admitted, 'Opinions on the quantity existing vary considerably.'[24] Even so, despite systematic German resistance and delay, by the end of 1920 the Commission calculated that it had destroyed 25,823 aircraft motors, or 90 per cent of the target figure, and 13,079 airplanes and seaplanes, or 92 per cent of the requirement, together with six dirigibles and quantities of cameras, wireless equipment and spare parts.[25] In January 1921, the Air Ministry told the Foreign Office, 'The aerial disarmament of Germany may be regarded as virtually accomplished and whatever material may still be concealed cannot be regarded as constituting a menace to the Allies.'[26] There remained a number of technical questions about how to distinguish between prohibited military machines and the civilian aircraft that Germany would be permitted to operate, but the Ambassadors' Conference (the allied ambassadors in Paris who acted as the main political organisation supervising treaty execution) decided, 1 February 1922, that the work of the Commission would be complete on 5 February.[27] On 5 May 1922, the Commission would cease to exist and Germany could begin civilian aircraft manufacture.[28] On 1 May, the German Government accepted the allied rules for distinguishing civilian and military aircraft and their proposals for the future surveillance of flying in Germany. As Lord d'Abernon, the first post-war British Ambassador to Germany, pointed out, taken together with naval disarmament, this went 'a long way to complete, from the English standpoint, the policy of protection against the principal dangers which menaced us'.[29]

Naval disarmament caused comparatively few inter-allied disputes, once the initial debates about how to dispose of the ex-enemy fleets were resolved. The Anglo-Americans took one basic position and the French another, the lesser allies falling somewhere between. The Americans proposed sinking all surface vessels in deep water, but accepted the

British alternative to break them up. France opposed both propositions because it wanted to incorporate German ships into its own navy. The Italians favoured destruction, but, should any ally be given ships for its own use, Italy wanted a similar proportion. Japan took a very similar position. There was a more marked division over the fate of Germany's submarines. All favoured their total destruction, except the French, who wanted the submarines distributed, with a free hand as to their subsequent use.[30]

Given that most Allies favoured destroying the enemy vessels, it is ironic that the German scuppering of forty-nine of their interned ships at Scapa Flow on 21 June 1919 precipitated a threat, in December 1919, to reopen hostilities in a quest to gain compensation for an incident privately described by the British Admiral, Wester Wemyss, as a 'real blessing'.[31] The Allies demanded the surrender of German floating docks and five of Germany's six permitted light cruisers, together with some other cranes, tugs and harbour equipment, but the matter became entangled with other potential German infringements and non-compliances which the Allies felt must be resolved before the treaty came into force. Clemenceau took a particularly hard line and alarmed the British Cabinet by a draft communication to Germany on 6 December which threatened to end the armistice unless Germany agreed to the allied demands. The text was modified, the Germans capitulated and the December crisis passed, though it strengthened Lloyd George's resolve to end the Paris Peace Conference and coloured his judgement about the effectiveness of the main British representative left in Paris, Sir Eyre Crowe.[32]

Eventually a British proposal about the fate of the German ships was accepted in December. All surface ships would be broken up, with the proceeds accruing to the Allies in proportion to their losses – 70 per cent for Britain, 10 per cent each for France and Italy, Japan 8 per cent and the United States 2 per cent. To compensate the French and Italians for their lack of a wartime naval construction programme each could incorporate five light cruisers and ten destroyers into its fleet. Each of the five major Allies could borrow a battleship, a light cruiser and three destroyers for a year, after which they too must be broken up or sunk.[33] Germany had surrendered 190 submarines at the end of the war, fifty-three had already been broken up, and forty-three were on loan to allied powers for propaganda purposes. Everyone except France wanted the rest broken up and eventually the French accepted the principle of destruction after the distribution of the German vessels in proportion to submarine losses (70 per cent for Britain, 18 per cent for France, 10 per cent for Italy and 2 per cent for the United States). France was again allowed to incorporate ten submarines into its fleet.[34]

The question arose whether the French and Italians could obtain the armament and equipment of the ships to be incorporated into their navies or, as the British argued, simply the hulls. Lord Derby, the British Ambassador in Paris, suggested a compromise in January 1920, very much in favour of France and Italy, whereby the equipment would be stored separately and only surrendered to the French and Italians if inspections of the vessels revealed any irregularities, but this was unacceptable to the Foreign Office and Admiralty.[35] At the San Remo Conference in April a similar proposal was agreed – the equipment for the ships should be stored until the French and Italian members of the Ambassadors' Conference agreed that the Germans had infringed the treaty, after which it would be surrendered. In June, unsurprisingly, they judged that infringement had occurred.[36] Only after repeated demands in 1920 and inclusion in the May 1921 ultimatum, did Germany hand over the bulk of the equipment, leaving a number of issues to be settled by arbitration.[37]

'There seems to be little doubt that the Allied authorities were guilty of considerable self-deception in recording the belief that by the end of 1924 the naval terms of the Versailles treaty had been carried out and that Germany was effectively disarmed.'[38] Stephen Roskill's verdict is harsh, the contemporary diplomatic exchanges and naval reports do not suggest that naval disarmament caused major difficulties for the Allies – battleships are difficult to hide. They knew of German attempts, sometimes without the knowledge or authority of the government, to infringe the treaty by smuggling equipment abroad or by undertaking construction for other countries. They were convinced that Germany was hiding equipment but, by the end of 1920, in terms of the really important articles limiting the size of the German navy in both ships and men, the Control Commission reported no obstruction by the German Government.[39] By the following October, the Foreign Office summary recorded that the disarmament of Heligoland, some minesweeping in the Baltic, and the delivery of certain war material would not be complete until 1922, some surplus ships under construction had not been destroyed and the compensation for the Scapa Flow scuttlings remained incomplete – hardly a damning indictment.[40] Some legal questions about whether the Allies had the right to limit the calibre and number of the guns on new German naval vessels were submitted to arbitration in late 1922 but, on 21 December 1922, Hardinge reported that the Ambassadors' Conference was cutting the Naval Commission to two officers per power from 15 January 1923, anticipating its rapid final withdrawal. The international complications caused by the occupation of the Ruhr in January 1923 delayed the actual withdrawal until September 1924 but the reality was that the bulk of naval disarmament was complete by mid-1921.[41]

The reduction of Germany's land forces produced the most inter-allied disagreements, with manpower issues causing much of the friction. In the main the British authorities, mindful of the needs of internal security but also aware that Germany's neighbours possessed much larger forces than its treaty army, were sympathetic to German requests for some relaxation of the limits, both of timetable and size, imposed by the settlement. The War Office believed that Germany should be allowed a larger army of between 150,000 to 200,000, at least for 1920. There was also sympathy for the German use of various paramilitary bodies, such as the *Einwohnerwehr* (civic guards), estimated to have between 300,000 to 400,000 men, the *Zeitfreiwilligen* (*Reichswehr* reserves) with 150,000 to 200,000 men, the *Sicherheitspolitzei* (security police) with 40,000 to 60,000 men and the *Technische Nothilfe* (technical volunteers) with 30,000 to 50,000 men. All were armed with rifles and machine guns, and the security police had trench mortars, artillery and aircraft. These, and other semi-official or private paramilitary organisations, constituted a continuing problem both for the Control Commission and the allied governments. All were banned by the treaty, and the allies had already required their disbandment but the British judged them important, at least in the short term, to German internal stability, and thus tended to be more receptive to German pleas for a relaxation of the treaty.[42]

The French did not agree, but Lloyd George persuaded their new premier, Alexandre Millerand, to allow Germany more time to reduce its army. Whereas the treaty demanded that the army be reduced to 100,000 men either by 31 March 1920 – the date specified by Article 160 – or by 10 April 1920 (three months after ratification as Article 163 required), the London Conference in February 1920 gave the Germans until 10 April to reach 200,000 men and until 10 July 1920 to arrive at the treaty level.[43] From the outset there were concerns that too rapid demobilisation to the treaty levels, combined with the unpopular requests for Germany to surrender political and military leaders accused as war criminals, and the gloomy economic situation, might well lead to the revolutionary overthrow of the new Weimar Republic.[44]

These fears seemed justified when, on 13 March, a right-wing putsch, nominally led by Gustav Kapp, drove the Government to abandon Berlin, and revealed the limitations of the Ebert–Groener pact of November 1918 when the threat to the republic came from the right rather than the left. German army commander, General von Seeckt, refused to use his troops to support the legitimate Government, declaring '*Reichswehr* does not fire on *Reichswehr*.'[45] Notwithstanding this, the putsch soon collapsed, but its aftermath led to considerable Anglo-French friction when the French Government decided, unilaterally and against the wishes of Britain, to occupy five German towns in retaliation for the German Government increasing troop levels above the numbers permitted in the demilitarised zone because it feared communist insurrection in the Ruhr district.[46] This first serious Anglo-French dispute over treaty execution was papered over at the San Remo conference held in Italy, 18–26 April 1920. Millerand promised no future French independent action but the allied leaders warned that, whilst they were aware of Germany's difficulties and were prepared not to insist upon a 'too literal interpretation of the Treaty', they demanded its execution and, if necessary, threatened further occupation of Germany. The Allies invited Germany to a conference at Spa, in Belgium, to discuss treaty execution and allowed it longer to evacuate the demilitarised zone.[47]

By the Spa Conference in July, Britain was less sympathetic to the German military requests. This was partly because of the efforts of Brigadier-General J.H. Morgan, the British representative on the Military Effectives Sub-Commission, who was always deeply suspicious of the Germans. Not a man to mince words, he had already declared, on 12 March 1920, 'It is clear that there exists a pre-conceived plan for defeating the application of the main principles of the Treaty.'[48] He now advised Kerr that the German threat came not only from the 340,000 men he calculated to be in its official and paramilitary forces but also from the continued existence of a legal framework for conscription and the failure of the *Reichswehr* to recruit a single long-term soldier.[49] Morgan's indictment was reinforced by a French report, circulated to the British Cabinet on 4 June, which showed that only Article 180, which dealt with the disarmament of the demilitarised zone, had been completely executed. Germany's lists of its own and captured allied weapons were totally unacceptable, no real progress had been made towards dissolving the *Zeitfreiwilligen,* the *Einwohnerwehr,* or the airforce and Germany had made no attempt to alter its legislation to comply with treaty requirements.[50] All this clearly impressed Lloyd George, who declared it was time for the Germans to 'hear the crack of the whip'. He agreed with Millerand that the German request for an army of 200,000 was unacceptable, though they would consider an increased police service.[51]

The Spa Conference, 15 to 26 July, the first post-war occasion when the Allies met German negotiators face-to-face, highlighted many of the key problems in disarming a major power after a total war: exactly how many weapons existed; how many were unaccounted for, whether by accident or design; how quickly armed forces could be cut to the much lower levels required; what would be reasonable levels for reserves of equipment and ammunition; how to judge the good faith, or otherwise, of a government and its agencies which were being forced to act against their own wishes? Foch and the French wanted to encourage German compliance by occupying the Ruhr district, an option that Lloyd George and his Government were normally anxious to avoid, not least because of deep suspicions of French motives and ambitions. With some reluctance Lloyd George accepted that the only way he could get Millerand to agree to allow Germany more time to disarm was to include the threat of occupation in case of non-compliance. Germany was given until 10 October 1920 to cut its army to 150,000 and until 1 January 1921 to complete the reduction to 100,000. The paramilitary organisations must be disarmed but Germany could keep a larger reserve of rifles and ammunition for the army, increase the number of civil servants in the War Office, whilst medical and veterinary officers need not be counted against the 4,000 army officers allowed.[52]

After the Conference, Walter von Simons, the Foreign Minister, admitted that Germany's Governments had not taken the treaty seriously: 'The Allies take it only too seriously, as was made quite clear to us at Spa.'[53] His Government now did so, introducing a legislative framework for the treaty army on 26 July and passing a law abolishing conscription and regulating the length of military service through all three stages on 31 July.[54] In reviewing progress that autumn, the British took a more sanguine view than the French; both accepted that the *Reichswehr* would, with some reservations, be cut to 150,000 men by 1 October but, whereas the British felt that sufficient numbers of machine guns, rifles and cannon had been surrendered, the French did not. The British tried to brush aside the lack of progress in disarming the *Einwohnerwehr* and *Sicherheitspolizei* but the French report, emphasising the failure of the Germans to fulfil this demand, was, as Eyre Crowe, the Permanent Under-Secretary at the Foreign Office, admitted, 'a formidable indictment [which] ... may foreshadow a French proposal for the occupation of the Ruhr'.[55] It did not, but the paramilitary forces, particularly in Bavaria, which became their main base once such groups were banned in Prussia, dominated the disarmament discussions in late 1920.

In Bavaria there were a number of complicating factors: the legacy of the brief communist regime in Munich and fear of a repetition; particularist or separatist sentiment tied in with relationships with the central Government; and an ambivalent French policy towards different aspects of treaty enforcement, which did little to allay British suspicions of French intentions in the Rhineland and catholic south.[56] The *Einwohnerwehr* and other paramilitary groups enjoyed popular support, with the *Orgesch*, a body led by Dr Escherich, the head of the Bavarian *Einwohnerwehr*, acting as a coordinating agency between these groups and the *Reichswehr*.[57] The Foreign Office feared that the French were encouraging the Bavarians to retain the *Einwohnerwehr*, either to promote separatism or to justify sanctions against Germany.[58] British policy was also torn, for, as Crowe pointed out, whilst 'It ought not to be our policy to oppose the unity of the German state ... we have everything to gain from promoting such particularist tendencies within Germany as may weaken the hegemony of Prussia in the state.'[59] Would disarming the *Einwohnerwehr* mean that the law-abiding surrendered their arms, whilst communist insurrectionaries retained theirs? Hardinge saw the paramilitaries as 'a real danger for the Allies' although d'Abernon, supported by the War Office, was less concerned and advised their regularisation in the short term.[60]

The French view emerging from Foch's Versailles Military and Naval Council continued to stress legal uncertainties about recruitment, the inadequate disarmament of civilians and paramilitary groups, concluding that the 'German Government ... has put itself in opposition both to the spirit and the letter of the Treaty'.[61] The War Office was much more positive in January 1921, judging that the destruction of weapons, apart from those held by paramilitary organisations, was nearing completion, that the German army had been reduced to treaty establishment and was manned by volunteers, and that 'Germany has ceased to be a military danger to the Allies for a considerable period of time.'[62] Disarmament played a lesser role in the dramatic events of spring 1921, when, in a series of measures of doubtful legality driven by exasperation at Germany's failure to pay reparations, the Allies occupied Duisburg, Ruhrort and Düsseldorf and imposed customs sanctions on Germany. This, and the subsequent ultimatum to Germany to force acceptance of the London reparations agreement in May 1921, helped to keep the pressure on Bavaria which finally published the central Government's ban on the *Einwohnerwehr* on 28 June 1921. Escherich warned his men that resistance would be futile and considerable quantities of arms were recovered, though he did add an ominous note, 'Our work has not been in vain, the seed has been sown and the harvest will surely come.'[63] In early summer 1921, however, another difficult problem seemed solved.

From early 1921, prompted originally by the rapid progress of the Air Commission, but encouraged by the naval and military reports, British attention turned to what would happen once the commissions declared Germany disarmed and what controls could be legitimately maintained on a sovereign state. Indeed, in June 1921, d'Abernon wrote that this was 'the most important and urgent question before European statesmanship'.[64] Britain realised that such future control would be the price for French approval to end the work of the present commissions and rapidly concluded that something beyond the vague provisions of Article 213 would be required.⁶⁵ In August 1921, in Paris, the British Foreign Secretary, Lord Curzon, suggested ending the present supervision arrangements and replacing them with extra-territorial expert commissions who would have the right to enter Germany.⁶⁶ This provoked a long debate with the French, who were not anxious to end control and were not receptive to the British contention that future arrangements, being additional to the treaty, would require German approval and hence concessions, which might include the evacuation of the three towns occupied in March. Curzon tried to establish firm dates for ending control, and to limit any new supervision only until 1925, but although the Air Commission was reduced from 240 to 37 officers in October and big cuts were expected in the Military Commission, reparations enjoyed a higher priority for the remainder of 1921 and no further progress ensued.⁶⁷

In February 1922, the Foreign Office produced an ambitious proposal: Germany should accept new allied air and military control commissions, to be paid for by the Allies, until the evacuation of the Cologne bridgehead (due 10 January 1925), after which their future would be negotiable. Naval supervision would be by the League under Article 213. The air commission would have sixteen officers (three per ally, with a British president) and the military twenty (seven French, including the president, four British, three each from Italy, Belgium and Japan). Only half the officers could be members of the present commissions and these must be replaced in three months by officers without a connection to the current control. Germany should be informed of outstanding military and naval obligations and notified that, upon their fulfilment, the military sanctions of March 1921 would end.⁶⁸ The French wanted the new arrangement to last for eight years, they were not receptive to ending sanctions or to bringing in new personnel and wanted to present the arrangement as an ultimatum.⁶⁹ Discussions continued intermittently over the spring and summer but the expectation was that the main work of the commissions would be complete by October 1922.⁷⁰ Working on the basis of a report from Nollet in May, the British authorities reduced his sixteen points requiring satisfaction before disarmament could be completed to four of vital importance, four of secondary importance and eight of no real significance.⁷¹ On 29 September 1922, the Allies agreed a text outlining the conditions under which military control would end and the Germans agreed in October to negotiate a replacement body.⁷² Problems did remain but many now accepted that Germany was disarmed. With the French now prepared to be party to a conditional withdrawal of military control, there would have been long odds in October 1922 that the Military Commission would continue until 31 January 1927, but this was what happened when the negotiations for its termination became a victim of the Ruhr occupation in January 1923.[73]

The disarmament of Germany revealed much about the differing perspectives of France and Britain in respect of their former enemy. The French saw a powerful neighbour, with massive resources of manpower, material and economic strength which would execute the treaty only in so far as it was forced to do so. Even that might not suffice; Foch declared, 'Disarmament gives us only a temporary, precarious, fictitious security. Weakness in your adversary does not create strength in you.'[74] France sought to break Germany's 'military spirit' and achieve 'moral disarmament' – an elusive, intangible conceit.[75] Such a French criterion was unattainable, given that Germany struggled to come to terms with the paradoxical concept of defeat in 1918 when it was clearly victorious in the east and, at the armistice, still fighting on enemy soil in the west. Unfairly, it was civilian politicians, branded as 'November criminals', not the military leaders, that many in Germany held responsible for this inexplicable outcome. Behind every German request to moderate the treaty terms or delay execution, the French saw a master plan for treaty evasion, bad faith and deliberate prevarication. Nor could it be claimed that they were entirely wrong. There is substantial evidence that Germany sought to preserve as much of the organisation of the old army as possible.[76] Britain concentrated much more on the destruction of German weapons and war-making capacity. It tended to believe that Germany could not, or perhaps should not, disarm as rapidly or completely France might wish, for internal and external German security reasons and, less openly stated, in the wider interests of balancing power on the continent.

The decision as to whether Germany was, or was not, disarmed was partly technical, partly political and partly philosophical. There was evidence of German treaty evasion, but it was clear, at least to d'Abernon, that 'Germany is incapable of entering upon a campaign against the *Entente*, or even against an isolated France with the smallest chance of success.'[77] Even within Britain two schools of thought existed. Major-General Sir Francis Bingham, president of the Armaments Sub-Commission, stressed the physical disarmament of Germany, a view that generally found favour with the British establishment. Critics like Morgan were more impressed by German reluctance to publish exact details of recruitment or to abandon an administrative structure for an army far in excess of 100,000 men. They shared French concerns about Germany's ultimate intentions and thought processes. Where Bingham stated, 'We can at any rate say that at present Germany is unable to raise up her head as a military power ... today she has seven divisions and 288 guns', Morgan stressed the depth of military tradition in Germany and that, 'after a most careful estimate by our experts in all the industrial districts of Germany, we found that, from the moment control is withdrawn it would take the German authorities only one year to attain their maximum war production in 1918 of guns and munitions'.[78] In the wake of the Locarno negotiations, it was decided that Germany was disarmed, even though not all observers agreed.[79]

The Allies reached this decision on a mixture of quantifiable and psychological grounds but they could console themselves that any future German rearmament on a significant scale could not be secret and it would then be for the British and French to take preventative action.[80] That they did not do so, particularly after Hitler began not only rearming but exaggerating the extent of German rearmament, was not the fault of the men who had, effectively, deprived Germany of its material capability to make war in the early 1920s.

NOTES

1. The Gulf Wars have reinvigorated the study of post-First World War disarmament. See the articles in the special edition of *Journal of Strategic Studies*, 29, 2 (April 2006), edited by Professor Martin Alexander, University of Wales, Aberystwyth and Professor John Keiger, University of Salford. A special edition of *Diplomacy and Statecraft*, 16, 3 (September 2005), edited by Professor Conan Fischer, University of Strathclyde, and the author, deals more generally with treaty enforcement. See also Philip Towle, *Enforced Disarmament: From the Napoleonic Campaigns to the Gulf War* (Oxford: Clarendon, 1997); Richard Schuster, *German Disarmament after World War I: The Diplomacy of International Arms Inspection 1920-31* (Abingdon: Routledge, 2006); and Alan Sharp, *Britain, France, Germany and the Execution of the Treaty of Versailles 1919-1923, with Particular Reference to Reparations and Disarmament* (Unpublished Ph.D. thesis, University of Nottingham, 1975).
2. David Stevenson, 'Britain, France and the Origins of German Disarmament, 1916–1919', *Journal of Strategic Studies*, 29, 2 (2006), p. 196, notes 3 and 4; Hew Strachan, *The First World War* (Oxford: Oxford University Press, 2001), vol. I, *To Arms*.
3. Articles 159–213 of the Treaty of Versailles, *The Treaty of Versailles and After: Annotations of the Text of the Treaty* (New York: Greenwood Press, 1968 reprint edn of an original US Government publication, 1944), pp. 319–65.
4. Stevenson, 'Britain and France', pp. 197–98.
5. For example, Articles 162, 173, 174, 175, 177, 179 and 183.
6. Quoted by Carolyn Kitching, *Britain and the Problem of International Disarmament 1919–1934* (London: Routledge, 1999), p. 9.
7. S.P. Tillman, *Anglo-American Relations at the Paris Peace Conference of 1919* (Princeton, NJ: Princeton University Press, 1961), pp. 166–75.
8. *Lord Riddell's Intimate Diary of the Peace Conference and After, 1918–1923* (London: Victor Gollancz, 1933), p. 42.
9. Lorna S. Jaffe, *The Decision to Disarm Germany: British Policy towards Postwar German Disarmament, 1914–1919* (Boston: Allen & Unwin, 1985), p. 214.
10. Stevenson 'Britain and France', p. 201.
11. Germany had to surrender 5,000 artillery pieces, 30,000 machine guns, 3,000 mortars, 2,000 aircraft and a considerable amount of road and railway material. In naval terms, Germany had to surrender 160 submarines, and allow most of its modern battleships and

battlecruisers to be interned. See David French, 'Great Britain and the German Armistice', in M. Boemeke, G. Feldman and E. Glaser (eds), *The Treaty of Versailles: A Reassessment after 75 Years* (Cambridge: Cambridge University Press, 1998), pp. 69–86. Geddes to Beatty, 11 November 1918, quoted by French p. 86. See also B. Lowry, *Armistice 1918* (Kent, OH: Kent State University Press, 1996).
12. 'Some Considerations for the Peace Conference before they finally draft their Terms', printed in *Papers respecting Negotiations for an Anglo-French Pact*, Cmd. 2169 (London: HMSO, 1924), p. 82.
13. *The Treaty of Versailles*, p. 309.
14. Ibid., p. 82.
15. Kitching, *Britain and International Disarmament*, p. 5. See Dick Richardson, *The Evolution of British Disarmament Policy in the 1920s* (London: Pinter, 1989); and two articles by Andrew Webster, 'Making Disarmament Work: The Implementation of the International Disarmament Provisions in the League of Nations Covenant, 1919–1925', *Diplomacy and Statecraft*, 16, 3 (September 2005), pp. 551–69, and 'From Versailles to Geneva: The Many Forms of Interwar Disarmament', *Journal of Strategic Studies*, 29, 2 (April 2006), pp. 25–46.
16. Paul Cambon, the veteran French Ambassador in London, regretted in 1920 that the British sought to use Germany to counterbalance France: 'The misfortune is that the English are not yet aware that Napoleon is dead.' Comte de Saint-Aulaire, *Confession d'un Vieux Diplomate* (Paris: Flammarion, 1953), p. 536.
17. Cmd. 2169, pp. 80 and 82.
18. Lord d'Abernon wrote in 1923: 'Many of the arguments which were valid in 1914 against Germany are valid today against France ... Anyone who supposes that a French Government dominating the Continent as Napoleon dominated it after Tilsit will remain friendly to England must be a poor judge of national psychology...Desiring the maintenance of the Anglo-French Entente, I am compelled to desire the existence of a strong Germany.' Lord d'Abernon, *An Ambassador of Peace*, 3 vols. (London: Hodder and Stoughton, 1929), 2, pp. 238–39. See also Alan Sharp and Keith Jeffery, '"Après la Guerre finit, Soldat anglais partit": Anglo-French Relations 1918–1925', *Diplomacy and Statecraft*, 14, 2 (June 2003), pp. 119–38.
19. Tillman, *Anglo-American Relations*, pp. 161–66.
20. H[eads of] D[elegation] Meeting 3, 9 July 1919, *Documents on British Foreign Policy, 1919–1939*, First Series (London: HMSO, 1947 onwards), I, pp. 52–57 [hereafter DBFP].
21. Articles 205 and 206. *The Treaty of Versailles*, pp. 356–57.
22. Masterman to Herr Mertens, Director of the Peace Department of the German Foreign Office, 24 June 1920, DBFP, X, p. 145.
23. Masterman to the German Minister for Foreign Affairs, 8 October 1920, ibid., pp. 396–97.
24. Masterman to Allied Military Committee of Versailles, 11 December 1920, ibid., pp. 455–56.
25. Report by Masterman, 28 December 1920, Enclosure 3 in Hardinge to Curzon, despt. no. 3897, 31 December 1920, ibid., pp. 488–90.
26. Report, 6 January 1921, ibid., vol. XVI, p. 620.
27. G. Pink, *The Conference of Ambassadors 1920–1931* (Geneva: Geneva Research Centre, 1942), passim.
28. Hardinge tel. 53 section 2, 1 February 1922, in FO 371/7448/C1633 in the National Archives, Kew [hereafter TNA].
29. D'Abernon tel. 109, 8 May 1922, TNA, FO 371/7450/C6733.
30. Balfour (Paris) despt. no. 1120, 30 June 1919, TNA, FO 371/4288/96822/32842.
31. Wemyss, 22 June 1919, quoted by Stevenson, 'Britain and France', p. 210.
32. See S. Crowe and E. Corp, *Our Ablest Public Servant: Sir Eyre Crowe, 1864–1925* (Broughton: Merlin, 1993), pp. 366–69.
33. H.D. Meeting 110, 9 December 1919, DBFP, II, pp. 514–16 and 526–29. It was

intended to use the borrowed vessels for experimental purposes. The United States sank the battleship *Ostfriesland* by bombing in July 1921 and Britain used another battleship, *Baden*, to check the efficency of its post-Jutland armour piercing shells. See Stephen Roskill, *Naval Policy between the Wars,* 2 vols. (London: Collins, 1968), I, *1919–1939* pp. 247–49.
34. HD Meeting 104, 2 December 1919, *DBFP*, II, pp. 471–72.
35. Derby tel. 107, 26 January 1920, ibid., pp. 2–5 and FO despt. 410, 2 February 1920, ibid., pp. 7–8.
36. I[nternational] C[onference] P[roceedings] 109, Minute 4, *DBFP*, II, pp.225–26 and Derby tel. 695, 11 June 1920, ibid., pp. 138–39.
37. Hardinge despt. 378, 15 February 1922, TNA, FO 371/7557/C2295.
38. Roskill, *Naval Policy*, p. 98.
39. See Curzon despt. no. 199 to Lord Kilmarnock, Berlin, 17 March 1920, *DBFP*, X, pp. 49–50, or Curzon tel. 80 to British representatives at The Hague, Berne, Copenhagen, Christiana and Stockholm, 27 April 1920, ibid., p. 73 and the report of the naval advisers for the Conference of Ambassadors, December 1920, enclosure no. 4 in Lord Hardinge, Paris, despt. no. 3897, 31 December 1920, ibid., pp. 491–94.
40. Enclosure No. 1 in Curzon to Hardinge, despt. no. 2796, 29 January 1921, ibid., XV, p. 936.
41. Phipps (Paris) tel.676, Section 3, 21 December 1922, TNA, FO 371/7455/C17547.
42. War Office Paper, 2 February 1920, 'The Present Situation in Germany', circulated to the Cabinet, 15 February 1920. C[abinet] P[aper] 632, in TNA, CAB 24/98.
43. ICP 35, Minute 4, *DBFP*, VII, p. 118.
44. See H.A.L. Fisher (President of the Board of Education) reporting his meeting with Lt. Colonel Stewart Roddie, who was based in Berlin, 4 January 1920, Lloyd George Collection (hereafter LGC), House of Lords Record Office, F/16/74/47; 'Report of the Army of the Rhine', 6 January 1920, TNA, FO 371/3770/170424.
45. Quoted by Erich Eyck, *A History of the Weimar Republic*, 2 vols. (New York: Science Editions, 1962), I, p. 150.
46. The French occupied Frankfurt, Darmstadt, Hanau, Homburg and Dieburg on the night 5–6 April 1920, Sir George Grahame (Paris) tel. 425, TNA, FO 371/3782/190061.
47. ICP 108, Minute 4, *DBFP*, VIII, pp. 199–204 and ICP 109, Minute 3, ibid., pp. 220–25.
48. *DBFP*, X, p. 36; see also J.H. Morgan, *Assize of Arms*, planned as two volumes, of which only one was published (London: Methuen, 1945).
49. Minute by Kerr, 12 May 1920, F/90/1/8 LGC.
50. TNA, CP1381 in CAB 24/108.
51. ICP 112, Minute 5 and Appendix 2, *DBFP*, VIII, pp. 357–58.
52. ICP 24, ibid., pp. 482–83.
53. Lord Kilmarnock (Berlin) despt. no. 621, 27 July 1920, TNA, FO 371/4740/ C2812.
54. Kilmarnock despt. no. 619, 26 July 1920 and 646, 31 July 1920, TNA, FO 371/4756/C1661 and C1974.
55. FO memo. 30 September 1920, TNA, FO 371/4757/C7611. Enclosure in Derby despt. no. 3215 and minute by Crowe, *DBFP*, X, pp. 403–07.
56. Hardinge minute, 'The French are determined to get Rhineland [*sic*]', ibid., IX, p. 71, n. 3.
57. George Saunders minute, 31 August 1920, TNA, FO 371/4757/C4933.
58. Lord d'Abernon, Berlin, despt. no. 1187, 23 November 1920, TNA, FO 371/4758/C921.
59. Crowe minute, 20 February 1920, *DBFP*, IX, pp. 60–61, n. 2.
60. D'Abernon despt. no. 1066, 6 November 1920, ibid., X, pp. 427–29, and despt. no. 1260, 28 December 1920, ibid., p. 451; Hardinge minute, TNA, FO 371/4833/C4050.
61. Report, 18 December 1920, *DBFP*, X , p. 487.
62. Report, 15 January 1921, *DBFP*, XVI, p. 611, n. 1.
63. William Seeds, Munich, despt. no. 124, 30 June 1921, ibid., pp. 916–17.
64. D'Abernon despt. no. 789, TNA, FO 371/5857/C13421.
65. See correspondence with the service departments in July 1921, *DBFP*, XVI, pp. 927–30.

66. ICP 208 Minute 2, ibid., XV pp. 666–67; Cheetham (Paris) desp. 2790, 14 October 1921, TNA, FO 371/5864/C19718.
67. FO despt. no. 2796 to Paris, 29 October 1921 and enclosure, *DBFP*, XVI, pp. 954–60.
68. FO despt. no. 535 to Paris, 22 February 1922, TNA, FO 371/7448/C2560.
69. Hardinge tel. 127, 4 March 1922, C3207, tel. 135, 9 March 1922, C3527, tel. 151 section 5, 15 March 1922, C3953, and FO despt. no. 840 to Paris, 23 March 1922, C4266, all in TNA, FO 371/7449.
70. Hardinge despt. no. 938, 14 April 1922, TNA, FO 371/7450/C5515.
71. FO despt. no. 2102 to Paris, 7 July 1922, TNA, FO 371/7450/C8493. The key issues were: reconstituting the police into local units, converting munitions factories, surrendering remaining unauthorised war material and providing documentation on the state of German war material in November 1918.
72. J. Addison (Berlin) despt. no. 773, 3 October 1922, C13952, and d'Abernon tel. 193, 30 October 1922, C14925, both in TNA, FO 371/7452.
73. John P. Fox, 'Britain and the Inter-Allied Military Commission of Control 1925', *Journal of Contemporary History*, 4, 2 (1969), pp. 143–69; Shuster, *German Disarmament*, pp. 131–81; Patrick Cohrs, *The Unfinished Peace after World War I: America, Britain and the Stabilisation of Europe 1919–1932* (Cambridge: Cambridge University Press, 2006), pp. 237–79.
74. J.C. King, *Foch versus Clemenceau: France and German Dismemberment 1918–1919* (Cambridge MA: Harvard University Press, 1960), p. 22.
75. See Andrew Barros, 'Disarmament as a Weapon: Anglo-French Relations and the Problems of Enforcing German Disarmament, 1919–28', *Journal of Strategic Studies*, 29, 2 (April 2006), pp. 301–21; and Peter Jackson 'France and the Problems of Security and International Disarmament after the First World War', ibid., pp. 247–80.
76. G. Craig, *Politics of the Prussian Army* (New York: Galaxy edn, 1964), pp. 381–415; J. Wheeler-Bennett, *Nemesis of Power* (Basingstoke: Papermac, 1967), pp. 95–153; Morgan, *Assize*, passim; B. Whaley 'Covert Rearmament in Germany, 1919–1939: Deception and Misperception', *Journal of Strategic Studies*, 5, 1 (1982), pp. 3–39.
77. D'Abernon, despt. no. 1184, 30 September 1921, *DBFP*, XVI, p. 946.
78. F. Bingham 'Work with the Allied Commission of Control in Germany, 1919–1924', *Journal of the Royal United Services Institute*, no. 69, 1924, p. 752. J.H. Morgan, 'The Disarmament of Germany and After', *The Quarterly Review*, no. 242 (1924), p. 447.
79. Morgan, *Assize*, pp. xi–xvii.
80. 'Une bonne part de l'organisation de guerre allemande a été brisée par la Commission ... Pour refaire ce qui a été détruit, l'Allemagne ne pourrer pas opérer en cachette.' Raymond Recouly, *Où en est l'Allemagne: Comment La Faire Payer* (Paris: Hachette, 1922), p. 154.

5

Sunk Before We Started? Anglo-American Rivalry at the Coolidge Naval Conference, 1927

CAROLYN KITCHING

The Coolidge Naval Conference of 1927 has famously been described as 'one of the most dramatically unsuccessful international gatherings of the twentieth century'.[1] The world's principal naval powers, the United States of America, Great Britain and Japan, met in Geneva in the ultimately mistaken belief that their cruiser strength could be limited along the same lines which the successful Washington Naval Conference, of 1921–22 had limited their strength in capital ships. The Conference which began in an apparent spirit of co-operation, ended in acrimony and recrimination on the part of the United States and Britain; a situation which continued to degenerate over the following two years to a point at which they were actually considering each other as potentially hostile powers against whom battle plans may well have to be formulated.

Although much has been written on the complex reasons for the failure of this initiative, the majority of these discussions have been part of a larger study of inter-war disarmament negotiations.[2] The more in-depth analyses of the Conference have been in the form of articles, the most detailed being David Carlton's 1968 study. In addition, there have been two more recent articles published: in 1993, Brian McKercher examined the politics of naval arms limitation, which included some analysis of the Coolidge Conference, and in 1996 Tadashi Kuramatsu looked specifically at the British preparation for the conference.[3] A definitive study of the Coolidge Naval Conference awaits an author.

This chapter, in tribute to Dick Richardson, examines the Coolidge Naval Conference in relation to an area not covered by previous studies: his theory of arms control negotiations. In evaluating the prospects of success or failure of disarmament and arms control negotiations, Richardson believed that the presence of five factors is necessary for any disarmament conference to succeed. These factors are: a belief in disarmament, both by governments and the individuals who comprise these governments; political leadership; political will; an understanding of the technical side of disarmament; and an appreciation of the same problems as seen through the eyes of other parties to the negotiations.[4] This chapter will take some specific examples from the Coolidge Conference and examine them in the light of these five factors, in order to identify whether, according to Richardson's thesis, it could ever have succeeded, or was it, in fact, sunk before it started? It will, however, also ask two further questions. First, should two further factors be included? One based on a theory put forward by Brian McKercher, namely the presence of an unacknowledged deeper, less obvious, agenda,[5] and the second, which emerges from this current analysis of Richardson's criteria, is the presence of *political necessity*. The second question is whether it is, in fact, essential that *all* of Richardson's five factors be present in order to reach a successful disarmament agreement?

In the aftermath of the First World War, a naval race appeared to be developing between the United States of America, Britain and Japan. The United States feared the expansionist aims of the Japanese in the Pacific, and Britain feared the loss of her naval superiority. The Americans also feared a renewal of the Anglo-Japanese alliance, formed in 1902 against Tsarist Russia, renewed in 1905 and 1911, and due to expire in 1921, seeing the original rationale for the alliance as defunct, and themselves as the only possible nation against which such an alliance could now be directed. The American President, Warren Harding, hastily called a conference of the leading naval powers in Washington in November 1921, in order to prevent the British taking the initiative. There was no prior consultation between the nine powers who eventually met at Washington,[6] and the American Secretary of State, Charles Evans Hughes, delivered what the leader of the British Empire Delegation, the former Prime Minister, Arthur James Balfour, described as a 'dramatic announcement';[7] the element of surprise appeared to work admirably, with agreement being reached quickly and amicably.[8] The success of Hughes' approach was to have serious repercussions in Geneva.

The conference at Washington in 1921–22 was judged to have been a resounding success, stabilising the naval building programmes, and the political relationships between the five major powers, Britain, the United States, Japan, France and Italy. Capital ships and aircraft carriers were limited in the ratio 5:5:3:1.75:1.75 respectively. Agreement on auxiliary combatant craft was, however, less easy to achieve. Britain had been quite prepared to accept the foregoing ratio for cruisers, provided that she could also possess 'a number of cruisers and auxiliary merchant cruisers ... over and above the proportion agreed upon for use with the fleet'.[9] An alternative proposal was that cruisers be limited to a maximum tonnage of 10,000 tons per ship, and Admiral of the Fleet, Earl Beatty, put forward the required number, for fleet and other purposes, at fifty (which was, in fact, less than the existing complement), although it was not intended to make this figure public.[10] Significantly, although no agreement was reached over the question of cruisers at Washington, this figure of fifty was to cause grave problems five years later. The French supported the British position over the limitation of cruisers, and the final Washington agreement was that no other 'vessel of war' – in reality, cruisers – was to exceed 10,000 tons or carry guns of more than eight-inch calibre.

The effect of the omission of any restriction of cruisers was to encourage the signatories of the Washington agreements to build vessels up to that tonnage. A further issue which was to have repercussions at the Coolidge Conference was the agreement reached between the United States and Japan that the former would not increase the fortifications of the naval bases at Guam, the Philippine Islands and Hawaii. The Washington Conference was a success primarily because agreement was vital to all governments concerned in order to halt the threatened naval race, and to stabilise relations between the powers in the Pacific. Because the political aspect was so important, the politicians overruled the naval representatives on a number of potentially contentious issues.

During the period 1922–27, all the major powers reviewed their naval programmes and strategy to take account of the political and armament position in the aftermath of the Washington Conference. In 1922, with its concentration of interests in the Pacific, the United States reoriented its sea power from the Atlantic. Japan was viewed as the major potential adversary, and, given the lack of adequate bases in the area, the General Navy Board wanted to obtain the greatest possible cruising range and firepower in future cruiser construction: there was thus a desire to ensure that all new vessels were built up to the full Washington standard, that is 10,000 tons with eight-inch guns. It was also in the American interest, so long as the 5:3 ratio with Japan in capital ships was maintained, in order to keep the number of cruisers as low as possible. The higher the number of Japanese cruisers, the greater the threat to American lines of communication.[11]

In Britain, following the abrogation of the Anglo-Japanese alliance, Japan also began to be viewed as the major potential adversary. From 1924 onwards, the Admiralty's war plans were based on a conflict with Japan and a figure of seventy cruisers was inserted into the war plan as additional justification for the Admiralty's claims. In Japan, the major potential adversary was seen as the United States. From February 1923 onwards, under the revised Imperial National Defence Policy, accepted by both the military and the navy, and based on Japanese perceptions of America's

Asian policy, war with the United States was seen as inevitable.[12] In naval strategic planning, however, unlike the British and Americans, the Japanese decided to concentrate not so much on cruisers but on large, high-speed submarines, whose objective would be to disrupt the American fleet on its passage across the Pacific. In this way, it was hoped, the strategic deadlock of Washington might be broken.[13]

Yet, at a political level, relations between the three major naval powers, more particularly the United States and Japan, improved dramatically in the years 1922–27, primarily because of the Washington agreements. In an atmosphere of improved relations, the perceived success of the Washington treaties, and the need, certainly in Britain, to effect economies in defence expenditure, conditions would seem to have been favourable for a discussion of a reduction in the classes of vessels excluded from the Washington agreements, in particular cruisers. Much of the success of the Washington Naval Conference can be attributed to the fact that it omitted the contentious issues, and the question of cruisers certainly came into this category. As Brian McKercher points out, 'cruisers were at once the chief naval weapon for attacking and for defending maritime lines of communication'.[14]

In December 1925, the League of Nations had established a Preparatory Commission in an attempt to draw up a draft disarmament agreement to which the world's powers could subscribe. The story of the Preparatory Commission has been told elsewhere,[15] but the important point to note here is that, like Washington before it, the commission was meant to address all forms of armaments – land, sea and air – but by early 1927 it appeared to be making little progress. In 1920, the United States' Congress had refused to ratify the Treaty of Versailles, and consequently to join the League of Nations. However, it was becoming obvious that no meaningful agreement could be reached without their participation, and an American delegation was despatched to Geneva, although President Calvin Coolidge was at pains to point out that '[P]articipation in the work of the preparatory commission involves no commitment with respect to attendance upon any further conference or conferences on reduction and limitation of armaments.'[16]

However, even American participation at the Preparatory Commission failed to break the stalemate which had developed between Britain and France, interestingly, partly over the issue of Britain's proposal that naval reduction should be based on limitation by numbers and classes of vessel as well as tonnage, and French insistence that limitation should be by total naval tonnage, irrespective of classes of vessel.[17] By the end of 1926, it had become apparent that America was more interested in conducting naval talks separately from negotiations at Geneva. This, according to Brian

McKercher, 'had nothing to do with the international situation, rather it was a reflection of domestic American politics'.[18] Driven by heavy Republican losses in the mid-term elections in November 1926, the US Administration felt that a coup in foreign policy could silence critics at home, and a successful international naval agreement, initiated by President Coolidge, could bring political and economic benefits. In his annual message to Congress on 7 December 1926, therefore, the President announced that his intention was to extend the Washington Naval Treaty to cover the smaller craft which the treaty had excluded.[19] On 10 February 1927, Coolidge issued an invitation to the five Washington powers to attend a conference in Geneva to address these outstanding issues, although France and Italy declined his invitation. Unfortunately, he failed to recognise that agreement had only been achieved at Washington because an 'unusual coincidence' of technical factors made it possible for the powers to agree a mutually satisfactory ratio and level of tonnage in capital ships.[20] The technical problems associated with limiting auxiliary categories of fighting ships were all too present at Geneva in 1927.

In order to analyse Richardson's criteria it is more important to examine the individual naval ambitions of America and Britain than to examine the detailed negotiations at the Conference itself. The British Admiralty feared the onset of renewed naval competition; their preference was to contain naval expenditure whilst still retaining British superiority. In December, three of the Sea Lords, Admirals Dreyer, Field and Chatfield, prepared proposals which they believed would answer the Navy's requirements. These proposals included the extension of the life of capital ships beyond that agreed at Washington, a reduction in the size and armaments of the smaller classes of warship, the introduction of a 5:5:3 ratio for the larger cruisers with eight-inch guns, until this class eventually became obsolete, and a reduction in the number of destroyers, provided submarines were likewise limited. Ultimately, the most significant of the Admiralty's proposals was the reduction of the maximum tonnage of cruisers from 10,000 to 7,500 and of their guns from eight-inch to six-inch.[21] This was the most appropriate configuration for Britain's requirements in order to police her Empire. Britain consistently maintained that her needs were different from those of other powers: the size of her Empire meant that her requirement in cruiser strength was absolute, and not relative to the strength of any other power.[22] In a significant jump from the figure of fifty cruisers, tentatively proposed by Beatty at Washington, the Admiralty now declared that they would need seventy cruisers, of which twenty-five would be for fleet work and the remainder for trade defence. By applying the same criteria to the United States and to Japan, they came up with figures of forty-seven and twenty-one respectively.

Obviously, in addition to the political coup which Coolidge hoped would result from his initiative, the US General Navy Board had its own policy aims. In the spring of 1927 it produced a large document which covered not only American aims, but also what it perceived those of the other four Washington signatories to be at that time. It concluded that Britain's aims included the 'maintenance of naval supremacy for the defence of the Empire', 'domination of world markets and world carrying trade' and 'opposition to the domination of the continent of Europe by any single power'.[23] The aims of the United States were cited as the maintenance of the Monroe Doctrine, and of the 'Open Door' policy with China, and, most significantly as far as the possibility of any agreement with Britain was concerned, they desired 'a Navy second to none'.[24] The final American proposal was that the classes of warship which had not been restricted by the Washington Treaty should be divided into three classes – cruisers, destroyers and submarines – and that the total tonnage in each category should be restricted.[25] They suggested that each nation should fill that tonnage in the way best suited to their own requirements, and that the relative strength of Japan to Britain and the USA in each of the three categories should be approximately the same as the ratios agreed at Washington. However, since the total tonnage proposed for cruisers was only from 250,000 to 300,000, it was obvious that this would not accord with the British Admiralty's own proposals.

The current chapter does not intend to examine in detail the proceedings of the Conference. As previously noted, this has been done elsewhere. For the purposes of this study it is sufficient to understand that it was over this disparity between the American proposal for total tonnage and the British requirement for numbers and sizes of individual cruisers that the Coolidge Conference was finally to collapse. Much of the detail of problematic discussions will be brought out in the discussion of Richardson's five criteria. The first of these pre-requisites is *belief in disarmament*. Both Richardson and the author of the present chapter have produced works covering the policy-making élites in Britain in the interwar period, and have concluded that there was no such belief.[26] Brian McKercher's conclusions are less condemnatory than Kitching's and Richardson's,[27] maintaining that the British policy makers did their best in a virtually impossible situation, but the current author remains convinced that there is ample evidence to demonstrate that the overwhelming majority of statesmen charged with implementing a multi-national disarmament agreement did not subscribe to the concept.[28] Certainly, in Britain's Conservative government of 1927, there were few supporters of disarmament in positions of power, the notable exception being Lord Robert Cecil, and he was completely overruled at Geneva in that year.

Cecil had threatened to resign on a number of occasions when his colleagues did not support his views, and eventually did carry out his threat in the aftermath of the failure of the Coolidge Conference. He stoutly declared that his Cabinet colleagues were 'not strong enough to resist the Admiralty',[29] and in his letter of resignation to the Prime Minister, Baldwin, declared that 'on the broad policy of Disarmament the majority of the cabinet and I are not agreed. To quote a well-known phrase, we "do not mean the same thing"'.[30]

A comparison of the attitudes of American and Japanese politicians and service personnel is more problematic, as studies of their respective disarmament policies appear to concentrate more on the diplomatic negotiations and policy objectives of the national governments and service departments, rather than on the views of the individuals who constitute these governments.[31] Nevertheless, conclusions can be drawn from their opinions and attitudes. Fanning, for instance, portrays Coolidge as a President who, despite subscribing to the popular belief that the First World War had been caused by the arms race prior to 1914, was a 'throwback to the "shadow presidents" of the late nineteenth century who viewed themselves more as administrators than as leaders directing legislation through the Congress'.[32] It has already been shown that his calling of the Conference was aimed more with an eye to the next election rather than to any real commitment to naval reduction, other than from an economic point of view. Such a man was unlikely to be able to stamp his authority on those within his administration who firmly believed in American naval superiority. Sadao Asada provides an equally negative view of belief in disarmament within the policy-making élite in Japan at this time. Baron Kato Tomosaburo, the chief Japanese delegate at the Washington Conference and later Prime Minister, was the only real supporter of the primacy of diplomacy in negotiations. His death in August 1923 allowed the supporters of a policy of parity with the United States to dominate the policy-making process, with potentially disastrous results for disarmament negotiations.[33]

It would appear from the foregoing that there is little evidence of the first of Richardson's criteria. The second of his criteria is the existence of *political leadership*. Were the politicians able to override the service personnel whose goals were obviously going to be in direct opposition to the goals of a conference designed to reduce, or at best, control the level of armaments? This was definitely the case at the Washington Naval Conference five years earlier and is one of the major reasons for its apparent success.[34] At Geneva in 1927, the situation was markedly different. The point to consider here is the nature of the negotiating teams which each of the three participants sent to Geneva. The British and

Japanese believed the Conference to be sufficiently important to send high-ranking officials. For Britain, the chief delegates were Lord Robert Cecil and Sir William Bridgeman, First Lord of the Admiralty, supported by Admiral Field, Chief of the Naval Staff, and other naval experts. The Japanese delegation was also from the 'highest naval and diplomatic circles'.[35] Admiral Saito Makato had served both as Minister of Marine and Governor-General of Korea. Viscount Ishii Kikijuro was currently ambassador at Paris, with a distinguished diplomatic record. Vice-Admiral Kobayashi and Rear Admiral Hara, both naval experts, along with Sadao Saburi, Chief of the Treaty Section of the Ministry of Foreign Affairs, completed the Japanese delegation.

The composition of the American delegation was somewhat more problematic. Initial proposals were to invite Mr Charles Evans Hughes, the former Secretary of State, whose handling of the Washington Conference had proved so competent and effective. However, Hughes was unavailable, and the Secretary of State, Frank Kellogg, confided to Hugh Gibson, the US delegate to the Preparatory Commission in Geneva, that the President and he did 'not know of anyone else to invite'.[36] They considered sending a 'good lawyer' to help in drafting the treaty. However, the Navy was to be amply represented by 'Admiral Schofield and some other assistants'.[37] Eventually, it was decided that the American delegation would be led by Hugh Gibson, the 'good lawyer', Allen Dulles, and Admirals Jones and Long. In this instance, the strength and authority of the naval delegates far outweighed that of the politicians.

The composition of this delegation was to cause problems, certainly as far as the British representatives were concerned. Bridgeman, for instance, commented that 'the personnel of the American delegation was not of sufficient authority or position' and they were unable 'to move without advice from home'.[38] Gibson was 'a plausible, but not very experienced diplomat' and Dulles, 'a former missionary', was 'more anxious to save face than get agreement'.[39] His opinion of the two Admirals was also very revealing: Long he considered a 'nonentity', and Jones, whilst being a 'very charming man' was 'absolutely determined to get everything the Big Navy party wanted, or nothing'.[40] Jones has also been described as viewing the world 'through a porthole':[41] perhaps an admirable quality for an Admiral, but less so for an objective negotiator. Bridgeman had only been in Geneva for a week when he wrote to Baldwin that the 'American delegates are men of very inferior ability and even their Naval Experts do not understand their business'.[42] A week later, his patience with the American delegation was almost exhausted: 'Job is my pattern in patience and G. Washington, whose virtues seem not to have descended on his countrymen, for truthfulness.'[43] Whilst these outpourings of frustration were obviously very personal to Bridgeman, they do indicate the contempt in which he held the American delegation, and hence contributed to his reluctance to compromise with them. It was not, however, only Bridgeman and the British delegation who considered the American delegation to be inferior. Bridgeman reported to Austen Chamberlain that conversations he had held with the Japanese delegation betrayed similar concerns. The Japanese, he declared, were 'greatly disturbed at the idea of an American presiding over the conference, partly because the man at present suggested, Mr Gibson, is so much inferior in rank to their delegates and ours, and partly because they are looking to us to protect them from any undue pressure which they fear the Americans may bring to bear on them'.[44]

Bridgeman's perception of the American delegation was accurate on another level. The delegation was scarcely able to move without advice from home: official exchanges between Geneva and Washington amply demonstrate their continual need to consult with their political superiors. Gibson, for instance, requested instructions from Kellogg on deferring discussion of capital ships until 1931,[45] and the following day repeated his request for instructions.[46] Kellogg's reply was to inform Gibson of the response he should make to Bridgeman's requests.[47] This is not to say that other delegations did not consult their political superiors on a number of matters, but the American delegation does seem to have been particularly dependent on instructions from home.

Although the British delegation may have been of a higher rank than that the American, they also were subject to the dictates of others, though in this case the 'others' were not always politicians. Beatty, for example, in a letter to his wife on the first day of the Conference, declared that, '[M]ercifully I have tied our naval representatives up so that they cannot give very much away without referring to me'.[48] Interestingly, he also commented in this correspondence that Baldwin 'seems to be imbued with a total distrust of the United States and yet hasn't the courage to agree to a very definite line on our part'.[49] Further evidence of the predominance of the Admiralty over the politicians lies in the admission by Beatty, on 19th July, two days after an Anglo-Japanese compromise was made public, that 'a week ago the Admiralty had completed a new scheme as an alternative to be put forward in the event of a breakdown on all the other proposals. They had sent it to Geneva in a sealed envelope, with instructions that it was not to be opened unless the need arose'.[50]

One politician who influenced the Cabinet and Bridgeman during the time that the delegation was brought home for consultation was the Chancellor of the Exchequer. Brian McKercher maintains that Winston Churchill played a key role in the Cabinets that 'forced Bridgeman and

Cecil to take the hardest line possible against the Americans', his purpose being 'to enhance his prestige both in the Cabinet and amongst the Conservative party generally'.[51] When Cecil resigned, he laid the blame for the failure of the conference on Churchill.[52] The point here is not that Churchill exercised political authority over the Admiralty, whose budget he was trying to curtail, but rather that he supported the Admiralty in their bid to retain naval superiority over the Americans. According to McKercher, Churchill argued that the Americans were 'out to secure naval supremacy on the cheap' and 'this had to be resisted at all costs'.[53]

There would thus seem to be little evidence of political leadership; the politicians on all sides appeared to bow to the views of their respective naval personnel. In order to test the element of *political will* in Richardson's theory, it is important to establish what each of the participants hoped to gain from a naval agreement at this time in order to establish their commitment to reaching such an agreement. It has been shown that Britain wished to retain her naval superiority and, at the same time, effect economies in military expenditure. Having already established parity in capital ships with the United States, and an acceptable margin over Japan, as a result of the Washington Conference, she had no intention of conceding such parity in auxiliary vessels.

The question of parity was one which was to cause considerable misunderstanding between the British and American delegations at Geneva. Almost immediately the Conference began, Balfour brought to the attention of his Cabinet colleagues 'evidence in the official telegram from the United States of America and in the Press [the significance of which will be demonstrated later] to show that American public opinion was determined to accept nothing less than a basis of parity with this country for all units of naval strength'.[54] Sir Maurice Hankey, the influential Secretary of both the Cabinet and the Committee of Imperial Defence, was vehement in his opposition to conceding parity with the Americans in the smaller class of cruiser. In a letter to Balfour he pointed out that, whilst Britain should agree at once to the battleship limitation as far as 10,000 ton cruisers with eight-inch guns were concerned, she should 'ask for limitation to 7,500 tons with guns not exceeding 6-inch, and in the first instance we should ask for no limitation in numbers'.[55] 'Time after time', he declared, 'we have been told that if we made this concession or that concession we should secure goodwill in America ... I have never seen any permanent result follow from a policy of concession. I would refuse either to be blackmailed or browbeaten and stand absolutely to our preconcerted plan.'[56] For his part, Balfour believed it to be essential that, if it were the policy of the Government not to oppose parity, 'it was essential to remove all misunderstanding by a public announcement to this effect'.[57] Further discussion within the Cabinet, however, resulted in a request that they should not adopt the principle of parity of naval strength 'in so many words, as this was contrary to previous policy and was believed to be strongly opposed by the Admiralty'.[58] A week later, Churchill put before his Cabinet colleagues a memorandum in which he declared that 'we ought not to let ourselves be netted in a scheme of parity with the United States in Cruisers and other Auxiliaries, since there can be no parity between a Power whose Navy is its life, and a Power whose Navy is only for prestige.'[59]

Even the meaning of parity became confused: the critics of the apparent concession of parity, with Churchill at their head, argued against the concept of what he termed 'mathematical parity' in favour of 'maritime parity' which would allow for Britain's greater requirements and deliver numerical superiority over the United States in fighting craft.[60] This idea became embodied in what the British began to call the 'doctrine of requirements' which attempted to justify their 'absolute need' for a fixed number of cruisers. This figure was translated as fifteen large cruisers and fifty-five of the smaller type, accounting for the Admiralty's absolute figure of seventy. Were the Americans to accept this idea, it would mean that they would be restricted to fifteen large cruisers, and would have to use the rest of their 'total tonnage' in the smaller cruisers for which they had no use. Their alternative to this was to forego the idea of parity, which they would never be prepared to do. In an attempt to explain this requirement, the British counteracted the American argument that one country's requirements must, of necessity, be relative to those of another, and put forward the suggestion that the smaller type were 'defensive' in character.[61]

The Americans maintained that Balfour had conceded the issue of parity in all classes at Washington, which a search through the records of that Conference disputed; parity had only been conceded in the classes of vessel under discussion at Washington, and 'did not apply to Cruisers required for the protection of trade'.[62] Confusion had arisen at Geneva because it appeared that Bridgeman had actually declared that Britain had 'no intention or desire to question American claim to parity'.[63] The problem as far as both Cabinet and Admiralty were concerned was that no-one knew exactly what Bridgeman had said. The *Times*' Washington correspondent stated that 'Mr Bridgeman has made some statement to Mr Gibson at Geneva, which has eased the situation in America' and 'there seems little doubt ... that he has in some shape or form conceded the principle of parity'.[64]

The issue of parity seemed to be one of the major stumbling blocks. Hankey informed Baldwin that if, as appeared likely, Bridgeman's statement had led the Americans to believe parity had been conceded:

a great difficulty was likely to arise in the number of Cruisers. The Admiralty insisted that 70 Cruisers were essential for the protection of the sea-borne communications and trade of the British Empire. If America accepted this figure it would involve a great increase in Cruiser construction, and the Americans would say that the Conference had only resulted in increased armaments. On the other hand, if the British total of Cruisers was reduced, the Admiralty could not guarantee the protection of trade routes. Moreover, if America insisted on building 70 Cruisers, Japan would demand 50, in which event the Admiralty would require more than 70 British Cruisers. It was also pointed out that, by securing parity, the American Navy really obtained a great superiority, since British Cruisers had to be spread for the protection of our world-wide communications, whereas the American cruisers could be concentrated at any point.[65]

Beatty's attitude was that it was important 'that we should not say that we accepted parity ... He himself would prefer to see the conference break down, even with the onus on us, rather than put the British Empire in a position of inferiority to the USA and in insufficient superiority to Japan.'[66]

Parity, of course, was essential as far as the United States was concerned. It believed this had been conceded at Washington in 1922, and, as stated earlier, President Coolidge believed it to be a relatively simple matter to merely extend the Washington ratios to other classes of vessel. Given that, in the most simplistic terms, America wanted a navy second-to-none and Britain wanted to retain her naval superiority, it is obvious that a considerable compromise would be needed to reach agreement. The political will to make steps towards this compromise was demonstrably absent. The Japanese position, of course, would have some bearing on any final ratio agreed, but whilst the two major powers were deadlocked, the Japanese factor appeared irrelevant. The US Navy Board had, in fact, produced a report similar to the one referred to above prior to the Washington Conference, and the Secretary of State, Charles Evans Hughes, had ignored it, 'to the considerable mortification of its authors'.[67] Lloyd George and Balfour had similarly overruled their naval advisers at Washington; this did not happen, on either side, at Geneva in 1927. Political leadership and political will obviously overlap in some areas, but given the fact that both Baldwin and Coolidge distanced themselves from negotiations, it would appear that the political will was not as strong as it had been five years earlier. In Beatty's opinion, the United States had set out to 'achieve command of the sea at no cost',[68] and Coolidge's initial concept of 'conversations rather than a formal conference' appeared to transform into 'the form of a regular conference'[69] almost without any real consideration of the implications, or preparatory exploration of how this 'navy second-to-none' was to be achieved. Whilst there must initially have been some political desire to make a success of this Conference, for 'Britain had gone willingly, indeed deliberately to the Geneva Conference',[70] and Coolidge, for reasons already discussed, wished for a successful outcome, this willingness seems to have begun to diminish almost immediately. Chamberlain himself declared that he had 'left the whole question of disarmament' in Cecil's hands.[71] As for Coolidge, it has been observed that he very soon lost interest in the Conference which was to bear his name when its form changed from his original intention, and he 'allowed naval people to dominate the conference'.[72] It is apparent that those who have been shown to lack political leadership also lacked the political will to compromise on issues which jeopardised a successful outcome, and this clearly demonstrates the absence of the third of Richardson's criteria.

The next factor to be considered is an understanding of the technical side of disarmament. The central point of disagreement at the Coolidge Conference related to the tonnage of cruisers and the size of the guns they carried. At the Washington Conference there had been no attempt to divide cruisers into two distinct classes: it was the whole issue of cruisers and other auxiliary craft which had caused problems, and the success at Washington was directly attributable to the decision to leave these out of the equation. Also at Washington, the majority of discussions were held in an open forum, whilst at Geneva the bulk of the work was done in the privacy of technical committees, and as such less amenable to the more open style favoured by the Americans.[73] At Geneva, the British demand that they retain freedom to construct as many smaller cruisers, that is under the Washington tonnage of 10,000, as they required, conflicted with the American desire to limit by tonnage whilst building only the 10,000 ton, eight-inch gun cruiser. They maintained that such cruisers 'could proceed from America throughout the whole line of American naval bases and could reach wherever the United States Government might desire to send them'.[74] But, as Carlton points out, American prejudice against small cruisers 'owed less to the sparseness of their Pacific naval bases than to fears that in a war such vessels might have an insufficient margin of superiority over the potentially armed merchantmen, which Great Britain possessed in such abundance'.[75] These fears became more apparent when, later in the conference, the Americans 'insisted that they must be allowed to arm their small cruisers with eight-inch guns'.[76] Williams believes that it was the eight-inch gun more than the cruising radius that appealed to the

United States, and supports the view that they saw this gun as being necessary to guard against the fleet of British merchant vessels, which could easily be converted into cruisers armed with six-inch guns.[77] The technicalities of which cruiser would most adequately do the job demanded of it, underpinned by American fear of the possibility of having to confront British armed merchantmen, ensured that agreement remained elusive, although it is questionable whether these were actually technical difficulties, or merely propounded as such in order to obtain the type of cruiser most suited to British and American demands.

The final point to be considered in Richardson's theory is that of an appreciation of the same problem as seen through the eyes of other parties to the negotiations, and this was demonstrably absent in Geneva in 1927. At this point, it is fair to say that only the views of Britain and America really need to be considered, because the Japanese were virtually left on the sidelines. Japan had come to the conference determined to increase the Washington ratio from 10:6 to a minimum of 10:7, and the Japanese delegation recognised that the Americans would prove strongly resistant to such a demand. However, as Sadao Asada points out, 'the worst did not materialize, and a head-on collision was narrowly avoided, because irreconcilable Anglo-American differences over the cruiser issue submerged the explosive ratio question'.[78] This fact also averted dissension in Tokyo: as Japanese Vice-Admiral Kobayashi wrote, 'The clash between the [Japanese] government and the navy did not occur, because Anglo-American differences broke up the conference'.[79] The Japanese were effectively relegated to the status of on-lookers while Anglo-American rivalry played itself out.

Each of these rivals saw the policies and aims of the other as being the main stumbling block. The differing requirements in type and number of cruisers stemmed from the different purposes for which these cruisers were to be used. The Americans believed they needed the largest possible tonnage with the largest possible armament, that is, 10,000 tons with eight-inch guns, the rationale for this being that they had far fewer naval bases in the Pacific for refuelling and docking purposes than the British had throughout the rest of the world. Britain, on the other hand, professed a need for a preponderance in, and no restriction of, the smaller type of cruiser needed to protect the lines of communication with the Empire. Instructions to the British Empire Delegation at Geneva were to 'insist constantly upon vital distinction between larger type of fighting cruisers and smaller type which we require for the purpose of our imperial communication. This distinction is as vital as that between battleship and cruisers.'[80] Whilst prepared to concede equality with the United States in the former, larger, class of cruiser, Britain could not surrender her 'freedom of action', though did not question the right of other countries 'to decide at their discretion upon their own arrangements'.[81] There was thus a very different perception of need: Britain concentrated on the 'doctrine of requirements',[82] whilst the American perception was that agreeing to the British programme would require her to substantially increase her expenditure if she were to achieve the 'navy second- to-none'.

Making much of the theme of potentially large savings, both Britain and the United States appealed to their own and each other's public opinion, in an attempt to portray their own case as the most sensible and economical. The US almost certainly fared better in this regard than did the British, both at home and on the other side of the Atlantic. The British were, as Carlton points out, 'widely – and correctly – suspected of seeking superiority over, rather than parity with, the United States in fighting craft' and 'withering scorn was poured upon the absence from the British proposals of any reference to a limitation of small cruisers'.[83] The campaign which the American press waged against the British proposals became one of the major features of the Conference. In a memorandum prepared by the Foreign Office in the wake of the collapse of the Conference, it was pointed out that during it, 'an anti-British campaign of considerable violence raged in the US press', and that this was 'the result of some two years of well-organised and persistent big-navy propaganda'.[84] Significantly, it was also pointed out in this memorandum that this type of propaganda had made very little headway when Charles Evans Hughes had been Secretary of State, but the 'advent of Mr Kellogg meant a change for the worse; instead of a firm and dominating personality at the head of the State Department, there appeared a weak, irritable and not too friendly politician lacking the courage required in the US to espouse firmly the cause of Anglo-American friendship'.[85] Thus the question of political leadership again raises its head; even the man to whom the American delegation to the Conference looked repeatedly for instructions, was seen to be a pale imitation of the former Secretary of State. The press campaign was significantly strengthened by the activities of W.B. Shearer, 'a creature in the pay of the Bethlehem Shipbuilding Corporation' and other large private American shipyards, who deliberately 'fomented dissension ... with a view to preventing ... agreement between Britain, America and Japan'.[86]

It can thus be seen that Richardson's five factors were noticeably absent from the Coolidge Conference. The belief in disarmament was missing, as was the political will and leadership. The technical difficulties were inextricably linked with the ability to appreciate the same problem as seen through the eyes of other parties to the negotiations. Technically, it was possible for the smaller cruisers favoured by the British to fulfil the requirements which the Americans asked of them, but their hearts were set on the largest cruisers they could afford within the total tonnage they had proposed. To allow the British to have freedom in the smaller cruisers, which they saw as vital to their imperial obligations, would have either meant an unacceptable increase in tonnage, or foregoing the 'navy second-to-none' – neither of which was acceptable to public opinion.

It has thus been shown that, according to Richardson's criteria for a successful disarmament agreement, the Coolidge Naval Conference was doomed to failure. However, rather than merely accepting the absence of these criteria it would perhaps be instructive to question whether it is, in fact, essential for all five to be present in order to achieve a successful outcome to disarmament negotiations. In this respect, it may be useful to compare briefly the emphasis within negotiations at Geneva in 1927 with those in Washington in 1921–22 and London in 1930. Fanning's assessment of the reason for success at Washington is succinct: the Washington treaties were a 'remarkable combination of arms limitation and political settlement' which 'succeeded because delegates had not attempted too much'.[87] In essence, the political imperative to reach agreement dominated proceedings, and because of this, politicians on all sides overruled their naval experts, even to the extent of shelving issues which proved too difficult, as in the question of cruisers and auxiliary vessels. Thus the criteria of belief in disarmament and ability to resolve technical difficulties did not enter into negotiations at Washington; the political imperative dominated. At the London Naval Conference in 1930 the lessons of Geneva had been learned. There was much prior discussion and negotiation, thus ensuring that the thorny technical issues were ironed out before the Conference began, and that each side understood the other's perspective. Both American and British leaders overruled their naval advisers and experts, and certainly as far as the British Labour Prime Minister, Ramsay MacDonald, was concerned, there was a greater degree of belief in disarmament *per se*.

Nevertheless, this still does not prove Richardson's theory conclusively. The current author would argue that the Washington Conference was a success not because of an ability to resolve technical issues, but because it *ignored* them, preferring to leave them out of negotiations altogether. There is also no evidence that a *belief* in disarmament was either present or essential: what was essential was a political imperative to reach agreement, and the personal beliefs of the delegates were irrelevant compared with this imperative, as were the strategic views of the naval personnel. The situation at the 1930 London Naval Conference was similar in some respects. Certainly MacDonald was a greater believer in disarmament than either Baldwin or Coolidge had been, but he also was driven by the political imperative, as was his American counterpart, Hoover, and thus the obstacles of technical difficulties and perceived requirements of Admiralty and Navy Board were dealt with, rather than ignored or allowed to dominate. Whilst in an ideal world the presence of Richardson's criteria would appear to favour successful agreement, a further factor could also be required, and that is the political *necessity* of reaching agreement.

Brian McKercher has brought yet another element into the discussion of the failure of negotiations at Geneva in 1927, which is the assumption that the agenda is reasonably obvious to all parties in the negotiations; a criterion which he believes was not necessarily present in the case of the Coolidge Conference. He points out that the Foreign Office 'concluded that the breakdown at Geneva stemmed from the incongruity of the British doctrine of maritime belligerent rights and the American theory of the freedom of the seas'.[88] Following discussions between the British Ambassador at Washington, Sir Esme Howard, and Coolidge's 'heir apparent', Hoover, the former concluded that the 'basic problem in Anglo-American relations stemmed from the political inability to square belligerent rights with the freedom of the seas'.[89] The Foreign Office believed this issue to be sufficiently serious for it to persuade the Cabinet to set up a Committee to consider it. The Admiralty, on the other hand, whilst recognising the problem, believed it to be nothing more than a 'diplomatic wrinkle'.[90] As McKercher points out, Rear-Admiral Sir Dudley Pound, assistant chief of the naval staff, declared that:

> We could never get the Americans to say why they wanted their cruisers but it is quite obvious what is at the back of their minds.
> a) They want 'Freedom of the Seas' by which they mean that when they are neutral no one shall interfere with their ships.
> b) To force us to agree to the 'F. of the Seas' they want 'parity'.
> c) They want to achieve 'parity' *on the cheap*, i.e. force us by treaty to come back to their level instead of having to build up to our level.[91]

McKercher presents a detailed analysis of the issue of belligerent rights versus freedom of the seas, but for the purpose of the current exercise it is enough to say that the British Cabinet finally accepted the Foreign Office view that a vicious circle existed – naval limitation, arbitration and belligerent rights – and that settling the belligerent rights issue 'was the key to breaking the circle'.[92]

If McKercher's view is accepted, the Conference was not about limiting the level of cruisers and auxiliary vessels for the present, but more concerned with future developments. The Great War, which was only nine years distant, had taught both Britain and America important lessons. For Britain, it highlighted the need to enforce a blockade where necessary or to break one if equally necessary. The employment of belligerent rights had ensured Britain's survival during the Great War. America, for her part, as a neutral for most of it, wished to retain the freedom to operate in all arenas. The freedom of the seas was crucial to her economic and foreign policy.

However, Kuramatsu disputes McKercher's view of the centrality of belligerent rights and maintains that the US State Department believed that this issue was 'a sort of smoke screen brought up by the British to make the Americans agree to the British claims for superiority in cruisers. The truth was that the Americans simply would not accept anything less than "a navy second to none"'.[93] Nevertheless, the seriousness with which the British government treated the issue of belligerent rights, in the months following the collapse of the Conference, appears to provide convincing evidence that McKercher's hypothesis deserves careful consideration. If he is correct, it would seem that all the cards were not on the table at the Coolidge Conference, further hampering its chances of success.

It is not the intention of this chapter to apportion blame for the failure of the Conference, though this has traditionally been laid at Britain's door, especially in the light of Cecil's resignation, but Kuramatsu disputes this contention and Allen Dulles could not avoid admitting, in June 1928, that the US wanted a big navy for prestige, and that types rather than tonnage wrecked the conference.[94] Dulles blamed the 'lack of knowledge of each other's intentions', and argued that the fact that Britain wanted seventy cruisers, at a time when she only possessed fifty, meant 'that any agreement would be fixing a limit for the future and not the present', which would in turn 'encourage rather than discourage building'.[95] Anglo-American rivalry, the insistence of the Americans on their right to arm all cruisers with eight-inch guns, and the British rejection of this claim, were what sank the Conference, and without the necessary preparation, and the understanding of each other's point of view, the Conference was almost certainly sunk before it started.

And yet, despite the Coolidge Conference being deemed the 'most dramatically unsuccessful' of international gatherings, it is arguable that it did play a large part in ensuring the success of the Conference which followed it less than three years later. The London Naval Conference of 1930 was judged to have been a resounding success because of the lessons learned in 1927. The Coolidge Conference had arguably cleared the ground for an Anglo-American agreement, brought about by the 'coincidence of favorable administrations in both countries'.[96] Prior to the

London Naval Conference, there was a great deal of consultation and preparatory work undertaken. The political leadership was present, with Ramsay MacDonald once again overriding Admiralty demands and accepting fifty rather than seventy cruisers, though with what effect on British prestige is perhaps a debateable point.⁹⁷

NOTES

1. D. Carlton, 'Great Britain and the Coolidge Naval Disarmament Conference of 1927', *Political Science Quarterly*, 83, 4 (1968), pp. 573–98.
2. Perhaps the most detailed of these analyses is R.W. Fanning, *Peace and Disarmament: Naval Rivalry and Arms Control 1922–1933* (Lexington, KY: University Press of Kentucky, 1995). See also C. Hall, *Britain, America and Arms Control, 1921–37* (London: Macmillan, 1987); C.J. Kitching, *Britain and the Problem of International Disarmament, 1919–1934* (London: Routledge, 1999); B.J.C. McKercher, *The Second Baldwin Government and the United States, 1924–1929: Attitudes and Diplomacy* (Cambridge: Cambridge University Press, 1984); Dick Richardson, *The Evolution of British Disarmament Policy in the 1920s* (London: Pinter Publishers, 1989); S. Roskill, *Naval Policy between the Wars* (London: Collins, 1968).
3. Carlton, 'Great Britain and the Coolidge Conference'; B.J.C. McKercher, 'The Politics of Naval Arms Limitation in Britain in the 1920s', *Diplomacy and Statecraft*, 4, 3 (1993), pp. 35–59; T. Kuramatsu, 'The Geneva Naval Conference of 1927: The British Preparation for the Conference, December 1926 to June 1927', *Journal of Strategic Studies*, 19, 1 (1996) pp. 104–21.
4. Dick Richardson, 'Process and Progress in Disarmament: Some Lessons of History', in V. Harle and S. Sivonen (eds), *Europe in Transition* (London: Pinter Publishers, 1989).
5. B.J.C. McKercher, 'Belligerent Rights in 1927–1929: Foreign Policy versus Naval Policy in the Second Baldwin Government', *Historical Journal*, 29, 4 (1986), pp. 963–74.
6. The nine were the United States, Britain, Japan, France, Italy, China, Belgium, The Netherlands and Portugal.
7. House of Lords Library, *Lloyd George Papers*, F/61/1/2, Balfour to Lloyd George, 14 November 1921, despatch no. 2.
8. For a detailed analysis of the Washington Naval Conference see E. Goldstein and J. Maurer (eds), *The Washington Conference, 1921–22: Naval Rivalry, East Asian Stability and the Road to Pear Harbor* (Ilford: Cass, 1994).
9. The National Archives, Kew [hereafter TNA], CAB 30/1A. 1st Conference of the British Empire Delegation, 13 November 1921.
10. TNA, CAB 30/1A, Balfour to Curzon, 29 November 1927.
11. US National Archives: General Board files, quoted in R.G. O'Connor, *Perilous Equilibrium: The United States and the London Naval Conference of 1930* (Lawrence, KS: University of Kansas Press, 1962). Paradoxically, if Britain were the projected adversary and the 5:5 ratio maintained, the General Board claimed it would be better to have a larger number of cruisers because of the putative potential of Britain's armed merchant cruisers.
12. T. Shimanuki, 'The Development of the Imperial National Defence Policy, the Estimate and Requisite Armament, and the Outline of Strategy since World War I', *Gunji shigaku*, 9, 1 (1973), pp. 65–74, cited in Sadao Asada, 'From Washington to London: The Imperial Japanese Navy and the Politics of Naval Limitation', in Goldstein and Maurer (eds), *The Washington Conference*.
13. On this point, see Asada, 'From Washington to London'.
14. McKercher, 'Politics of Naval Arms Limitation', p. 43.
15. See, for example, Kitching, *Britain and the Problem of International Disarmament*; McKercher, *Second Baldwin Government*; B.J.C. McKercher (ed.), *Arms Limitation and Disarmament: Restraints on War, 1899–1939* (Westport, CT: Praeger, 1992); Richardson,

The Evolution of British Disarmament Policy.
16. *Papers Relating to the Foreign Relations of the United States* [hereafter *FRUS*], I, 1926, (Washington; Government Printing Office, 1941), Coolidge, message to Congress, 4 January 1926, pp. 42–44.
17. See earlier references to proceedings at the Preparatory Conference.
18. McKercher, *Second Baldwin Government*, pp. 58–59.
19. *FRUS*, 1926, I, pp. vii–xxx.
20. Carlton, 'Great Britain and the Coolidge Conference', p. 574.
21. See Roskill, *Naval Policy*, p. 499.
22. See, for example, TNA, CAB 23/54, CC38(27), 4 July 1927; Roskill, *Naval Policy*, p. 500.
23. Cited in Roskill, *Naval Policy*, p. 501
24. Ibid.
25. Ibid., p. 502.
26. See Kitching, *Britain and the Problem of International Disarmament*; and Richardson, *The Evolution of British Disarmament Policy*.
27. McKercher, *Second Baldwin Government*.
28. For an in-depth discussion of the British policy-making élite during the inter-war period, see Kitching, *Britain and the Problem of International Disarmament*, ch. 3.
29. British Library, Cecil Papers, ADD.51073, 26 July 1927.
30. Ibid., ADD.51080, 9 August 1927.
31. See discussions of negotiations in publications previously referred to in this chapter for an impression of such attitudes.
32. Fanning, *Peace and Disarmament*, p. 19.
33. Asada, 'From Washington to London'.
34. For an analysis of all five major powers' policies at the Washington Conference, see Goldstein and Maurer (eds), *The Washington Conference*.
35. McKercher, *Second Baldwin Government*, p. 65.
36. *FRUS*, 1927, I (Washington; Government Printing Office, 1942), 500.A15a 1/182b: tel. Kellogg to Gibson, 13 April 1927.
37. Ibid.
38. Salop County Records Office, Bridgeman Papers, p. 143.
39. Ibid.
40. Ibid.
41. B.H. Williams, *The United States and Disarmament* (Port Washington: Kennikat Press, 1973), p. 166.
42. Cambridge University Library, Baldwin Papers, Volume 130, Bridgeman to Baldwin, 25 June 1927.
43. Ibid., Bridgeman to Baldwin, 1 July 1927.
44. Birmingham University Library, Austen Chamberlain Papers, AC/54/54, Bridgeman to Chamberlain, 3 July 1927.
45. *FRUS*, 1927, I, 500.A15a 1/136, tel. Gibson to Kellogg, 23 June 1927.
46. Ibid., 500.A15a 1/324, tel. Gibson to Kellogg, 24 June 1927.
47. Ibid., 500.A15a 1/322, tel. Kellogg to Gibson, 24 June 1927.
48. B. McL. Ranft (ed.), *The Beatty Papers*, vol. 1 (Navy Records Society, 1989), p. 350, No. 196 [BTY/17/77/108-111] to his wife, 21 June 1927.
49. Ibid.
50. Report. Proceedings and Memoranda of Cabinet Committee on Further Limitation of Naval Armaments, LNA (27) Series, 3rd Meeting, 19 July 1927, TNA, CAB 27/350.
51. McKercher, 'Politics of Naval Arms Limitation', p. 48.
52. Ibid.
53. Ibid.
54. TNA, CAB 23/54, CC37(27)10, 29 June 1927.
55. British Library, Balfour Papers, ADD. 49704, Hankey to Balfour, 29 June 1927.
56. Ibid.
57. TNA, CAB 23/54, CC37(27)10, 29 June 1927.

58. Ibid.
59. Ibid., CC38(27)5, 4 July 1927.
60. Carlton, 'Great Britain and the Coolidge Conference', p. 578.
61. Ibid., p. 580.
62. Ibid.
63. Ibid.
64. Baldwin Papers, Hankey to Baldwin, 1 July 1927.
65. TNA, CAB 23/54, CC38(27)5, 4 July 1927.
66. TNA, CAB 27/350, Report, Proceedings and Memoranda of Cabinet Committee on Further Limitation of Naval Armaments, Geneva Conference, LNA (27) Series, 2nd Meeting, 18 July 1927.
67. Ibid.
68. McL. Ranft, *The Beatty Papers*, p. 355.
69. *FRUS*, 1927, I, 500.A15a 1/169, British Ambassador at Washington, Howard, to Secretary of State, Chamberlain, 6 April 1927.
70. K. Middlemas and J. Barnes, *Baldwin: A Biography* (London: Weidenfeld and Nicolson, 1969), p. 369.
71. British Library, Cecil Papers, ADD.51079, Chamberlain to Cecil, 10 August 1927.
72. Kuramatsu, 'The Geneva Naval Conference of 1927', note 41.
73. Williams, *The United States and Disarmament*, p. 167.
74. TNA, FO 411/6, memorandum by Austen Chamberlain, 11 July 1927.
75. Carlton, 'Great Britain and the Coolidge Conference', p. 582.
76. Ibid.
77. Williams, *The United States and Disarmament*, p. 175.
78. Asada, 'From Washington to London', p. 168.
79. Ibid.
80. Telegram from Chamberlain to BED [British Empire Delegation], cited in Carlton, 'Great Britain and the Coolidge Conference', p. 580. Carlton provides evidence to show that this telegram was, in fact, drafted by Birkenhead.
81. Ibid.
82. Ibid.
83. Ibid., p. 576.
84. TNA, CAB 24/189, CP293(27), Memorandum by Foreign Office 'Respecting the Future of Anglo-American Relations', 17 November 1927.
85. Ibid.
86. Richardson, *The Evolution of British Disarmament Policy*, p. 3. For a more detailed description of the activities of Shearer, see Fanning, *Peace and Disarmament*, pp. 65–67.
87. Fanning, *Peace and Disarmament*, p. 159.
88. McKercher, 'Belligerent Rights', p. 964.
89. Ibid., p. 965.
90. Ibid.
91. Pound to Keyes [Commander-in-Chief of the Mediterranean Fleet], 10 August 1927, KEYES [Churchill College, Cambridge], 15/20, cited in ibid.
92. Ibid., p. 972.
93. Kuramatsu, 'The Geneva Naval Conference of 1927', p. 116.
94. TNA, CAB 21/321, Registered Files, Transcript of Notes by Major Casey, Australian Liaison Officer, 12 June 1928.
95. Ibid.
96. Williams, *The United States and Disarmament*, p. 168.
97. See McKercher, *Politics of Naval Arms Limitation*, p. 52.

6

Arms Control and the Anglo-Soviet Naval Agreement of 1937

KEITH NEILSON

The Anglo-Soviet naval agreement of July 1937 has until recently been an under-researched topic.[1] Conventional accounts of British naval arms limitation tend to end with the signing of the Anglo-German Naval Agreement (AGNA) of June 1935 and to ignore all subsequent efforts at naval disarmament.[2] Greg Kennedy has shown that such an approach is unfortunate, both because it ignores the fact that the implementation of the AGNA was in fact dependent upon the Anglo-Soviet Agreement and because it fails to see that British naval strategy was conditioned by naval arms limitation generally and not just with respect to Germany. There is, however, another matter that the Anglo-Soviet Agreement illustrates and that is the matter of what is required for success in arms-control discussions. As Dick Richardson pointed out, for successful negotiations to occur, at least five conditions must be met. Two of these – the need for both parties to want the talks to succeed and the ability of both sides to see the other's circumstances and to adjust policy accordingly – are nicely illustrated by the naval arms control negotiations between Britain and Soviet Russia in 1936–37.[3]

Soviet Russia was extremely displeased when Britain signed the AGNA. For the Soviets, the agreement seemed to block the way for any potential cooperation between Britain and Soviet Russia to check German aggression. Also, it was viewed as a reneging on the promise made by Anthony Eden, then Secretary for League of Nations Affairs, when he had visited Moscow in 1935, at which time he had declared that no such agreement was possible.[4] However, despite this disappointment, Britain and Soviet Russia began naval talks a year later in May 1936. The reasons for this were varied. The British realised that they needed an agreement with the Soviets when Japan left the London Naval Conference early in 1936. Faced with the possibility that naval arms control would collapse entirely, the British decided to attempt to negotiate bilateral agreements with France and the United States. These were to be followed by an agreement with Germany and a further accord with Soviet Russia. Soviet concurrence was particularly important, for if an understanding could not be reached with Moscow, and the Russians began to build in a fashion incommensurate with existing bilateral agreements, this would cause the other Powers to react. Soviet building could spur Japanese building and Japanese building would lead to American construction. Further, Germany would be unlikely to accept an expansion of the Soviet fleet, particularly because of the signature of the Franco-Soviet Pact in May 1935. Thus, an Anglo-Soviet agreement was critical for the success of Britain's complicated efforts to ensure her naval position by means of arms control. For the Soviets, the position was more straightforward. They did not trust either Japan or Germany to observe any arms limitation agreements. Instead, they put their faith in new building programmes, but were willing to negotiate arms control at the same time as increasing the size of the Soviet fleet.[5]

This position was driven home in the Anglo-Soviet naval arms control talks that began in May 1936. At that time, the Soviets had made it clear that, in any Anglo-Soviet naval agreement, Moscow would reserve the right to build a fleet sufficient to defend its coasts and its rights in the Far East.[6] After meetings later in the month, further complications emerged. The Soviets also were unwilling to 'exchange information regarding vessels in the Far East', and argued that it was necessary to pursue a qualitative building race with the Japanese because the latter's fleet was, in the words of the Soviet Ambassador to Britain, Ivan Maisky, 'all-powerful, whilst the Soviet Far Eastern Navy hardly existed'. It was evident, as the Director of Plans at the Admiralty, Captain T.S.V. Phillips, noted, that such Russian reservations 'will undermine the whole basis of a naval treaty'.[7] Admiral Sir William James, the Deputy Chief of the Naval Staff, agreed, but added that, as any Soviet naval building 'cannot seriously disturb the balance of naval power ... we might just as well accept what we can get' from Moscow. He was, however, not impressed by pursuing an Anglo-Soviet treaty that would be 'a very hollow and one-sided affair'. He concluded that 'I see little object in pursuing a Treaty on these lines; but I admit that I am completely distrustful of the Russians and all their sinister works, and look on Russia as the evil genius of Europe today'. The First Sea Lord, Ernle Chatfield, was more practical, and called for further discussions.

These occurred in London on 4 June 1936.[8] Here the Soviets argued against any limitation of their gun calibres on battleships to fourteen inches, as France and Italy had already begun constructing ships with fifteen-inch guns, while others, most likely Japan, might equip their ships with sixteen-inch weapons. In addition, the Soviets informed the British that they had begun construction of three 10,000 ton cruisers mounting 7.1-inch guns, and that ten were pending. Although no compromises were arrived at during the talks, there was hope that the Soviets might agree to refrain from stepping outside the qualitative limits if others would do likewise. But, Phillips noted, some important points had emerged. First, it was clear that Russia was prepared to go to considerable lengths to build up her navy in the immediate future. Second, the dispute over gun calibres was not going to be resolved easily. The French and Italian building programmes were in progress and the Germans were also building two fifteen-inch gun ships, something which Phillips feared would stiffen Soviet attitudes when they learned of it. Third, as to cruisers, the Admiralty was not opposed to the Soviets building 'a certain number', perhaps seven, but it was hoped that they might be persuaded to equip them with six-inch guns and to limit their displacement to 8,000 tons. The British were in fact willing to supply the guns in order both to solve the difficulties that the Soviets said they had building such weapons and to prevent the construction of the larger cruisers. Most significantly, however, there was the realisation that some of the Soviet concerns must be taken into account, because if the Soviet treaty were lost this would probably 'mean losing that with Germany and consequently the whole qualitative agreement'.

In June, progress was made. The Soviets agreed both that they would adhere to qualitative limits, providing others, principally Japan, did so too, and that they would inform the British of all building in Europe, although not in the Far East.[9] Yet the Russians were still insistent about cruisers, and Phillips noted that the fact that three were being built 'already imperils the "cruiser holiday" and may give Germany the excuse she desires to build her additional eight-inch cruisers'. This impelled the naval talks into the wider political waters.[10] On 19 May, the Foreign Office's principal naval arms control negotiator, Sir Robert Craigie, had held talks with Captain Erwin Wassner, the German naval attaché in London.[11] Have, in what the Permanent Under-Secretary to the Foreign Office, Sir Robert Vansittart, termed a 'shocking breach of faith', Wassner stated that the Germans would build the five eight-inch gun cruisers – which they were permitted under the Anglo-German Naval Agreement – despite their earlier assurances that they would build only three if, in Craigie's words, 'a general agreement could be reached to stop the construction of this type of cruiser'. The reason adduced for this change of heart was the ratification of the Franco-Soviet Pact, which, the Germans asserted, meant that the Soviet and French fleets should be considered as one.

Craigie felt this excuse to be 'thread-bare' and believed that it was simply a 'try-on' by the Germans that would be abandoned when the latter realized that such a policy would merely result in France and Russia increasing their building programmes. Vansittart was more indignant with the German's bad faith. Their justification was 'the same old stalking-horse [the Franco-Soviet Pact] that we have all unanimously rejected, but which has yet been used to cover the breach of the assurances given at Stresa – a breach which has culminated in the remilitarisation of the Rhineland, and all its illimitable consequences for Europe. (We are only at the beginning of these.)' Eden, now Foreign Secretary, agreed that the German action was 'serious' and that the 'pretext' for it, the 'Franco-Soviet Treaty ... is of the flimsiest'.

The German use of the Franco-Soviet Pact to block naval negotiations quickly became a sore point. When Joachim von Ribbentrop, Hitler's Ambassador-at-large, used this argument again in early June, Vansittart's earlier irritation was shared by Ralph Wigram, the head of the Central Department at the Foreign Office.[12] Wigram rejected Craigie's contention that the problems had arisen from Hitler being personally unaware of the earlier German promises. Instead, he pointed out that the Pact also had been used earlier by the Germans to avoid discussing 'air limitation, [the] Eastern pact and Locarno, & probably soon [will] be taken in the matter of military effectives', all of which Hitler had 'personally backed'. In fact, Wigram simply believed that Hitler was using the Franco-Soviet Pact as he used other excuses, to gain time and manoeuvring space for his own nefarious purposes.[13] While an immediate German back-down and a return to a figure of three cruisers allowed Craigie to write a smug self-congratulatory minute, Vansittart issued a prescient warning. He feared that the respite was only temporary, and 'that when the Soviet Govt's plans are made known Germany will declare her intention to lay down the five cruisers'.[14]

Craigie immediately began to try to whittle down the Soviet demands.[15] On 17 June and again, five days later, he attempted to persuade the Soviets to build only seven cruisers, with smaller guns, but they were concerned that design changes might delay construction. Only a hope that the French might cancel their cruiser programme, in light of the Soviet plans, gave Phillips any optimism that the Germans might not build to their full limit of five cruisers. When Eden raised the matter at Geneva with the Soviet Foreign Minister, Maxim Litvinov, the latter 'seemed to know very little of this subject', but suggested that 'if we were able to reach an agreement on the Straits question, then he felt that it would be easier to fall in with our views in respect of the cruiser construction'.[16] Eden rejected any connection between the two topics, but a linkage was clear. In fact, other, related aspects of Anglo-German-Soviet naval relations were raised at

Montreux during July, where the Germans argued that Soviet construction of a Black Sea fleet, while the Straits were closed to German vessels, would upset the naval balance. But on the 23rd of that month, Craigie achieved what Eden termed a 'useful step forward'. The naval negotiator persuaded the Soviets to agree to build only eight cruisers on condition that they could mount sixteen-inch guns on future battleships.[17] Craigie played for time on this latter point, contending to Maisky on 29 July that the views of the French and Germans needed to be obtained.[18] Ironically, both of the latter opposed the Soviet conditions, causing Phillips to note that it 'will be interesting if a situation arises in which both France and Germany will be exercising pressure on Russia in the same direction'.

Little occurred in August and early September. But, in October, the Germans again attacked the Anglo-Soviet negotiations, reiterating the argument that the Montreux settlement had worsened their naval circumstances.[19] Using arguments provided by the Admiralty, Craigie was able to trump the German contentions about the adverse impact of Montreux, although there was fear that rumours of a Soviet–Turkish agreement might alter matters; for this reason the Turkish Government was advised not to make one. But, nonetheless, the German press continued to make 'the most out of the Soviet bogey' by arguing that Soviet ships built for the Far East could be used in Europe – something counter to the actual proposed Anglo-Soviet agreement.[20] The Germans also contended that the British naval 'concessions' to Soviet Russia were based on strategic grounds; that 'the Soviet fleet will act as a check on Japan and Germany and add to British security'.[21] While some at the Foreign Office argued that this contention was 'ridiculous', Laurence Collier, the head of its Northern Department, was much more accurate when he noted that 'I think a strong Soviet fleet in the Baltic would indirectly help against the Germans'.

At the end of October, Craigie returned to his negotiations.[22] On the 29th, he attempted to bring the Germans onside. He noted that the British rejected the German contention that the Franco-Soviet Pact was a 'military alliance', and also pointed out that, contrary to German assertions, Soviet naval building in the Far East was bound by qualitative restrictions, providing that Japan also observed them. With regard to technical matters, Craigie stated that it would be 'useless' to attempt to convince the Soviets not to demand mounting sixteen-inch guns in their battleships in light of the fifteen-inch guns being installed in German, French and Italian ships. As to cruisers, Craigie made the point that, '[a]fter months of negotiation', the British had persuaded the Soviets to build only eight cruisers instead of ten. If the Germans were to use this as a reason to build five, instead of three, cruisers, then the Soviets would revert to their larger programme.

While no agreement was reached, the position seemed hopeful. Such a feeling was reinforced on 30 October, when Craigie met with Maisky.[23] Craigie informed the Soviet Ambassador of what had taken place in the talks with Germany and dangled the possibility that Japan and Germany might agree to limit their gun calibres to fourteen-inches if Russia would limit herself to fifteen-inch weapons.[24] Maisky said that achieving the latter was 'doubtful', reiterating what Craigie himself had told the Germans, that on the cruiser issue there was no room for manoeuvre. If the Germans were to build five cruisers, Maisky was adamant that Soviet Russia would build ten. However, there was room for optimism. Maisky professed himself 'anxious to push on with our naval negotiations as quickly as possible', and suggested that it might be possible to sign an Anglo-Russian treaty independent of an Anglo-German one, with the provision that the former would come into effect upon the signing of the latter. Such optimism was augmented on 20 November when the German representatives agreed that a compromise could be reached on the vexatious cruiser issue.[25] Four days later, the Soviets agreed, leaving the issue of gun calibres as the major remaining point of contention.[26]

At this point, however, wider international politics intruded into the discussions. On 28 November, Admiral V.M. Orlov, the Chief of the Soviet Naval Forces, gave a speech to the Eighth Congress of Soviets, in which he stated that, due to the on-going naval rearmament in Germany and Japan, Soviet Russia was proceeding to build a large, blue-water navy.[27] While Adrian Holman, one of the naval negotiators in the American Department at the Foreign Office, viewed this speech as 'unfortunate', he pointed out that the 'publicity' given to the recent agreement signed by Japan and Germany outlining their mutual hostility to the Soviet Union – the so-called Anti-Comintern Pact – made such a development understandable. Craigie was less sympathetic. Faced with the likely collapse of both his Anglo-German and Anglo-Soviet negotiations, he vented his displeasure at length:

> The trumpeting of the Soviet Government's naval intentions is about the worst policy they can pursue. They think it will frighten Germany & Japan. Actually it will give the pretext for large increases in the German & Japanese navies and put a serious strain on the Anglo-German Naval Agreement of 1935 – to say nothing of its effects on the agreements we are now trying to negotiate.

In his view, the Soviets were proceeding foolishly: 'The only hope Russia has of increasing her relative naval strength is to go about the job quietly, even though resolutely'. Already unhappy about the impact that the Franco-Soviet Pact was having on Britain's policy generally, Vansittart simply noted that the 'Soviet government seem to have lost all political sense of late'. Only Collier supported Holman's, and by extension, the Soviet position: 'the Russians can hardly be expected not to use this sort of language after the German–Japanese pact & its secret annexe (of which they are as well aware as we are)'.

Collier's disagreement with Craigie became even more pronounced in early December during further discussion of Orlov's speech.[28] In a report from Moscow, Chilston, the British Ambassador argued that it was unlikely that any concerns about arms limitation would deter the Soviets if they felt that an agreement about naval restrictions with Germany was 'impossible of fulfilment'. One of the clerks in the Northern Department considered that the Soviet building programme might have been inspired by the Soviets being 'unable, le cas échéant [should the occasion arise], to intervene effectively in Spanish waters, or even to protect their transports against insurgent raiders enjoying foreign support'.[29] Further, he pointed out that the Soviet attempts to buy large turbines in the United Kingdom 'leads one to think that the Soviet Govt. are contemplating the construction of a number of very large capital ships, but it may be doubted whether it is in the interests of this country for the S.[oviet] S.[tate] to do this'.[30] Collier was in no doubt his remarks underlined his appreciation of the value of the Soviets to the British position:

> Personally, I think it would be to our interest that this development should be carried out with British materials since it is clear that it will take place anyhow (though perhaps more slowly without such material), if, as seems likely, the Germans persist in their objections to the Anglo-Soviet Naval Agreement and thus give the Russians good reason to think that they might as well be hanged for a sheep as a lamb, since the Soviet Navy could hardly be used against us, and since anything which would keep the Germans and Japanese preoccupied and at the same time provide an additional market for our engineering products should suit our book.

He dilated on the potential value of Soviet military strength. 'Like the Soviet Army, the Navy seems fated to remain of defensive value only, in most respects; but in a few years' time its submarines and destroyers might be able to make things very awkward for the Germans in the Baltic.'

Sir Lancelot Oliphant, an Assistant Under-Secretary at the Foreign Office and a long-time observer of the Russians, agreed with Chilston about the Soviets' intentions: 'My belief is that they intend to build just as much & as quickly as they can.' However, Craigie's objection to Orlov's speech related to tactics rather than substance. The head of the American Department argued two things: first, a reiteration of his earlier contention that building 'a fleet with a flourish of trumpets' was counter-productive and, second, that 'the Russian Government have an interest in preserving the Anglo-German Naval Agreement'. Craigie's reasons for the latter reflected his views both of Soviet naval capabilities and possible Soviet assistance for Britain. 'The Russian fleet', he contended, 'never has been efficient in the past ... and is unlikely to become much more so in the future. Therefore the lead which we hope to maintain in good British ships under the Anglo-German treaty is far more valuable to us than the problematical assistance of a re-constructed Russian navy.' While Vansittart agreed with this, Oliphant did not. His contrary view was based on his estimate of Soviet attitudes and motivations:

> The Soviet's motto is 'Charity begins at home', and if they think they can build a big fleet and rally their people, neither our beaux yeux nor the risk of 'busting' the Anglo-German Naval Agreement will ... stop them. It is then my firm conviction that (whether we care to hope for sense or not) we must be prepared and not surprised to find the Soviet ignoring what might in the long run be to their interest and going full steam ahead with the construction of big ships and big guns.

While Craigie thought that 'we have a little more "leverage" with the Russians' than Oliphant believed, it was evident that Soviet policy could have a profound effect on Anglo-German naval matters.

The whole issue over the matter of possible Soviet orders with British firms for naval armaments was also raised.[31] On 9 December, the Admiralty informed the Foreign Office that they had blocked several firms from accepting Soviet naval orders on the basis that to permit them to do so would annoy the Germans and Japanese. This was not view of some in the Foreign Office, and Collier observed that the 'Admiralty's incursions into foreign policy always fill me with alarm. This time they fill me with consternation!' He pointed out that to accede to the Admiralty's argument would mean accepting 'the thoroughly vicious principle of allowing our policy in these matters to be dependent upon the good will of either the Germans or the Japanese Government'. He felt that the Admiralty's arguments were based 'on the strange assumption that "the stabilisation of Europe and the Far East" is assisted by the German and Japanese navies keeping their present overwhelming superiority over the Russian navy'. In any case, Collier still held to his earlier view that British firms should work on 'getting a footing in the Russian armament market' in general.[32]

Craigie rejected this approach. For him, the point was the same as it was for the Admiralty: anything that might induce Germany to build beyond the levels of the Anglo-German Naval Agreement was to be avoided. 'It is not that we need worry about the <u>political</u> aspect of repercussions in Germany, but about the possible repercussions on the <u>naval</u> situation.' All agreed that, despite an earlier decision by the Committee of Imperial Defence that Russia should not be given access to British technology through munitions orders, every assistance, including technical assistance, should be given to the Soviets in an effort to get them to adopt a fifteen-inch gun.[33] Whether the Soviets could be persuaded to limit their gun calibre remained problematical. Litvinov informed Chilston that Soviet Russia 'could not afford to be less powerfully armed than other powers ... and added that the German-Japanese agreement had not exactly encouraged confidence in any reduction of armaments'.[34]

The intertwined nature of foreign policy and the naval aspects of these negotiations could not be denied, despite Craigie's contention. On 17 December, Ribbentrop once again noted the pernicious impact of the Franco-Soviet Pact on Germany's naval position. He hinted that, as a result of the Pact, the 35 per cent limit might have to be reconsidered, rejecting a British argument which denied that the agreement was directed against Germany.[35] Ribbentrop's action caused real concern at the Admiralty, where Hoare, the First Lord, noted on 6 January 1937 that he was 'very nervous' about the possibility that the Anglo-German Naval Agreement might be 'prejudice[d]'.[36] Chatfield, in fact, waxed fulsomely about the Anglo-German Naval Agreement and its importance: it had the 'greatest benefit not only from a military standpoint but from a Political and International one. Its loss would be serious therefore for both reasons. It was undoubtedly a <u>most</u> friendly gesture to us' by Germany, and he claimed that it was a 'remarkable agreement, unique in world history'. What import Russian considerations in such a case?

The fact was, however, that Soviet concurrence was necessary. And, in fact, as Litvinov informed Chilston on 28 December, the Soviet Government viewed the entire situation as 'uncertain' due to the constant German objections.[37] The Soviet Foreign Minister suggested that a general naval conference be called to deal with the issue, a call reiterated by Maisky on 6 January 1937.[38] This provoked ire at the Foreign Office. Eden remarked that, as 'Soviet suggestions are seldom conceived in a constructive spirit', he wished for Craigie to give his views. These were unequivocal. The Russian proposal was 'thoroughly a bad one'. The British had previously explained to the Soviets that no conference was possible, both because the French would not treat with the Germans, and because the British had always intended to proceed in a piecemeal fashion before they might 'risk' a general conference. Given that 'practically all the difficulties in negotiations with Russia and Germany' had 'been eliminated' – except the issue of gun calibres, about which, in any case 'the

Japanese are going to force upon the world the general adoption of the sixteen-inch gun' – '[t]his Russian move is particularly irritating'. At the Admiralty, Phillips characterised the Russian proposal as 'merely another example of Soviets' delaying tactics'.

Nonetheless, it had to be dealt with, and, to do so, Craigie made his points to Maisky on 12 January and attempted to chivvy the Germans to move more quickly.[39] By the beginning of February, the Germans had settled on a further naval agreement, confining themselves to the observation that they objected in principle to the Franco-Soviet Pact.[40] On 5 February, Craigie outlined the German position to Maisky, and pressed the Soviet Ambassador to expedite matters.[41] That this was unlikely was presaged by Maisky's remark that the Soviets had already laid down battleships with sixteen-inch guns and that any changes, all of this being dependent on Japan's attitude, might cause unacceptable construction delays. Further evidence of possible Soviet intransigence came on 15 February when Chilston reported that Admiral Orlov had stated that no compromise over calibres was possible, prompting Craigie to complain that the Soviets were 'behaving very unreasonably', a remark that Vansittart echoed, adding '& very provocative'. This must have been doubly galling to Craigie, for, in January and early February, he had attempted to use the anticipated settlement with Russia and Germany to induce the Japanese to reduce their demands with respect to gun calibres, making clear to Tokyo the linkage between such an agreement and the possibility of better Anglo-Japanese relations.[42] A Soviet refusal meant that all his carefully laid plans were in danger of collapse.

However, Orlov's remarks were not a formal denunciation of the possibility of a treaty, and Craigie continued to negotiate with the Soviets and Germans throughout the rest of February and early March.[43] In fact, on 5 March, while Craigie complained that it had been 'exceedingly difficult to obtain any definite replies from Moscow' due to the 'almost incredibly slow and obstructive' attitude of the Soviets, he was confident that 'we may now consider that we are in agreement on all points of substance'. This was not so. On 8 March, Maisky informed Craigie that Moscow would not sign any agreement with Germany, as the Russians had no confidence in German promises and because Japan 'remain[ed] entirely outside any limitation treaty'.[44] In such circumstances and given 'recent events' – the Germans in Spain and the Anti-Comintern Pact – 'it was now clear to the Soviet Government that for the defence of Russian territory they must depend on their own forces and their own forces alone'. The Ambassador returned to his demand for a general naval conference and for all building programmes to be verified by inspection.

This was shattering news. Craigie termed it a 'flagrant breach of faith', and searched for the underlying reasons. Unable to conceive that it could result from the technical details of the negotiations (for which he praised himself), he saw the 'deeper' causes as likely stemming from Russia's desire for a 'qualitative agreement' rather than a quantitative one and two wider issues: first, that the Soviets felt 'that they can place no further reliance on France or ourselves'; second, 'the isolated position into which the Soviet Government have manoeuvred themselves in connexion with the Non-Intervention negotiations'. He then made practical suggestions: a 'severe remonstrance to Moscow', the elimination of any further 'technical aid in naval matters' to Soviet Russia, and an attempt to induce the Germans to sign a treaty irrespective of the Soviet position. Sir Alexander Cadogan, one of the Deputy Under-Secretaries at the Foreign Office and a former British Ambassador to China, found the episode 'very deplorable and maybe disastrous'. He believed that the Russians did not see their own advantage clearly in the matter, as he doubted that they were in any position 'to challenge the other naval Powers to a race in qualitative armaments ... from their own point of view, their behaviour is as senseless as it is disgraceful'. He agreed with Craigie's practical steps ('though we can have little hope that that will do any good') and desired that the 'well-deserved odium' would, in Vansittart's phrase, fall squarely on Moscow.

At the Admiralty, views were similar. Phillips suggested that, as the Soviet objections were 'clearly only excuses', the best course would be to attempt to induce the Germans to sign without a parallel Anglo-Soviet agreement.[45] Chatfield and Hoare agreed, and both hoped that the Soviet actions would receive widespread bad publicity. Hoare also wanted more. He wrote to Eden, asking the Foreign Secretary to make a further attempt to induce the Soviet Union to agree to a treaty.[46] The consequences of failure were profound: 'Without an agreement with Russia we cannot hope for one with Germany. Unless we can get Russia to change her mind it seems to me that the whole fabric of limitation which we have built up may collapse and that we shall be faced with the prospect of unlimited building by all countries.' Eden concurred, and, while pointing out that it would be dangerous to give wide publicity to the Soviet refusal because of its adverse effect on gun-calibre discussions with Tokyo, stated that he would take the matter up with Maisky. He did so on 15 March.[47] The Soviet Ambassador was unmoved. When Eden mentioned that, at the beginning of the talks, the Soviets had been willing to sign an agreement with Germany, Maisky simply reiterated his earlier remarks about the changed world situation. A deadlock was at hand.

Eight days later, Maisky reversed himself, and declared that Soviet Russia was now prepared to sign an Anglo-Soviet naval agreement.[48] This was termed a 'most satisfactory and not a little surprising change of heart'.

The reasons for it remain obscure – although in Cabinet Eden credited the 'strong representations which he had recently made to Moscow' for the Soviet reversal,[49] – but one can speculate that the temporary refusal might been a bargaining tactic to put pressure on London to quicken the pace of approval for orders of naval equipment that Soviet Russia was attempting to place in Britain.[50] Whatever the case, matters moved quickly. By June, the Admiralty was helping the Soviets procure six-inch guns and turrets in order that the Soviet cruisers to be constructed would not stir German building, and other cooperation over naval orders flowed.[51] This eagerness reflected the Admiralty's continuing fear that a collapse of the talks would lead to an unrestricted naval building race, which would in turn doom its plans for dealing with a two-front naval conflict against Germany and Japan.[52] By 21 June, both the Soviets and Germans had agreed to draft treaties. These were duly signed early in July, marking what Eden termed 'an excellent piece of work by all concerned and a reward for perseverance'.[53]

What had this naval incident demonstrated? First, but least significantly, it had served as another in the series of irritants between London and Moscow that made cooperation between the two difficult. The British found the Soviets difficult negotiators, inconsistent in their positions and often unwilling to consider what the British felt were the wider aspects of the discussions. The second point is related to this last matter, and was more important. The Anglo-Soviet naval discussions demonstrated that, since Soviet Russia had decided to end its self-imposed exclusion from Great Power relations and to put its actual and potential military strength in the scales of the international balance of power, it could not be ignored in the formulation of British strategic foreign policy. No policy with respect to Germany or Japan could be made without considering Moscow, and the latter was unwilling to act as a British puppet in any way.

The third matter that the Anglo-Soviet discussions makes clear is that arms-control discussions are rarely negotiated in a vacuum, and that they are affected by a variety of things not directly involved in the talks themselves. Both within the Foreign Office and between that body and the Admiralty there were a variety of opinions and positions that affected the nature of the negotiations. At the Foreign Office, Craigie represented those who felt that the importance of the AGNA was so great that other considerations of policy should be subordinated to its achievement. For him, the Soviets were merely an irritant that needed to be overcome. On the other hand, Collier saw the Anglo-Soviet talks in the wider context of Britain's policy. For him, the Soviets were a potential barrier to the threats posed by both Germany and Japan. Collier felt it unwise to attempt to coerce the Soviets into signing a naval arrangement that would affect their security adversely, in the hope that the Germans would honour the AGNA. For him, this might serve to drive a wedge between Britain and Soviet Russia, something that would have an adverse effect on Britain's position generally. There was a similar gap between the Foreign Office and the Admiralty. The latter was concerned about its own task: maintaining Britain's naval supremacy. Soviet Russia could not threaten it, nor, in the Admiralty's view, could a resurgent Red Navy help maintain it. The other, non-naval, ways that Soviet Russia was important to Britain's global position were of little import in comparison. As a result, until Soviet intransigence drove home the point that Moscow could not be ignored, the Admiralty preferred to go full-steam ahead, regardless of the Russian position.

The final point is what the Anglo-Soviet discussions reveal about arms-control negotiations generally. Richardson's point that arms-control agreements can be reached only when both sides want the talks to succeed remains true, but needs to be considered carefully. What must be emphasised is that, while both sides may want an agreement, it still may be that a suitable arrangement cannot be found. This can be due to the fact that the underlying assumptions of each side about the aims and nature of arms control are incompatible or because the attainment of what one side feels is essential to an agreement vitiates what the other side hopes to obtain from the same talks.

In the Anglo-Soviet talks, the basic British assumption was that it was essential to avoid a naval arms race. This derived from a number of beliefs: a general one that arms races were intrinsically bad because they led to war, and the more specific one that Germany's naval growth, if it could not be prevented, had to be limited by agreement in order that British naval security could be maintained until the political will to build a larger fleet could be found. The Soviets shared only part of these assumptions. On the one hand, for Moscow, arms races were not necessarily wrong; in fact, they were an unavoidable consequence of the inevitable friction between communist and capitalist states. On the other hand, the Russians shared the British hope that the Germans might be persuaded to limit naval construction while Soviet Russia hurried along its own building programme. Thus, while the basic assumptions of the two countries were not congruent, they posed no insuperable barrier to an agreement.

It was with respect to what was to be obtained via the agreement that British and Soviet views were largely incompatible. The British desire for a comprehensively qualitative, as well as a quantitative, naval agreement was based on strategic and technological considerations that did not apply to Soviet Russia. The British wanted a large number of smaller cruisers in order to defend their maritime lines of communication. This reflected the wider needs of a maritime empire. The Soviets lacked a such an empire and merely wished to be able to control the narrow waters around Soviet Russia that were threatened by Germany and Japan. For this purpose, larger cruisers with larger calibre guns were ideal – although not essential. However, should the Soviets choose to build such ships, so, too, would both the Germans and the Japanese, and the latter's doing so would also stimulate an American response, further complicating matters. All of this would force the British to respond in kind. But such a necessity would necessarily mean (due to cost) that Britain could build fewer cruisers, and, fewer cruisers would not be sufficient to provide for the naval security of empire. This problem, caused by the differing requirements of security, could be overcome only if either side could find a way to meet its concerns in a fashion compatible with the requirements of the other. The resolution of the Anglo-Soviet impasse reflected Richardson's second general point: the requirement for one or both sides in a negotiation to see the other's requirements and to adjust policy accordingly. While the British never agreed with the Russian evaluation of how Soviet security needs could best be met (indeed, the British always thought they could see the answer to Soviet concerns more clearly than could Moscow), and the Soviets were quite unwilling to build as the British prescribed, London was able to find a way to permit a settlement to be reached. By providing technical expertise and equipment sufficient such that the Soviets could build smaller cruisers more rapidly and with less expense than would have been the case if larger cruisers had been insisted upon, the British were able to provide off-setting advantages to Moscow that made the Anglo-Soviet agreement possible.

While the Anglo-Soviet agreement turned out to be of limited importance, given that just after its signature the Japanese embarked on full-scale war with China and abandoned any pretence of naval arms control while the Germans attempted to avoid any observation of the AGNA,[54] it provides a useful example of the complexity and difficulty of arms-control negotiations. This is not surprising, for the ramifications of unsuccessful or, perhaps even more significantly, successful but flawed, negotiations are profound, given that the stakes can often be national existence itself.

NOTES

1. The exceptions are Greg Kennedy, 'Becoming Dependent on the Kindness of Strangers: Britain's Strategic Foreign Policy, Naval Arms Limitation and the Soviet Factor, 1935–1937', *War in History*, 11, 1 (2004), pp. 34–60; David K. Varey, 'The Politics of Naval Aid: The Foreign Office, the Admiralty, and Anglo-Soviet Technical Cooperation, 1936–1937',

Diplomacy and Statecraft, 14, 4 (2003), pp. 50–68; and Keith Neilson, *Britain, Soviet Russia and the Collapse of the Versailles Order, 1919–1939* (Cambridge: Cambridge University Press, 2006), pp. 204–5.
2. Joseph A. Maiolo, *The Royal Navy and Nazi Germany, 1933–1939: A Study in Appeasement and the Origins of the Second World War* (London: Macmillan, 1998), pp. 11–37; Claire M. Scammell, 'The Royal Navy and the Strategic Origins of the Anglo-German Naval Agreement of 1935', *Journal of Strategic Studies*, 20, 2 (1997), pp. 92–118.
3. As discussed in Carolyn Kitching, *Britain and the Problem of International Disarmament 1919–34* (London: Routledge, 1999), p. 12. Kitching is referring to Richardson's unpublished *A History of Arms Control and Disarmament*.
4. Kennedy, 'Becoming Dependent', pp. 37–39; Neilson, *Britain, Soviet Russia*, pp. 132–35.
5. See Jürgen Rohwer and Mikhail S. Monakov, *Stalin's Ocean-Going Fleet: Soviet Naval Strategy and Shipbuilding Programmes 1935–1953* (London and Portland: Cass, 2001), pp. 221–24; Lennart Samuelson, 'The Naval Dimensions of the Soviet Five-Year Plans, 1925–1941', in William M. McBride (ed.), *New Interpretations in Naval History* (Annapolis: Naval Institute Press, 1998), pp. 221–24; Gunnar Åselius, 'The Naval Theaters in Soviet Grand Strategy During the Interwar Period', *Journal of Slavic Military Studies*, 13, 1 (2000), pp. 68–89; and Alexander Hill, 'The Birth of the Soviet Northern Fleet 1937–42', *Journal of Slavic Military Studies*, 16, 2 (2003), pp. 65–82.
6. Outlined in Maisky's note of 13 May, sent by Craigie to Phillips (Director of Plans, Adm), 14 May 1936, The National Archives, Kew [hereafter TNA], Adm 116/4053.
7. Minute by Phillips, 2 June 1936, TNA, Adm 116/4053. The following quotations are from the minutes by James (3 June) and Chatfield (3 June).
8. What follows is based on PD 05742/36, 'Record of the Third Meeting between Representatives of the Soviet Embassy and the United Kingdom, which was held in Mr. Craigie's room at the Foreign Office at 4 p.m. on Thursday June 4, 1936', ns, TNA, Adm 116/4053 and the minute by Phillips (8 June).
9. PD 05758/36, 'Record of the Fourth Meeting between Representatives of the Soviet Embassy and the United Kingdom, which was held in Mr. Craigie's room at the Foreign Office at 4 p.m. on Friday, 12th June', 1936, ns, and Phillip's minute (16 June), ibid.
10. For the German side of the naval talks, see Maiolo, *Royal Navy and Nazi Germany*, pp. 48–56.
11. What follows is based on Craigie's account of this talk and the minutes: Craigie (20 May), Vansittart (24 May) and Eden (25 May), all TNA, FO 371/19838/A4708.
12. His minute (5 June) on Craigie's account of an interview with Ribbentrop, 3 June 1936, TNA, FO 371/19838/A4773.
13. See his general remarks on this point in his minute (27 May) on Phipps to FO, tel. 183, confidential, 26 May 1936, TNA, FO 371/19906/C3879.
14. The minutes by Craigie and Vansittart (both 11 June) on Craigie's account of an interview with Wassner and Prince von Bismarck (German Ambassador, London), 11 June 1936, TNA, FO 371/19838/A5038.
15. 'Record of the Fifth Meeting between Representatives of the Soviet Embassy and the United Kingdom which was held in Mr. Craigie's room in the Foreign Office at 10.30 on Wednesday, June 17th', 1936, TNA, Adm 116/4053 and the minute by Phillips (25 June).
16. Eden to FO, tel. 76, 27 June 1939, Eden Papers, TNA, FO 954/24.
17. Craigie's untitled minute, 23 July 1936, TNA, FO 371/19840/A6266 and Eden's minute (25 July).
18. 'Record of the Sixth Meeting ... on Wednesday, July 29th 1936, TNA, Adm 116/4053 and the minute by Phillips (n.d., but c. 1 August); 'Record of a Meeting between the Representatives of the German Embassy and the United Kingdom ... July 30th, 1936', TNA, FO 371/19840/A6431.
19. Untitled report of an interview between Craigie and von Bismarck, 12 October 1936, Adm 116/3378 and the minute by Phillips (3 November); the FO minute, 14 October 1936, TNA, FO 371/19840/A8178.
20. For the arguments, see Phillips to Allen (clerk, American Department), 17 September 1936,

TNA, FO 371/19838/A7550 and the Admiralty's later amplification, in the untitled minute by Phillips, 16 October 1936, TNA, Adm 116/3378 and Phillips to Craigie, 2 November 1936 and enclosure, TNA, FO 371/19839/A8672. The fears about Turkey are in the minutes and attachments on TNA, FO 371/1839/A8671. The quotation is from the minute by Holman (American Department), 26 October, on Phipps to FO, despt. no. 1114, 16 October 1936, TNA, FO 371/19840/A8369.
21. The minute by Holman (26 October) on Phipps to FO, despt. no. 1134, 21 October 1936, TNA, FO 371/19840/A8450 and the minute by Collier (2 November).
22. 'Record of a Meeting between Representatives of the German Embassy ... on 29th October 1936', ns, TNA, FO 371/19839/A8735.
23. Craigie's account of a meeting, 30 October 1936, TNA, FO 371/19840/A8790 and his minute (nd). The Admiralty also rejected this view of the Franco-Soviet Pact, fearing that it would be used to challenge the 35 per cent limit of the Anglo-German Naval Agreement; see the minutes on Craigie to Phillips, 17 November 1936, TNA, Adm 116/4053.
24. This hope was also found at the Admiralty; see the minute by Phillips, 26 November 1936, TNA, Adm 116/4053.
25. Craigie's untitled minute of the meeting, 21 November 1936, TNA, FO 371/19839/A9340.
26. 'Record of a meeting between the United Kingdom and Soviet Delegations ... November 24th, 1936', ns, FO 371/19840/A9424. At the Admiralty, opinion was very much of the view that the Soviets ought to compromise; see the minutes on PD 06003/36, a report on the German discussions of 20 November, TNA, Adm 116/4053.
27. Chilston to FO, tel. 202, 29 November 1936, TNA, FO 371/19840/A9420 and the minutes by Holman (30 November), Craigie (30 November), Vansittart (2 December) and Collier (8 December). The British Military Attaché had suggested that this was so, earlier in the year; see Chilston to FO, despt. no. 463, 8 August 1936, TNA, FO 371/20344/N4119 and enclosures. In fact, the Soviet decision had been taken late in 1935, in response to the Japanese and German threats; see Rohwer and Monakov, *Stalin's Ocean-Going Fleet*, pp. 221–24 and Lennart Samuelson, 'The Naval Dimensions of the Soviet Five-Year Plans, 1925–1941', in William M. McBride (ed.), *New Interpretations in Naval History* (Annapolis: Naval Institute Press, 1998), pp. 221–24; for the context and expenditures on the Soviet Navy, Lennart Samuelson, *Plans for Stalin's War Machine: Tukhachevskii and Military-Economic Planning, 1925–1941* (Basingstoke: Macmillan, 2000), pp. 176–83.
28. What follows, except where otherwise noted, is based on Chilston to FO, despt. no. 683, secret, 1 December 1936, TNA, FO 371/20344/N6018 and the minutes by Walker (ND) of 3 December, Collier (9 December), Oliphant (9 and 18 December), Craigie (15 and 19 December), Vansittart (16 December).
29. The idea that the Spanish Civil War inspired the building of the Soviet fleet has been debunked; see Rohwer and Monakov, *Stalin's Ocean-Going Fleet*, pp. 64–66.
30. For Soviet attempts to purchase naval material in the United States, see Malcolm Muir, Jr., 'American Warship Construction for Stalin's Navy Prior to World War II: A Study in Paralysis of Policy', *Diplomatic History*, 5, 4 (1981), pp. 337–51.
31. Adm to FO, 9 December 1936, TNA, FO 371/20354/N6142 and the minutes by Walker (14 December), Collier (15 December), Craigie (17 December) and Vansittart (21 December).
32. His minute (28 October) on Adm to FO, secret, 26 October 1936, TNA, FO 371/20354/N5293.
33. For the Admiralty's concurrence, see the minutes by Phillips (26 November 1936) and Hoare (2 December 1936) on PD 06003/36, TNA, Adm 116/4053 and the account of a meeting with the Soviet Naval Attaché to discuss this point on 21 December 1936, attached to Seal (Adm) to Collier, secret, 23 December 1936, TNA, FO 371/20657/A1987; for the earlier decision, see 'Proposed Technical Aid Agreement between the Government of the U.S.S.R. and Imperial Chemical Industries, Ltd', FCI 96, E.F. Crowe (Comptroller-General, DOT), 10 November 1936, TNA, CAB 48/4 and the minutes, 284th meeting of the CID, 19 Nov 1936, CAB 2/6.
34. Chilston to FO, tel. 212, 11 December 1936, TNA, FO 371/19840/A9851.
35. See the account in Eden to Phipps, despt. no. 1425, 18 December 1936, TNA, FO 371/19839/A9986; 'Memorandum communicated to the Counsellor of the German Embassy

by Sir R. Craigie, December 15, 1936', TNA, FO 371/19839/A10085 and 'Record of Meeting ... on December 15th 1936', TNA, FO 371/19839/A10124.
36. The minute by Phillips, 23 December 1936, on PD 06029/36, most secret; the minutes by Hoare, 6 January 1937 and Chatfield, 8 January 1937, all TNA, Adm 116/3929. Chatfield is also in '[Record of Interview between Sir R. Craigie and the German Ambassador', TNA, Adm 116/3596.
37. Chilston to Craigie, 29 December 1936, TNA, FO 371/20657/A263.
38. Maisky to Craigie, 6 January 1937, TNA, FO 371/20675/A349; Vansittart's minute of a discussion with Maisky, 6 January 1937, TNA, FO 371/20657/A394 and the minutes by Eden, Craigie and Vansittart (all 7 January); minute by Phillips (11 January) on Craigie to Adm, 11 January 1937, TNA, Adm 116/4053.
39. Craigie's minute of a conversation with Maisky, 12 January 1937, TNA, FO 371/20657/A395; Craigie to Phipps, 26 January 1937, TNA, FO 371/20652/A695.
40. 'Record of a Meeting ... 1st February 1937', ns, TNA, FO 371/20652/A894.
41. Craigie's minute of a conversation, 5 February 1937, TNA, FO 371/20657/A1221.
42. This can be followed in Craigie to Phillips, 14 January 1937, and the minutes, which yield FO to Clive, tel. 7, pink, 15 January 1937 in that sense, TNA, Adm 116/3382; Eden to Clive, tel. 41, 18 January 1937, TNA, FO 371/20645/A449.
43. Summarised in Craigie's untitled memo., 5 March 1937, TNA, FO 371/20652/A1984. The following quotation is from this source.
44. Craigie's interview with Maisky, 8 March 1937, TNA, FO 371/20658/A2080 and the minutes by Craigie, Cadogan and Vansittart (all 9 March).
45. The minutes by Phillips (9 March), Chatfield (11 March), and Hoare (11 March), all TNA, Adm 116/4053.
46. Birmingham University, Avon Papers, AP 13/1/56 and 56A, Hoare to Eden and reply, 12 and 13 March 1937.
47. Eden's discussion with Maisky, 15 March 1937, as reported in Eden to Chilston, despt. no. 135, 15 March 1937, TNA, FO 371/20657/A2062. Eden's position was drafted for him by both the FO and Adm, 'Draft Aide-Mémoire', ns, 12 March 1937 and minutes, TNA, FO 371/20658/A2081.
48. Holman's account of Eden's meeting with Maisky, 23 March 1937, TNA, FO 371/20658/A2284 and the minute by the former (24 March).
49. TNA, CAB 23/88, CC 13(37), 24 March 1937.
50. For an indication of the difficulties and their resolution, see Seal (Adm) to Collier, 20 April 1937 and the minutes, TNA, FO 371/21090/N2149.
51. Kennedy, 'Becoming Dependent', pp. 58–59.
52. For evidence of these fears, see 'A New Standard of Naval Strength', DP(P) 3, Board of Adm, 26 April and circulated by Hoare, TNA, CAB 16/182.
53. His minute (3 July) on Craigie's untitled minute, 3 July 1937, TNA, FO 371/20653/A5236.
54. J.A. Maiolo, '"I believe the Hun is Cheating": British Admiralty Technical Intelligence and the German Navy', *Intelligence and National Security*, 11, 1 (1996), pp. 32–58.

7

Disarmament and Peace Movements in British and US Feature Films of the Inter-War Period

DAVID DUNN

A common assumption is that the inter-war years produced a largesse of anti-war or pro-peace films. Despite their number being comparatively few, 'they eclipse the thousands of pro-war features and shorts in quality and impact'.[1] A chronological survey of great anti-war films made between the world wars might proceed as follows. Just after the fighting but before the Armistice, Abel Gance's first film version of *J'accuse* was released. (He remade the film with sound in 1938.) Scripted jointly with Blaise Cendrars, its finale depicted a victory parade with soldiers returning from the front as their dead comrades rise up from their graves to confront civilians with their guilt.[2] King Vidor enjoyed success with *The Big Parade* in 1925, although it was criticised by French critics for being too emotive,[3] and by elements of the British press for suggesting that Americans won the war.[4] In 1930, the *annus mirabilis* of anti-war film, James Whale's *Journey's End*, Lewis Milestone's *All Quiet on the Western Front* and G.W. Pabst's *Westfront 1918* appeared. The release of three high-quality films from Britain, the USA and Germany in the same year allowed audiences to compare national pacifist sentiments, as well as providing a barometer of international anti-war public opinion.

Hollywood, it is claimed, was:

> especially flexible in its coverage of the War. By 1930 even those US producers who had previously supported intervention – such as Carl Laemmle, head of Universal Pictures which made *All Quiet on the Western Front* – were at the forefront of the pacifist cause. Nor was it just the traditional war picture that made this its message: the 'forgotten man' sequence in the Busby Berkeley musical *Gold Diggers*

of 1933 was critical of conflict, while the War's responsibility for unemployment and its link to crime and gangsterism was shown in *I am a Fugitive from a Chain Gang* and *The Roaring Twenties*.[5]

James Whale's *Frankenstein* (1931) reflected the condition of many veterans with its themes of disfigurement, trauma and social displacement, while *The Black Cat* (1934) starred Boris Karloff as a famous architect, Hjalmar Poelzig, who built his modernist house on the site of one of the Great War's most bloody battlefields.

Other international nominees for inclusion in the list of great anti-war feature films of the period include the Swedish film *En Natt [One Night]* (1931),[6] Aleksandr Dovzhenko's *Arsenal* (1928) from Russia, G.W. Pabst's *Kameradschaft* (1931) from Germany and Ivor Montagu's *Peace and Plenty* (1939) from Britain.[7] Many have also rated highly *The Story of an Unknown Soldier* (1932) from Belgium producer, Henri Storck. Its eleven and a half minutes of documentary-cum-satire with no spoken commentary, simply juxtaposed images, made it ideal for international distribution. Yet while there has been no short supply of candidates or critics to nominate the great anti-war films of the 1920s and 1930s, their impact as agents of peace is debatable. Jean Renoir, whose classic feature of 1937, *La grande illusion*, expressed 'all [his] deep feelings for the cause of peace' and demonstrated how class, religion and language caused war, noted that his film failed to stop world war breaking out within two years.[8] On the other hand, public opinion, especially on the issue of aerial bombardment, indirectly influenced the conduct of British foreign policy, and Harold Macmillan's recollection that Britons in 1938 'thought of air warfare rather as people think of nuclear warfare today' (that is, as a means of total destruction) is frequently attributed to the impact of one film, *Things to Come* (1936), showing bombers meeting ineffective fire from the ground while they obliterate 'Everytown' on Christmas Eve, 1940.[9]

Film, however, is often constrained in its critique of international politics. States use censorship as a means to curtail the ambitions of film-makers, especially those seeking to question a government's pursuit of the national interest through military means. The focus on German militarism during the First World War in films such as *All Quiet on the Western Front* and *Westfront 1918* led to a backlash within Germany, where after 1931 only patriotic war films were permitted. Because of the damage it might cause to Anglo-German relations, Britain had already banned *Dawn*, a 1928 bio-pic about Edith Cavell, the British nurse who helped British soldiers escape from German-occupied territory and who was executed. (Herbert Wilcox remade the film in 1939, when the international climate had changed.) Keen not to offend German and Turkish sensitivities, British censors aborted an Alexander Korda project on T.E. Lawrence. Through the Hays Code, Hollywood effected similar control over materials likely to cause Germany distress. Even while alarm bells were sounding about Nazi anti-semitism, re-militarisation and territorial absorptions, films such as *The Road Back* (1937), the sequel to *All Quiet on the Western Front*, and *Three Comrades* (1938) had their coverage of Germany suppressed at the request of the German Government, working through the Hays Office.[10]

On the false premise that it contained War Office footage, Paul Rotha's 1936 polemical film, *People of Britain*, (aka *Peace of Britain*), variously dubbed by the press the 'New Anti-War Film' and the 'Peace Film', was initially censored. The British Film Institute catalogue describes it as:

> PROPAGANDA. Caption urging people to work for peace. Slogans superimposed on pictures of warships, tanks, troops, people in gas masks etc. Commentary impresses the fact [sic] that there is no defence against aerial warfare, mentions the effects of gas attacks and so on. Four people each comment on war – none of them wants war, one suggests that the League of Nations should be able to mediate ... Final slogans encourage viewers to write to their MPs.[11]

For a 'Peace Film' lasting only three minutes, the conflict it produced was considerable. The British Board of Film Censors initially refused to licence it for general exhibition but, after protests, relented and gave it a 'U' certificate. Adverts then began appearing in the trade press, beneath a photograph of two adversaries in military uniform with gas masks, exhorting exhibitors to book the film: 'Will you help to maintain international peace? Let the screen speak to the people of Britain.' Such emotive endorsements were responding to a new battle line: whether or not distributors should show the film. Some CEAs (Cinematograph Exhibitors' Associations), such as Bolton's, declined, arguing that they were 'entertainment caterers' and 'it was policy to avoid showing anything which might tend to cause argument among patrons'.[12] The trade press reported that the Bristol CEA, among others, received a letter from the League of Nations – almost certainly a letter written by the British-based League of Nations Union, the largest and most influential organisation in the British peace movement – over the CEA's decision to advise its members not to show the film. The letter only served to confirm in the mind of the organisation's chairman that the material contained in the film must therefore be propaganda. Spirited debate between the chairman and some of the members raised a comparison with the ten-minute short, *Death on the Road*, which the Association was recommending for screening that week. The chairman emphasised that the branch opposed films of a controversial nature – even though it was pointed out to him that *Death on the Road* 'aimed to save some 1000s of lives [while] the peace film aimed at saving millions of lives. There was also propaganda in the newsreels.'[13]

Films with anti-war messages could be box-office poison: 'Ernst Lubitsch made a minor masterpiece (which was a major financial disaster) in *The Man I Killed* (1932), about the search for forgiveness by a Frenchman for having killed a German soldier in battle.'[14] Yet *All Quiet on the Western Front* had been a sell-out from its Easter 1930 opening in New York, and within two weeks it was evident that Universal would more than recoup its $1.2 million investment.[15] Reinforcing the cinematic exploitation catch-phrase that there is no such thing as bad publicity, one entrepreneurial Bristol cinema-owner used the activism of the pro-peace lobby to increase the size of audiences for a showing of *All Quiet on the Western Front* in 1937. He secured the cooperation of various peace societies in the city by providing a special preview to their leaders. He then circulated handbills to clergy, university students, women's guilds, railway workers and other trade unionists, announcing that the film was being shown 'at the urgent request of many societies whose object is the promotion of Peace'.[16] Across the Atlantic, where the appeal of isolation and non-interventionism was growing ever stronger, a re-released *All Quiet on the Western Front* found huge audiences in the capital, Washington, DC. In Columbus, Ohio, during Armistice Day week, it attracted full houses for three days, with audiences of 6,000 people.[17] Ironically, because of the initial censorship and then refusals by some local cinemas to show Paul Rotha's *People of Britain*, it was discussed widely in the national and trade presses and was seen at 570 cinemas, free of charge, by 4,300,000 people across the UK.[18]

In 1929, William Marston Seabury published a tome of more than 400 pages on *Motion Picture Problems: The Cinema and the League of Nations*. In his introduction detailing the forthcoming sections, he wrote:

> The first step in the organization of an effective world peace in support of the anti-war Treaties of August 27, 1928 [Kellogg–Briand pact] will necessarily be the formulation of appropriate ways and means to induce all of the instrumentalities of public communication and influence to 'scrap' the war mind and to think in terms of world peace, and the first of the instrumentalities of public communication and influence to be appropriately controlled and made amenable to a reasonable and universally beneficial use of its immense power to influence the masses of the world, is the motion picture.[19]

John Sydney, five years later, concluded a lecture on 'Films and Peace' before an anti-war organisation with a similar plea, that 'the League of Nations and other peace organisations should make it not the least important of their functions to expose the patriotism bogey and to show up war in its true colours and in this, one of the strongest weapons to their hand is undoubtedly the film'.[20]

At least two films were made by the League of Nations, which also distributed several 'peace' films and cooperated in the making of others.[21] For example, in 1926 the League of Nations Non-Partisan Association distributed the five-reeler, *Hell and the Way Out*, which advocated the USA joining the League of Nations.[22] Two of the non-commercial films made by the League, *The World War and After*, a four-reeler, and the one-reeler, *Lest We Forget*, were for use in elementary schools, but copies had ceased to be available by 1934. (It is unclear whether the League made a third film looking at international economic interdependence.)[23] The building and organisation itself was the site and subject of Alberto Calvacanti's promotional short for the GPO Film Unit, *Message from Geneva* (1937), which showed how a BBC broadcast could be made from the League's headquarters via the Post Office's land lines.[24] Resolutions passed by the *Comité d'entente des grandes associations internationales*, a League conference held in Paris in the summer of 1937, endorsed its ambition to be more active in using films and radio for peace.[25] Like so many League initiatives, it had strong rhetorical foundations. Meanwhile, Britain, Germany, the Soviet Union and the USA continued to develop effective means to promote their national interests using celluloid and radio.

It was part of the progressive culture of the 1930s for 'thinking people' to reflect on the educational role of cinema. Many valued the most didactic and socially responsible films – 'What Films Have Done for World Peace' was not an uncommon way to construct a cinematic survey.[26] E.G. Cousins, in November 1936, argued that every year another opportunity to make a great anti-war film was lost. Cousins hoped that someone would make a film laying the blame for the Great War, and indeed all war, on its causes. These he listed as: a) the munitions' manufacturers; b) secret diplomacy (attempts to win a theoretical advantage over another country); c) imperialism, and d) dictatorship. Cousins, in idealistic language so resonant of the early 1930s, warned that such a film would begin a cycle of productions that would lead society away from box-office profit to a 'profit for the whole world'.[27] His primary target, munitions' manufacturers, echoed the mid-1930s revival of the 'Merchants of Death' controversy in Britain.[28] The public and press had a long-standing fascination with the political intrigues and associates of Sir Basil Zaharoff, popularly known as the 'mystery man of Europe', who reportedly had interests in Krupp, Skoda and other armaments' manufacturers. Moreover, one of the five questions on the 1935 Peace Ballot that aimed to discover the British public's attitude towards the League of Nations and collective security asked: 'Should the manufacture and sale of armaments for private profit be prohibited by international agreement?' Almost ten and a half million people answered, 'Yes'.[29]

Andrew Buchanan, who was one of the consultants for Associated Realist Film Producers, an organisation set up to liaise between documentary film-makers and potential sponsors, when interviewed for *Sight and Sound* in July 1939, replied to the question of what was 'the most vital need of the day for the screen' without hesitation: 'the putting forward of a constructive way to peace ... a full length film of the magnitude of *All Quiet*, but with a peace theme ... a sort of 1940 Sermon on the Mount ... The location of the film should be "anywhere" and it should be released simultaneously in all countries'.[30] However worthy such sentiments, by mid-1939 they were not in keeping with public opinion, and, furthermore, as will be shown later in this essay, they ran counter to the preoccupation of feature film makers.

At this point it is worthwhile relating Buchanan's comment to Martin Ceadel's *Pacifism in Britain*, covering the period 1914 to 1945.[31] Ceadel identifies two faiths: pacifism which considers war wrong in all circumstances, and 'pacificism', which believes war to be irrational and inhumane but controllable by armed force. Pacificism dominated British thinking between 1918 and 1931 and supported the League of Nations' policy of collective security as the major deterrent to further war. By 1936, the League's inadequacy as a peace-keeper, the successful establishment of fascist regimes in Germany and Italy and the outbreak of the Spanish Civil War had left pacifism as a faith rather than a policy. Buchanan's proposal for a Christian-framed peace film echoed Dick Sheppard's Peace Pledge Union, in contrast to the albeit-reluctant, socialist-cum-Communist Party exhortations from some of his documentary film-making colleagues.

In discussing the impact of Abel Gance's *J'accuse* (1919) and King Vidor's *The Big Parade* (1926), Manuela Gheorghiu-Cernat, in *Arms and the Film* (1983), cautioned that ten years after the end of the war, with newsreel pictures of the front lines being taken from the archives to illustrate avowedly anti-war films, 'more than once the makers' intentions were belied by the spectacular images and the grandiloquent commentary, both demanded by the jubilee context'.[32] It is only, he claimed, with the virtually simultaneous shooting and release of Lewis Milestone's *All Quiet on the Western Front* and G.W. Pabst's *Westfront 1918* in 1930 that 'for the first time film, as works of art, no longer represented the views of the dominating culture of the Establishment'.[33] Rod Kedward made a similar point when he wrote, 'it was not until the end of the 1920s that film even began to approach the written and spoken word in its contribution to peace. The great feature films about peace were all made after 1928.' However, he admitted to some exceptions, 'particularly the American peace films of 1915–16 and isolated ventures elsewhere', principally from Soviet Russia.[34]

It is not surprising that most writing on the inter-war period, by contemporaries and thereafter, valued the power of the written word to persuade and inform, and applied these criteria to film, the single most powerful new medium of the twentieth century. But audiences were not so different from those of today, and, despite the recent revival of interest by mainstream cinema-goers in political documentaries, independent features and political thrillers such as *Syriana* (2005) and *The Constant Gardener* (2005), we know that the majority of modern-day audiences pay to watch films whose morality does not make a contribution towards a better world. In 1917, the Report of the Commission set up by the National Council of Public Morals to investigate cinema gathered considerable evidence from the industry as well as viewers, noting that 'cinemas for commercial and competitive reasons did not promote films of an instructive nature'.[35] And so, in a roundabout fashion, I arrive at the purpose of this essay: to explore the 'peace' and 'disarmament' themes in the feature films that the 18.5 million weekly ticket-purchasers in Britain are most likely to have watched, in order to better understand how cinema may have (mis)informed them.[36]

My initial focus is on scenes and narratives of diplomats, disarmament conferences, the League of Nations, pacifists and peace activists. These were not the only aspects of diplomacy, interstate relations and world events covered by cinema between the wars – in fact they were in the minority. Robert W. Gregg, in *International Relations on Film*, argued that:

> diplomacy encompasses three tasks. One is negotiation. The picture of the diplomat that most people carry around in their heads is that of a negotiator, someone sent abroad by his or her government to persuade another government to enter into an agreement on terms favourable to the diplomat's country. A second task of diplomacy is that of representation, or communicating to other governments a country's policy objectives and official position on issues; this is what ambassadors and their staffs routinely do. The third task of diplomacy most frequently involves espionage, and that is the task of gathering information and reporting it back to the diplomat's home government. The problem that necessitates – or at least invites – espionage is that sovereign states typically do not wish other states to know everything there is to know about their capabilities and their intentions.[37]

One does not have to agree fully with Gregg's analysis to concur that the public's perception of diplomacy is often framed in this tripartite fashion, particularly in the age of quota quickies, where film-makers, despite an almost unlimited canvas of narratives, characters and choice of *mise-en-scène*, painted mostly by numbers. As well as traditional diplomatic activity, my survey is extended to include one of the most regularly occurring treatments of international relations in film: peace-time espionage.

I have omitted biblical or religious references to peace, and deliberately not included any films that are set in wartime. This means, for example, the exclusion of *The Spy in Black* (aka *U-Boat 29*) (1939), directed by Michael Powell and starring Conrad Veidt and Valerie Hobson, which focused on the First World War, and *The Last Barricade* (1938) where, during the Spanish Civil War, a journalist falls in love with a local senorita whose father is a spy planning to blow up a garrison full of soldiers. The 'anti-war war films' are best covered in Manuela Gheorghiu-Cernat's *Arms and the Film: War and Peace in European Films*. Furthermore, given that 'by 1939 the ordinary British filmgoer knew only the English-speaking stars of British and American pictures',[38] I have ignored foreign-language films. The countries of origin for my review are therefore the USA and the UK.

It is necessary to provide some caveats. First, newsreels were a stable item on a cinema's menu, and, it might be assumed, made available the current international political context, informing viewers' judgements on world events. However, British newsreels and the US *The March of Time*, in particular, focused on personalities and entertainments, apart from major political events which they also framed as celebrity politics – a point that I return to in my conclusion. Second, it is impossible to assess any film's popularity and impact without more information on its distribution and reception, the composition of audiences, and what their reading and other viewing habits were. Third, I know from researching historically based topics using predominantly paper-based searches, that being comprehensive – even if one is ruthless in applying one's criteria – is impossible. The main paper-based records that I have consulted are the *American Film Institute Catalogue* and David Quinlan's *British Sound Films: The Studio Years 1928–1959*.[39]

The League of Nations and world peace featured in only five US films of the immediate post-war decade, and these were all made between 1919 and 1924. *The Spirit of Lafayette* (1919) began with scenes of armistice parades in New York and moved into the biography of Lafayette, the Frenchman who volunteered to serve in the American Revolution. Returning to the present, the storyteller concludes that Lafayette would have wished for the League of Nations. US President Woodrow Wilson, who was greeted in Paris in mid-December 1918 with great enthusiasm on his second trip to the French capital, took a pre-release copy of *The Spirit of Lafayette* to view as he sailed across the Atlantic.[40] Wilson's ideals for a permanent League of Nations are said to have inspired *Whom the Gods Would Destroy* (1919), a film that was endorsed by League of Nations societies throughout the USA, and the American branch of the League to Enforce Peace. It told of a young explosives' inventor being courted by a German university. He becomes disillusioned and moves to Belgium. During the war, he suffers horribly. At the Paris conferences, the former belligerents harness their energies towards world peace.[41]

Mutt and Jeff, two popular animated cartoon characters, attend the Paris Peace Conference in *Sir Sidney* (1919) and offer off-the-wall advice to world leaders Woodrow Wilson, David Lloyd George and Georges Clemenceau: 'Gentlemen of the Peace Congress – First – I think we should annex Patagonia to Sweden...' A poster for the short urged proprietors to 'do some annexing yourself – profits', by showing the film at their cinema.[42]

Uncle Sam of Freedom Ridge (1920) told of a former soldier who determines that his son's death in the Great War will not be in vain. The ex-serviceman so strongly endorses the League of Nations that, when the Senate refuses to ratify the treaty, he takes his own life and, in the throes of death, composes a plea in support of the League. This film was seen as providing non-partisan support for the League of Nations, and was shown at Democratic Party campaign rallies.[43]

Distributed in 1924 by Vitagraph, *Two Shall Be Born* was based on a short story published at the turn of the century. A dying Polish count, head of a committee working for permanent peace among the countries of Europe, instructs his daughter, Mayra, to deliver vital papers to New York. Mayra is kidnapped and tortured by a renegade Polish baron but refuses to disclose the whereabouts of the papers. Since this is melodrama, the story also has her falling in love with and marrying an Irish traffic cop who had been disinherited by his millionaire father for not marrying a blue-blood socialite. Myra is rescued by her husband, who is then reconciled with his father.[44]

The bell-weather British peace picture of the 1920s, variously described by reviewers as 'imaginative' and 'a kind of English *Metropolis*', had a league of women attempting to prevent the Second World War. *High Treason* (1929), directed by Maurice Elvey and produced and distributed by Gaumont, was based on a 1927 play by Noel Pemberton-Billing, a noted supporter of air power. During the First World War he had consistently advocated the creation of a separate air force, not connected to either the army or the navy, and urged the Government to make aerial attacks on German cities.

High Treason was set in a futuristic world of the 1940s in which the Channel Tunnel already existed, television news dominated print journalism, and aeroplanes landed on the roofs of tall buildings. England was part of a United Europe in conflict with a United America. With its publicity tagline, 'The Peace Picture', the film portrayed millions of women within a Peace League trying to stop the two governments from embarking on a cataclysmic war. They determine that the only way conflict can be avoided is by killing the leader of one of the superpowers, and so they assassinate the leader of United Europe. This was one of the first British sound movies and, in conjunction with Alfred Hitchcock's *Blackmail* of the same year, led to claims in some quarters of Britain leading the world in film-making.[45] Notwithstanding the story's anticipation of technological advances and the Greenham Common women's peace movement of the 1980s, the heralding of British superiority in film-making, like the morality of peace through assassination, was ill-conceived.

The 1930s began promisingly for British espionage thrillers. George King directed the quota quickie, *Midnight*, which had a young woman assisting a British agent in preventing secret plans from falling into the hands of enemy agents. *The Last Hour* depicted a nest of foreign spies who steal the blueprint of a death ray in order to terrorise British ships and planes. *The Price of Things*, however, from a novel by the film's Channel Island director, Elinor Glyn, was distinguished only by featuring real-life twins playing screen twins, as a spy ring attempts 'to gain possession of a secret document from one of the twins, a duke, with the help of a *femme fatale*'.[46]

1931 saw three British films involving inventions, thefts and spies. *The Wickham Mystery* had a necklace and blueprints for a revolutionary aeroplane stolen by villains hoping to sell the plans to a foreign power. In *A Honeymoon Adventure* (aka *Footsteps in the Night*), directed by Maurice Elvey, the husband-inventor of a honeymooning couple is kidnapped, and *No Lady*, directed and starring Lupino Lane, had him mistaken for an international master criminal. The film climaxes in a glider race that a foreign power is determined to win by any means possible. Of variable quality, these films were described by David Quinlan respectively as 'creaky', 'zippy' and 'a comedy vehicle which made up in pace and get-up-and-go what it lacked in subtlety'.[47]

The League of Nations provided the backdrop for the British feature film, *After the Ball* (1932), starring American Esther Ralston and South African-born Basil Rathbone. Quinlan describes this as 'familiar early 1930s' comedy stuff, but done with sparkle and poking some pertinent fun

DISARMAMENT AND PEACE MOVEMENTS IN FEATURE FILMS   139

at the League of Nations'.[48] In Geneva, a diplomat's wife flirts with a handsome courier by posing as her own maid.

Espionage drove the plot of two other British comedies of 1932. In *Josser Joins the Navy*, one of three films in which Ernie Lotinga played Jimmy Josser, he enlists 'in order to track down a mysterious Chinaman ... and his confederate ... a treacherous officer who has stolen a secret formula'.[49] In *The Silver Greyhound*, a British secret agent meets a woman in Paris and falls in love. She turns out to be a spy who drugs him and makes off with a valuable document, but his superior reclaims the document, and he, the girl.[50]

FPI (1933) was filmed in Germany with an all-British cast, a 'futuristic drama about a giant floating aircraft carrier which a group of financiers conspire to destroy'. Quinlan concluded: 'Not much liked even in its time and pretty creaky now'.[51] Two other British entries for 1933 were *The Right to Live*, in which a scientist invents a neutralising agent for poison gas which is then stolen by spies, and *I Spy*, in which a playboy, mistaken for a spy, falls in love with a woman who really is a spy. Quinlan rates each of these films as '2', signifying 'pretty awful'.[52]

Reflecting on recent events such as the London Naval Disarmament Conference, the US comic character Krazy Kat brought peace to a jungle whose animals were war-weary after years of trench-style conflict in the animation *Disarmament Conference* (1931).[53] In 1932, Louis de Rochemont, who went on to create the monthly US newsreel, *The March of Time*, in 1934, edited a sixty-five minute, social-political documentary from Movietonews footage. *The Cry of the World* showed the devastation wrought by the First World War. Featured in its coverage was the international movement towards permanent peace, and the League of Nations and World Court in session. The *New York Times* 'remarked that the film contained some "ironical turns" including the placement of scenes of fighting in Shanghai after scenes of disarmament speeches, and the showing of military and naval maneuvres of various countries following scenes of the reduction of armaments conference'. The film failed commercially.[54] In the *RKO* picture, *Diplomaniacs* (1933), from a story and screenplay by Joseph L. Mankiewicz, dimwits Willy and Hercules are offered a million dollars to represent the oil-rich Adoop Indian tribe at the Geneva Disarmament talks. In a vaudeville-style of mayhem, the final stages of the plot, according to the *AFI Catalogue*, unfolded as follows:

> At last in Geneva, Hercules and Willy are spied upon by Winklereid [an evil conspirator] and his cohorts, Schmerzenpuppen, Puppenschmerzen, Schmerzenschmerzen and Puppenpuppen. Protected by the omniscient Adoops, Willy and Hercules, who have prepared an impromptu peace treaty, survive the conspirators'

assassination attempts and arrive safely at the conference. During their unique 'harmony-among-nations' speech, Winklereid tosses a bomb into the room, which explodes and blackens the faces of all present. After the war-loving delegation sings a song of peace, Winklereid, determined to ensure a continuing market for his employer's explosive bullets, steals Willy's treaty and forges the names of the delegates on it. Willy and Hercules, believing they have succeeded, return to America, only to discover that war has been declared and that they have been drafted.[55]

The Man Who Knew Too Much (1934) was credited with being the thriller that re-established Alfred Hitchcock's reputation. Its detailed treatment of espionage created considerable suspense as a secret agent is murdered in St Moritz, but, before dying, he manages to pass on information about a planned assassination attempt to be made on a foreign diplomat in London. *The Return of Bulldog Drummond*, from a novel by Herman C. McNeile (aka 'Sapper'), has the detective busting a gang of 'political crooks' who have kidnapped his wife.[56] *Thunder in the Air*, a thirty-five minute UK short by Hans Nieter, was an 'experimental movie which, alternating newsreel extracts with acted scenes, strongly condemned the munitions industrial profiteers'.[57]

How's Chances? (1934) was typical of the period, with marital infidelity played out among the diplomatic classes. In this musical comedy, a young British ambassador negotiating a treaty to be signed by two diplomats has to fight off the amorous attentions of their wives. In *Once in a New Moon* 'an English village is hurled into space through the collision of a dead star with the Moon. The science-minded postmaster… is unwillingly elected President of the "new" country, but a government of Conservatives is set up by the nobs of the village and civil war threatens until the slice of land is returned to Earth.'[58] Although not strictly falling within either of my categories, of espionage or peace, this Fox-British science fantasy may have allowed audiences to ponder, albeit at an allegorical level, some of the wider issues raised by the League.

In 1935, Hitchcock directed *The 39 Steps*, based on the novel by John Buchan. Starring Robert Donat and Madeleine Carroll, this was arguably the best version of the familiar tale of handcuffed flight from both police and spies, ending back in the music hall where the story started. *Handle with Care* was at the opposite end of the quality spectrum. Quinlan included quotations from contemporary reviewers when he described this film as an '"extremely unfunny" farce about a couple of reformed crooks, a brace of spies and a country house wrestling match which one of the ex-crooks wins by taking a "strength pill"'.[59] Marginally better were the knock-about *Jimmy Boy*, in which a gang of foreign agents plots to blow up London, and the thriller, *Expert's Opinion*, where enemy agents try to extract the design of a new aircraft gun from a ballistics expert. The musical comedy *Heat Wave* probably lies outside my criteria as it involves a greengrocer who is mistaken for a gun-runner and thwarts a South American coup.[60] However, its international stereotypes, particularly near the start of a Civil War in Spain, may have had some impact on the attitudes of the British viewing public.

The US cartoon character, Krazy Kat, attempted musical diplomacy in Columbia's 1935 *Peace Conference*.

> Three world-power representatives (animals in top hats and pinstripe tails), after being relieved of their weapons, dance together to a conference to discuss world peace. But as soon as they start to slice off their shares of a world globe, they begin to quarrel. Alerted by the doves of peace, Krazy Kat enters the melee in a tank and shoots a shell from which Bing Crosby emerges. His crooning pacifies the delegates, but only briefly. With Uncle Sam now in attendance, the conference again gets under way when a giant from Mars crashes into earth and disrupts the meeting. The delegates and Krazy Kat, with a Rudy Vallee-loaded shell, another Crosby shell, and a big-band shell, unite to restore world order.[61]

Another US cartoon of 1935 addressed the destructive role of munitions' manufacturers. *Neighbours* pitted a hitherto happy pair of roosters against one another after a crow spreads lies about each of them and then sells them arms. The roosters wipe one another out, and their ghosts bemoan false prophets and profiteers.[62]

British feature film, particularly into the mid-1930s, can be to seen tapping into national preoccupations with aviation, merchants of death, and questionable League practices. By this time, visits to Germany for ex-servicemen, as well as cultural exchanges with schools, were being encouraged by the Nazi regime. *Men of Yesterday* (1936) was, according to Quinlan, 'an intelligently written, poignant plea for peace'. 'Ex-Major Radford devotes his spare time to the welfare of ex-servicemen. Currently, he is working hard on a "reunion" that will bring English, French and German veterans of the First World War together. When he loses his job, Radford ... loses his enthusiasm and even contemplates suicide, but his ex-batman ... pulls him round, and his "reunion" dream comes true.'[63]

The Secret Voice (1936) was more formulaic: foreign agents kidnap the sister of an inventor of a non-flammable petrol to force him to reveal its formula, which he has sent to the League of Nations. In *Wolf's Clothing*, a naïve British diplomat is despatched to France where spies mistake him for an assassin. *Guilty Melody* has a British agent proving the innocence of a singer whose treacherous husband is sending out coded messages on her records.[64]

George Arliss's career was in decline when he made *East Meets West* and *His Lordship* (aka *Men of Affaires*) in 1936. In *East Meets West* he is the sultan of a small country with a harbour of strategic importance to both Britain and an Eastern power. In *His Lordship*, he helps a friend accused of murdering a middle-eastern emir to escape to England. His twin brother, the Foreign Secretary, will not assist so Arliss kidnaps and impersonates him, trapping two sheiks into confessing their role in the killing, and thus preventing war.[65]

The Spanish Civil War inspired a number of features films,[66] as well as compilation films such as Ivor Montagu's *Defence of Madrid* (1936) and *Peace and Plenty* (1939).[67] Ingenious screenwriters and directors may have adapted plots to a Spanish context or, as is more likely in the case of Arthur Behrend, had their novel optioned because of its Spanish setting. *The House of the Spaniard* (1936) told of a Lancashire clerk discovering that his boss is both a counterfeiter and a revolutionary. The clerk is kidnapped and taken to Spain but rescued by his boss's daughter, whom he later helps to escape.[68]

The year 1937 introduced *The Road Back*, the sequel to *All Quiet on the Western Front*, and Jean Renoir's *La grande illusion*, showing the senselessness of old aristocratic codes of honour and chivalry in the age of mass war. It was also the year of Frank Capra's *Lost Horizon*, which opened with Ronald Colman, playing Robert Conway, an author and a diplomat, rescuing British subjects from a revolution in China. It ends with him climbing the mountains, in sight of the pass to Shangri-La, where he hopes to join the mission of spreading peace to the world.[69] However, peace through armed deterrent was a more popular theme. *Blake of Scotland Yard*, a feature-length version of a fifteen-part, US-made serial, started with Sir James Blake of Scotland Yard demonstrating, for the League of Nations at his London home, a death ray that is able to destroy boats two hundred miles out at sea. Blake, hoping his invention will end war, thwarts theft, kidnapping and skulduggery by enemy agents, before handing the weapon over to the League.[70]

In Britain, the 'Crazy Gang' series was launched with *Underneath the Arches*. Down-and-outs Bud Flanagan and Chesney Allen find themselves in South America, thwarting revolutionaries intent on stealing a 'peace' gas. In *Holiday's End*, a revolutionary is found to be responsible for the murder of the science master in a British boarding school after the boy king from a small European country starts his new term. *Bulldog Drummond at Bay* had the eponymous hero defeating foreign spies who use a 'peace club' to hide their attempts to steal an inventor's new radio-controlled aeroplane.[71] The infiltration of the peace movement, as a theme in feature film, could be seen as reflecting a growing disenchantment with pacifism, although an attack on the gullibility of the peace movement is consistent with Bulldog Drummond's political orientation. A wealthy former officer, now a private detective, Drummond in Sapper's novels is a crude version of the imperial adventurer: a chauvinist, racist and anti-Semite.[72]

'An international armaments ring plans to bomb London. A suspicious reporter is killed before he can discover the truth, but his friends, a cartoonist and an agony columnist, discover the plotters' underground laboratory and, although some bombs are dropped, smash the controls and end the raids.' Thus Quinlan summarises *Midnight Menace* (aka *Bombs over London*).[73] In *Wife of General Ling*, a Secret Service agent investigates how British arms are being smuggled into China. A gentle old antiques dealer turns out to be the spymaster of the gang planning to kill a scientist with an explosive timepiece in *The Fatal Hour*. British and foreign agents fight over a valuable document aboard an east-west train in *Passenger to London*. Broadly satirical of the Hitchcock and John Buchan styles, the eponymous hero in *Mr Stringfellow Says 'No'* witnesses a car crash, is told a secret by the dying driver, and then pursued by spies of several nationalities, kidnapped, and forced into a plane. He escapes by parachute, is captured and locked in the Tower of London, then given a knighthood and elected to Parliament.[74]

Alfred Hitchcock's *The Lady Vanishes* (1938) was a spy mystery imbued with delightful character studies of British eccentricity – foreign agents may pose difficulties but they will inevitably be outwitted by Anglo-Saxon common sense and breeding! That same year, in a comedy called *Lightning Conductor*, a bus conductor, the inventor of a new type of gas mask, visits the Air Defence Office just as a theft of vital plans occurs. The boys' adventure flick, *Luck of the Navy* (aka *North Sea Patrol*), had a gang of foreign spies stealing the secret orders given to a British naval commander. He purses and destroys their Q-ship. The farce, *Many Tanks Mr Atkins*, saw Private Nutter's plans for a supercharged tank attract the attention of German agents.[75] Although the enemy had been ambiguously portrayed throughout the 1930s – German? Bolshevik? Middle Eastern? – from 1938 his homeland was clearly identified as Germany.

'Tim ..., a war correspondent, tracks down but falls in love with Jacqueline ..., accomplice of armaments monger Zubova ..., who had supposedly committed suicide. Tim is captured and forced to watch Zubova sinking a ship which he hopes will start a war. Jacqueline shoots Zubova but is herself fatally wounded and dies in Tim's arms. Fast-moving melodrama on stereotyped lines' was Quinlan's assessment of *Mr Satan*[76] which tapped into the various intrigues surrounding Zaharoff and the Merchants of Death.

Old Mother Riley was the alter ego of Arthur Lucan – the Danny La Rue or Dame Edna Everage/Barry Humphries of her/his day. In *Old Mother Riley in Paris*, s/he's mistaken for a spy and ends up earning a medal for counter-espionage. Another successful comedy starred Tom Walls as a British agent who is called back from his honeymoon to uncover a nest of spies in *Strange Boarders*.[77]

The Warner Brothers animation, *A Feud Was There*, was released during the Munich crisis of 1938. 'It portrays Egghead as the much-abused "peacemaker" between two feuding mountain families. Fortuitously, perhaps, the Egghead character sported a stiff collar and bowler hat – sartorial symbols associated with Britain's prime minister and appeasement advocate, Neville Chamberlain.'[78] Then in November, Walt Disney's *Ferdinand the Bull* appeared. Michael Shull and David Wilt have commented on its significance:

> The allegorical implications of the bull who would rather sniff flowers than fight are debateable but take on weight in the context of the troubled times in which it was released. The bull, for instance, could be interpreted as representing a powerful America refusing to live up to its international responsibilities, particularly with regard to the refusal to aid Republican Spain's struggle against Franco's fascist rebels. (Following the Christmas 1936 release of the children's book by Munro Leaf on which the cartoon was based, there were widespread accusations that the book was a pacifist tract.)[79]

In 1939, cinema reflected the quickening pace towards war, both in the quantity and content of its output. British film-makers also debated on screen the government, media and public's preoccupation with aircraft as a force for good or evil. In *Meet Maxwell Archer* (aka *Maxwell Archer Detective*), a pilot accused of murder appeals to the eponymous sleuth who is tracking a gang of foreign agents. *Spies of the Air* saw schemers about to pass the designs for a new plane to an overseas country. *Q Planes* (aka *Clouds over Europe*) starred Ralph Richardson, Valerie Hobson and Laurence Olivier in a spy thriller about bombers being brought down by a radio beam while on test flights.[80]

Valerie Hobson starred as a Bosnian in *The Silent Battle* (aka *Continental Express*). With her father in prison, she is compelled by an armaments manufacturer to assassinate the president. Dissuaded by her fiancé and what turns out to be a secret service agent, she is kidnapped, but later rescued by them.[81]

> Rival spies are after the formula for a new cartridge which is in the hands of a German chemist. A British agent and his sister arrive in Berlin and, by playing up to the chemist's son Max, she gets the formula, although she and Max have fallen in love. He pursues her and stops her train, but at the last moment he is unable to hand her over to the authorities. Risible spy thriller.

Thus writes Quinlan of *Secret Journey* (aka *Among Human Wolves*). *The Four Just Men* (aka *The Secret Four*) had a plot to block the Suez Canal, stopping the movements of all ships and troops to the East. Old Mother Riley/Arthur Lucan returned for two farces: *Old Mother Riley Joins Up*, in which she prevents secret papers from falling into German hands, and *Old Mother Riley MP*, in which she is appointed Minister for Strange Affairs, forcing the Emperor of Rocavia to pay a £50 million debt to the UK.[82]

Traitor Spy (aka *The Torso Murder Mystery*) showed a freelance spy escaping to a hideaway after he has photographed secret papers. German agents pressure him, and the British cordon off the building. *Spy for a Day* pitted a northern farm-worker against British and German agents because of his similarity to an infamous German spy, until he helps the British locate the enemy agent, and finds the courage to ask the village postmistress to marry. In *Sons of the Sea*, the routines of navy life were shown in colour as backdrop to a plot about the son of a naval commander suspected of treason. The real espionage mastermind is finally apprehended. *Hell's Cargo* (aka *Dangerous Cargo*) was a remake of a French film in which Russian, French and English naval commanders chase a murderer across the high seas. The villain releases a chemical, producing a deadly gas threatening shipping. The French captain saves the day: the Russian dies. Read as prophecy, the film anticipated the inclusion of Russia among the Allies and the considerable extent of its losses. In *All at Sea*, British comedy stalwart, Sandy Powell, played a messenger from a chemical factory. Spies pursue him after he accidentally joins the navy while carrying a powerful explosive about his person.[83]

Warner Brothers began production on *Murder in the Air* in mid-September 1939, the fourth and final of its 'Secret Service' films. (The film was released in the spring/summer of 1940.) It starred Ronald Reagan who, as a US Government agent, impersonates a foreign spy who is, in fact, dead, and is then ordered by his controller to board an airship with a new weapon, an inertia projector, which can cut out all electrical supplies. Reagan meets his contact, who is posing as a secretary to a member of the League of Nations, and is ordered to destroy the airship while the spy makes off with the blueprints for the projector.[84]

The Columbia cartoon, *Peaceful Neighbours*, released in January 1939, was similar to a number of earlier Warner Brothers animations, but, despite the increase in international tension, was more optimistic than the aforementioned *Neighbours* of 1935. When rival families of chickens start to engage in open warfare, ingenious doves of peace stuff the shells and bombs with flowers, sweets and perfume, leading the chickens to stop fighting, eat, rebuild their homes, and then play and dance together.[85] Although not distributed until December, three months into the war, *Peace on Earth* is worth mentioning because it is claimed to be the only cartoon ever nominated for the Nobel Peace Prize; however, it does not appear on the nomination database. It was produced by Metro-Goldwyn-Mayer and directed by Hugh Harman. Set in a post-apocalyptic world, squirrels sit around on Christmas Eve, with the youngsters asking the meaning of the word 'men' in the phrase 'Peace on earth, good will to men'. Their grandfather describes the savage history of humankind and its extinction.[86] The film was remade by William Hanna and Joseph Barbera in 1955 as *Good Will to Men*.

Conclusion

Some may view a miscellany of B-movie plots as unedifying, particularly given the caveats I mentioned earlier. These are threads of an incomplete tapestry, and there is more that could be researched about the creation, distribution, promotion and reception of such films, furthering our understanding of the links between what people saw on screen and how these translated into political messages. Yet, even without that information, we can draw some conclusions.

Many genres of film in the later inter-war years, for example historical dramas such as *Fire over England* (1937) and science fiction such as *Things to Come* (1936), allowed audiences to draw parallels with contemporary world events. Such films may also have played a role in turning Americans away from isolationism, and realising the dangers of the looming war and the importance of siding with the British cause.[87] The increase in the numbers of spy pictures in 1939 certainly made audiences aware that international rivalry and tension were on the increase. Yet, as far as feature-film depictions of the League of Nations and the related issue of peace activism is concerned, there are recurring images.

The League was always a showcase, a public spectacle. The radio and the press, which featured photographs as well as editorials and commentary, covered the League's activities extensively for public consumption. The newsreels shown in cinema to accompany each performance provided partial, episodic updates on international affairs. What feature films chiefly instilled in the public's consciousness of the workings at Geneva was the display of celebrity and contradiction. The world's most famous diplomats with their top hats and cravats, exactly as they were portrayed and described in *The March of Time* newsreels, could be identified directly with celebrities from the studios, the stars. To the standard contradiction of an organisation that discussed peace while aggression prospered (a familiar theme of newsreels, particularly *The March of Time*), feature film's plots of espionage and marital infidelity offered partial explanations.

On occasions when film-makers created images of peace organisations other than the League, these were mostly 'peace leagues' and 'peace clubs' comprising well-intentioned do-gooders whose association had been infiltrated by spies intent on subverting its purpose and stealing their 'peace gasses'. In feature film – as in the real life of the League – idealism was invariably corrupted by cynicism, power politics and evil ambitions. However, so frequently did this theme occur in film that in the popular mind the idealistic 'peacenik' ceased to appear harmless and naïve, becoming as dangerous a threat as the radical or foreign spy. This reflected the broader shift in public opinion during the late 1930s, particularly the hardening of attitudes, in the last twelve months of peace, and suggests that such films anticipated – and may have helped to create – public attitudes since feature films take several months to produce.

It would be fashionable to conclude with film theory, suggesting that each member of an audience in the 1920s and 1930s was capable of negotiating their own interpretation of disarmament and peace movements; after all, they had other sources on which to draw, including collective memories, discussions about the newspapers they had read and the films and newsreels they had seen. However, cinema embellished and made crude versions of the reality that increasingly framed other media's commentaries and hence the popular consensus. In the earliest years after the Great War, feature films' portrayal of the League was a League of *Notions*, well-intentioned but not fully endorsed. From 1924 to 1929, it would have been difficult to challenge the tangible evidence that the League really was working, which may account for the dearth of League-themed feature films from Britain and the USA in the period.

By the early 1930s the *Notions* had become dismembered and half-baked; and by the late 1930s disarmers and peace-seekers were being crudely exploited as by-words for dupes and lackeys. We often claim that films reflect the times in which they were made. The inability of feature films' narrative to capture positive aspects of the League's work or the achievements of peace campaigners is scarcely the sole responsibility of the film-makers.

NOTES

I am exceedingly grateful to Adrian Smith for his detailed comments on an earlier version of this essay, and to my editors Keith Hamilton and Edward Johnson.

1. Andrew Kelly, 'Trench Footnotes', *Sight and Sound*, 7, 12 (December 1997), p. 25.
2. Manuela Gheorghiu-Cernat, *Arms and the Film: War and Peace in European Film* (Bucharest: Meridane Publishing House, 1983), p. 99.
3. Ibid., p. 100.
4. Andrew Kelly and Edward Lawrenson, 'W for War', *Sight and Sound*, 8, 4 (April 1998), p. 30.
5. Kelly, 'Trench Footnotes', p. 25.
6. Nominated by John Sydney, 'Films and Peace: A Survey and a Plea', *Sight and Sound*, 3, 11 (October 1934), p. 110.
7. H.R. Kedward, *Images of Peace 1916–1923* (Oxford: Oxford University Press, 1972), p. 6.
8. Cited in Kelly and Lawrenson, 'W for War', p. 29.
9. See, for example, Vincent Orange, 'The German Air Force is Already "The Most Powerful in Europe": Two Royal Air Force Officers Report on a Visit to Germany, 6–15 October 1936', *Journal of Military History*, 70 (October 2006), p. 1014.
10. Kelly and Lawrenson, 'W for War', p. 28. For details of the T.E. Lawrence–Korda case, see Andrew Kelly, Jeffrey Richards and James Pepper, *Filming T.E. Lawrence: Korda's Lost Epic* (London: Tauris, 1996).
11. ftvdb.bfi.org.uk/sift/title/13176?view=synopsis (accessed 14 June 2006).
12. 'Peace v. Peace Film', *Today's Cinema*, 47, 3416 (22 September 1936), p. 1.
13. *Today's Cinema* (27 May 1936), 46, 3319, p. 32.
14. Kelly, 'Trench Footnotes', p. 25.
15. John Whiteclay Chambers II, '*All Quiet on the Western Front* (1930): The Antiwar Film and the Image of the First World War', *Historical Journal of Film, Radio and Television*, 14, 4 (1994), p. 392.
16. 'Peace Campaign for War Film: Bristol Societies Circularised' (aka 'Peace Propaganda Used by Exhibitor showing "All Quiet on the Western Front"'), *Kinematograph Weekly*, 1557 (18 February 1937).
17. 'Peace Films Are Box Office in USA', *The News Letter*, 2, 6 (1 April 1937).
18. *Sight and Sound*, 5, 18 (Summer 1936), pp. 30–31, cited in Rachael Low, *The History of British Film*, vol. 5, *1929–1939: Documentary and Educational Films of the 1930s* (London: Allen and Unwin, 1979), p. 99. A few local and regional British 'peace films' are now available for viewing at www.movinghistory.ac.uk/homefront.
19. William Marston Seabury, *Motion Picture Problems: The Cinema and the League of Nations* (New York: Avondale Press, 1929), p. 14.
20. Sydney, 'Films and Peace', p. 112.
21. For brief details of the League's support for 'educational' cinema, see Low, *The History of British Film*, vol. 5, pp. 13–14.
22. *The American Film Institute Catalogue of Motion Pictures Produced in the United States*, vol. F2, *Feature Films, 1921–1930* (Berkley, CA: University of California Press, 1997), p. 336.
23. Sydney, 'Films and Peace', p. 110.
24. Low, *The History of British Film*, vol. 5, p. 112.
25. *Today's Cinema*, 14 July 1937.
26. *Picturegoer* (9 November 1935), 5, 233, pp. 10–11.
27. E.G. Cousins, 'A Great Film Lost', *Kinematograph Weekly*, 1542 (5 November 1936), p. 4.
28. See David G. Anderson, 'British Rearmament and the "Merchants of Death": The 1935–36 Royal Commission on the Manufacture of and Trade in Armaments', *Journal of Contemporary History*, 29 (1994), pp. 5–37.
29. en.wikipedia.org/wiki/Peace_Ballot (accessed 19 February 2007).

30. Arthur Vesselo, 'Theme for Peace' (Interview with Andrew Buchanan), *Sight and Sound*, 8, 30 (1 July 1939), p. 61.
31. M. Ceadel, *Pacifism in Britain 1914–1945: The Defining of a Faith* (New York: Oxford University Press, 1980).
32. Gheorghiu-Cernat, *Arms and the Film*, p. 117.
33. Ibid., p. 122.
34. Kedward, *Images of Peace*, pp. 6–7.
35. Quoted in ibid., p.7.
36. The figure of 18.5 million comes from Rachael Low, *The History of British Film*, vol. 7, *Film Making in 1930s Britain* (London: Allen and Unwin, 1985). p. 1.
37. Robert W. Gregg, *International Relations on Film* (Boulder, CO: Lynne Rienner Publishers, 1998), p. 90.
38. Low, *The History of British Film*, vol. 7, p. xv.
39. D. Quinlan, *British Sound Films: The Studio Years 1928–1959* (Totowa, NJ: Barnes and Noble Books, 1985).
40. *The American Film Institute Catalogue of Motion Pictures Produced in the United States*, vol. F1, *Feature Films, 1911–1920* (Berkley, CA: University of California Press, 1988), p. 874.
41. Ibid., p. 1032.
42. Michael S. Shull, and David E. Wilt, *Doing Their Bit: Wartime American Animated Short Films, 1939–1945* (Jefferson: McFarland, 1987), p. 20.
43. *AFI Catalogue*, vol. F1, 1988, p. 964.
44. *AFI Catalogue*, vol. F2, 1997, p. 840.
45. www.csie.ntu.edu.tw/~b2506017/sf/4h.htm (accessed 27 July 2006).
46. Quinlan, *British Sound Films*, pp. 113, 97 and 131.
47. Ibid., pp. 174, 83 and 121.
48. Ibid., p. 33.
49. Ibid., p. 92.
50. Ibid., p. 146.
51. Ibid., p. 71.
52. Ibid., pp. 137 and 89.
53. Schull and Wilt, *Doing Their Bit*, p. 21.
54. *The American Film Institute Catalogue of Motion Pictures Produced in the United States*, vol. F3, *Feature Films, 1931–1940* (Berkley, CA: University of California Press, 1993), p. 434.
55. Ibid., p. 509.
56. Quinlan, *British Sound Films*, pp. 135–36.
57. Gheorghiu-Cernat, *Arms and the Film*, p. 133.
58. Quinlan, *British Sound Films*, pp. 85 and 125.
59. Ibid., p. 79.
60. Ibid., pp. 92, 65 and 80.
61. Shull and Wilt, *Doing Their Bit*, pp. 23–24.
62. Ibid., p. 24.
63. Quinlan, *British Sound Films*, p. 112.
64. Ibid., pp. 143, 176 and 78.
65. Ibid., pp. 62 and 82.
66. See Majorie A. Valleau, *The Spanish Civil War in American and European Films* (Ann Arbor, MI: UMI Research Press, 1982).
67. www.britmovie.couk/bio/m/009.htm (accessed 24 January 2007).
68. Quinlan, *British Sound Films*, p. 84.
69. *AFI Catalogue*, vol. F3 (1993), pp. 1235–1237.
70. Ibid., p. 180.
71. Quinlan, *British Sound Films*, pp. 167, 83 and 44.
72. en.wikipedia.org/wiki/Bulldog_Drummond (accessed 21 February 2007)
73. Quinlan, *British Sound Films*, p. 113.

74. Ibid., pp. 174, 67, 128 and 116–17.
75. Ibid., pp. 99–100, 105 and 109.
76. Ibid., p. 116.
77. Ibid., pp. 124 and 154.
78. Shull and Wilt, *Doing Their Bit*, p. 26.
79. Ibid.
80. Quinlan, *British Sound Films*, pp. 111, 151 and 133.
81. Ibid., p. 146.
82. Ibid., pp. 143, 71 and 124–25.
83. Ibid., pp. 164, 151–52, 150, 80 and 33.
84. *AFI Catalogue*, vol. F3 (1993), pp. 1439–40.
85. Shull and Wilt, *Doing Their Bit,* pp. 72–73.
86. en.wikipedia.org/wiki/Peace_on_Earth_(1939_film) (accessed 24 January 2007).
87. Kelly and Lawrenson, 'W for War', p. 28.

8

Britain and the Provision of Arms to Finland, 1936–1940

GLYN STONE

In view of the significance of arms exports as an instrument of foreign policy, in achieving strategic objectives, converting potential allies and influencing foreign governments, it is surprising that so little attention has been paid by historians to this subject in the context of British rearmament in the later 1930s. They have tended, instead, to focus on strategic policy and imperial defence, Treasury and other constraints on the extent and pace of rearmament and the performance of the armaments industries in rearming and preparing for war.[1] This neglect is not for want of relevant material or potential case studies. British arms companies, such as Vickers and the Bristol Aeroplane Company, supported by British diplomats were engaged in a range of negotiations with countries across Europe. Arms exports were on the agendas of the Cabinet and, from September 1939, the War Cabinet, the Defence Policy Requirements Committee (DPRC), before September 1939 the Committee of Imperial Defence, the Chiefs of Staff Committee, the Deputy Chiefs of Staff Committee, the Foreign Arms Order Committee and its successor, the Allied Demands Committee. The Foreign Office played a crucial role in providing the political dimension to the export of arms and munitions, recognising that participation in the European arms trade in the later 1930s could not be avoided, partly for commercial reasons but mainly because conceding the field to Germany and Italy would result in a dangerous loss of influence and prestige. Advised by the Foreign Office, the DPRC took the decision in October 1936 that it was important not to discourage foreign arms orders, and this remained the policy beyond the outbreak of the Second World War.[2] With this policy decision in mind officials in the various European departments supported by the Assistant Under-Secretaries, the Permanent and Deputy Permanent Under-Secretaries and the Foreign Secretary expended considerable time and effort in trying to persuade the extremely reluctant service departments to release arms to foreign countries at a time when they considered stocks to be grossly inadequate for Britain's own defences.

In the absence of abundant supplies of weapons and munitions it was essential to establish which countries should receive priority in their provision. A Foreign Office memorandum, drawn up by the Permanent Under-Secretary, Sir Robert Vansittart, for the DPRC in late September 1936, revealed that the priority for arms exports to European countries was directed towards southern Europe, notably Portugal, Greece and Turkey.[3] Subsequent priority lists produced by the Foreign Office and the Chiefs of Staff confirmed the southern emphasis with the inclusion of Romania and Yugoslavia along with Portugal, Greece and Turkey.[4] In contrast with the southern orientation of British arms export policy, northern Europe, including Finland, came low down on the priority lists drawn up by the Foreign Office and the Chiefs of Staff because there was no immediate perceived German or Soviet threat to British interests. Despite its low priority, the focus of this essay is on the provision of British arms to Finland because of all the countries seeking British arms in the late 1930s it was only Poland and Finland which became engaged in an actual war before 1940 and Poland's participation during September 1939 was over before her British and French allies could organise anything in the way of effective material assistance. Instead, it was Finland's war with Soviet Russia in the winter of 1939–40 which provided the first real test of the capacity of the western allies to supply effective material assistance to another country threatened by conflict. What it demonstrated subsequently was the clear limitation of British (and French) arms provision and the absolute priority of Britain's own defence programme in the conflict with Nazi Germany, which doomed Finland from the outset despite the heroic resistance of her armed forces.

II

In 1937, when the Foreign Office drew up a priority list for arms exports based on political considerations, Finland was placed only eleventh out of the top twenty countries, followed immediately by Estonia, Latvia and Lithuania.[5] Later, in July 1939, when the Deputy Chiefs of Staff produced a priority list based on the relative strategic importance of countries requiring arms from the United Kingdom, Finland was omitted altogether from both the general priority order of the top fifteen countries and separate naval, land and air priorities.[6] The Nazi–Soviet Pact in late August 1939, the demise of Poland in September and its aftermath did little to transform the priority assigned to British arms exports to Finland until the outbreak of the Russo-Finnish War on 30 November 1939 propelled her to the top of the priority list for arms exports other than those to the French, the Turks and Dominion allies. Indeed, as late as 7 November 1939 the

Deputy Chiefs of Staff placed Finland within category C (countries at present of little importance) for naval, land and air armaments. The Finns were assigned tenth place overall for naval armaments and nineteenth for both land and air armaments.[7]

The Finns' only potential enemy was Soviet Russia, and this was confirmed in the mid-1930s by a series of warnings from Moscow. In June 1935 the Finnish Government was warned that if war should erupt between the Soviets and Germans, the Red Army would concentrate on forward defence and occupy Finland immediately and in January 1936 the ill-fated leader of the Red Army, Marshal Mikhail Tukhachevskii, accused Helsinki of building air bases in eastern Finland to enable Germany to strike at Soviet territory. Later in 1936, the Leningrad party chairman, Andrei Zhdanov, publicly warned Finland and the Baltic States not to compromise their neutrality by making security agreements with Germany.[8] Confronted with the Soviet threat, the Finns increased their own rearmament programme and placed orders with Britain for aircraft (Blenheim bombers) and engines amounting to nearly £400,000 and a further order for thirty-two Vickers tanks, while the leading military figure in Finland, General, later Field-Marshal Carl Gustav Mannerheim, visited Britain in September 1936 and was permitted to attend specially arranged tank manoeuvres and to visit a number of armament factories, including Vickers-Armstrong and the Bristol Aeroplane Company.[9] Earlier in the year, in January, he had met the British Foreign Secretary, Anthony Eden, on the occasion of King George V's funeral and prior to that he had visited the Hendon air show in 1934. In 1936 also, the Air Ministry for the first time appointed an air attaché to Finland and the Baltic States to advise, amongst other duties, on the sale of aircraft.[10] At the same time, the Finns diversified their arms orders by purchasing dive-bombers and fighter aircraft from the Dutch Fokker Company rather than Germany and Bofors guns from Sweden rather than Vickers.[11]

Rather than rely entirely upon arms imports, the Finns were determined to become more self-sufficient, particularly in the production of aircraft, including the manufacture of Bristol Blenheims and aero engines under licence in Finland. By the end of 1938, according to the British Legation in Helsinki, progress had been retarded and the Finnish Minister of Defence had publicly referred to the shortage of tanks, anti-aircraft guns and field artillery.[12] For their part, British arms companies were slow in fulfilling their orders for tanks and aircraft as priority was given to home defence or to countries higher on the priority list than Finland, such as Turkey, Greece and Portugal. When in June 1939 the 'conspicuously pro-British and anti-Nazi'[13] Chief of the Finnish Air Force, Major-General Jarl Lundqvist, expressed an interest in purchasing thirty

Spitfire fighters, he was quickly discouraged despite the possibility that the Finns might turn to Germany to purchase Messerschmitt fighters or alternatively to the United States. Moreover, when it was suggested that Lundqvist might visit the United Kingdom during July, the Air Ministry was less than enthusiastic and preferred to focus on the visit of military delegations from Poland, Romania and Turkey, countries 'which are of real importance to us in war'.[14] In view of the attitude of the service departments towards Finland's armaments needs it was hardly surprising that the Foreign Office should note in July 1939 that 'there have been signs recently of a definite cooling of Finnish opinion towards this country'.[15] On the other hand, the successful private visit of General Sir Walter Kirke, a former military adviser to the Finnish armed forces and recently appointed Commander of the Home Forces, to Helsinki between 18 and 22 June, compared favourably with the frosty reception given to the visit of the German Chief of Staff, General Franz Halder, a week later and led the Foreign Secretary, Lord Halifax, to comment that although the Finnish General Staff were 'undoubtedly somewhat pro-German' they were 'by no means beyond the reach of other influences'.[16]

The outbreak of the Second World War and the rapid and overwhelming defeat and partition of Poland between Germany and Soviet Russia naturally induced considerable apprehension and fear in Finland and also Latvia, Lithuania and Estonia. Indeed, under the terms of the secret protocol to the Nazi–Soviet Pact of 23 August 1939 the Baltic States and Finland were assigned to the Soviet sphere of influence. Between 28 September and 10 October 1939 Estonia, Latvia and Lithuania signed mutual assistance pacts with Moscow leaving Finland isolated and compelled into entering negotiations with the Soviets in their capital.[17] While the British Government was highly critical of, and deplored Soviet bullying of these small northern states, they did not expect the Soviets to invade Finland, but they remained resolved that should such an event take place it was not a sufficient *causus belli* to declare war on Soviet Russia. At the end of October the Chiefs of Staff were adamant that the invasion of Finland itself would involve no military threat to Britain and France who were in no position to take on additional burdens by declaring war on Soviet Russia; an action which would certainly 'consolidate the alliance between Germany and Russia'. If the War Cabinet decided to confront Soviet aggression in Scandinavia the Chiefs advised that it should only be undertaken when it was 'clear beyond all doubt that Russia intends to invade Sweden or Norway. No assurance of support should be given to Finland alone, or to Sweden in connection with the threat to Finland.'[18] Later, on 21 November the Chiefs of Staff, in response to a Foreign Office request for advice on the military implications of providing assurances of support to Scandinavian countries in the event of German or Soviet aggression, insisted that Britain and France could afford 'no assistance to Finland against Russian aggression', that 'no assurance should be given to any Scandinavian State as regards Russian aggression' and that it was essential 'to avoid any action likely to consolidate the alliance between Germany and Russia'.[19]

The British military authorities were certainly consistent. When the Foreign Secretary, Lord Halifax, sought to persuade the service departments to offer Finland and the Baltic States 'every inducement to maintain a firm front towards both Germany and the Soviet Union', the War Office was singularly unimpressed and insisted that the six remaining Vickers tanks, outstanding from the order placed with Finland in 1937, should be retained in the United Kingdom in view of the likelihood that they would be required by Turkey or some other ally or prospective ally, for whom it was essential to have war material available.[20] Eventually, at the beginning of November 1939, under pressure from the Foreign Office, the War Office relented.[21] At a meeting of the War Cabinet on 4 November the Prime Minister himself, Neville Chamberlain, expressed the hope that 'all possible steps would be taken to expedite the despatch of these tanks to Finland'.[22] But by now the Finns had got the message and purchased twenty-five Fiat fighters from Italy with the promise of immediate delivery. According to Lundqvist, the price was low, the aircraft had been taken from first-line Italian squadrons and Mussolini had wished to help the Finns against the Bolsheviks.[23]

No doubt the lukewarm attitude of the British military authorities towards the Finns would have continued, despite their knowledge that Germany was facilitating the passage of war material to Finland, were it not for the outbreak of the Russo-Finnish War on 30 November 1939.[24] The Soviets suspended their talks with the Finns in late November and took the decision to invade because above all, as Josef Stalin, the Soviet dictator, recollected one month after the end of the war against Finland, war was necessary to protect Leningrad by seizing the Karelian Isthmus. Between 30 to 35 per cent of the Soviet defence industry was concentrated in the Leningrad region, and as the second city of Russia, its safety and the safety of the country were indivisible; in Stalin's words, 'Leningrad's security is our country's security'. He feared that 'a breakthrough to Leningrad and the formation there of, say a bourgeois White Guard government would provide a serious basis for a civil war inside the country against the Soviet Government'. Stalin also admitted that with the three western powers locked in 'deadly combat' the moment had been opportune to settle the Leningrad problem 'when other countries were busy elsewhere, so this was the best moment to strike'. Moreover, expectations of a short victorious war were high, as Stalin reflected: 'We expected to bag an easy win. We were terribly spoiled by the Polish campaign.'[25] Recent investigations in the Soviet archives have failed to support the argument that Moscow intended to annex Finland; rather, they confirm the view that Soviet Russia wanted to acquire a part of Finnish territory and to strengthen Soviet influence in Finland by means of a 'preventive war' and to insulate itself from the threat of military intervention from Germany or Anglo-French forces.[26]

III

Within days of the outbreak of the war the Finnish Government had made an appeal to Britain to provide them immediately with thirty fighters and twelve Blenheims, which had been ordered previously, in order to prevent the complete Bolshevisation of their country. It was understood that the British Government would probably be unable to supply Spitfires and Hurricanes but that it might be able to spare some Gloster Gladiators which could be flown to Finland by Finnish pilots.[27] Before the War Cabinet could discuss the Finnish request, the Air Ministry turned it down flat so as not to denude their own air forces.[28] When the War Cabinet met on 2 December they had agreed that, unless the Soviets committed further acts of aggression in south-eastern Europe, there was nothing to be gained by intervening militarily in Finland which could outweigh the additional strain on Allied resources and the certainty that Soviet Russia and Germany would be united against a common enemy.[29] But the political consequences of doing nothing could not be ignored. At the War Cabinet meeting of 4 December, Halifax stressed that from the political point of view it would be in Britain's interest to respond positively to the Finnish request for aircraft. He added that while it was advantageous that 'Russia should be causing embarrassment to Germany' it was important to recognise that the Soviet invasion of Finland could in time prove 'very embarrassing to ourselves, particularly through its repercussions on the Scandinavian countries'. Chamberlain himself was inclined to the view that 'every effort should be made to give the Finns at least a measure of support'. He argued that the political effect of such a gesture could be very considerable, particularly on the Swedes, and support for Finland would 'conform with the policy of throwing in our resources in places where they would be of most value'. The Secretary of State for War, Leslie Hore-Belisha, added that support for Finland could produce 'a good moral effect on the United States', help to prevent Sweden from being 'thrown into the arms of Germany' and 'hold up the Russian advance [which] would be of great importance' in keeping the Soviet menace from coming 'dangerously close to us'.[30] The following day, the Air Ministry, 'in view of the manifest desire of the War Cabinet to go some way to meet Finland's request for fighter aircraft' and despite the fact that from the military point of view 'there was no case for supplying Finland with fighters since we had insufficient for our own needs', proposed the dispatch of twenty Gladiators to Finland.[31]

Clearly, the Finns were in a desperate position and heavily reliant on Britain and France for most of their arms supplies because Germany was doing very little to support them. Indeed, the first straw in the wind as to Germany's attitude was a speech by the Führer, Adolf Hitler, as early as 6 October 1939, when he omitted Finland from a list of states with which Germany enjoyed friendly relations.[32] As the War Cabinet soon learned, the Director General of the Finnish Foreign Ministry told the British Minister at Helsinki only ten days after the outbreak of Soviet-Finnish hostilities that 'Germany was hand in glove with Russia' and he had information that Germany would recognise the Soviet puppet [Otto] Kuusinen government of the 'Finnish Democratic Republic', installed at Terijoki, just inside the Finnish border, as soon as the Finns suffered reverses on the Mannerheim Line, which lay across the neck of the Karelian Isthmus, an area of crucial strategic interest to both Finland and Soviet Russia. Moreover, the Finnish Minister at Berlin was being treated as a pariah and the Germans were no more helpful unofficially than they were officially.[33] Indeed, early in the war, and despite the pro-Finnish attitude of the German Legation at Helsinki, all 'important' German diplomatic missions were instructed to express sympathy for the Russian standpoint in conversations and to refrain from any expression of sympathy for the Finnish position.[34] As State Secretary Ernst von Weizsäcker explained to the German Minister at Helsinki, Wipert von Blücher, Germany's situation as it had developed over the previous six months did not permit it 'to appear to equivocate vis-à-vis the Russians. An unexposed flank towards the east means a great deal to us at the present time.'[35]

Confirmation of the German attitude was received on 12 December from British Legation sources in Stockholm when it was revealed that six of the twenty-five Italian fighters were held in cases at Sassnitz harbour in north Germany, one had reached Stockholm and one was at Malmo, and that the transit of the remaining seventeen was held up, probably by the Germans who, it was believed, feared offending the Soviets.[36] Furthermore, on 20 December the Legation at Helsinki learned that Germany had held up an order for fifty-four howitzers which the Finns had ordered from German factories, and the British Minister, Thomas Snow, took this as more evidence of German complicity in the Soviet invasion.[37] Previously, on 10 December, the War Cabinet had been informed by the First Lord of the Admiralty, Winston Churchill, that a German warship on 3 December had stopped a Swedish tanker in Swedish territorial waters and revealed that the German Navy had orders to stop supplies of oil from reaching Finland.[38] Halifax, however, was not fully convinced that Germany was pursuing a entirely anti-Finnish policy. Despite Finnish protestations and reports from the British Legation at Helsinki, he believed it was likely that Germany was pursuing 'a double policy – stopping certain consignments of arms ostentatiously and, at the same time, surreptitiously giving indirect assistance to Finland.'[39] Moreover, he warned the French Ambassador, Charles Corbin, that it must not be forgotten that one of Germany's essential aims was 'to push us [Britain and France] into a war with the Russians'.[40] The Foreign Secretary's suspicions of German assistance to Finland were not entirely unfounded. According to 'reliable information' received by the British Legation in Oslo, between 120 and 150 30mm guns had been supplied by Germany to Finland a few days before the outbreak of the Russo-Finnish War.[41] In addition, according to the Finnish Minister at Rome, who told Italian Foreign Minister Galeazzo Ciano personally, Germany had supplied arms to Finland, 'turning over to her certain stocks, especially from the Polish war booty'.[42]

On 14 December Soviet Russia was expelled from the League of Nations and the recommendation was made for the procurement of war material for Finland.[43] Prompted by the French Government, on 22 December the Cabinet discussed the extent to which assistance could be rendered to Finland, with particular reference to the dispatch of technical missions and the supply of war material, and how Norway and Sweden might be persuaded to provide assistance to their Finnish neighbour.[44] Meanwhile, the increasingly desperate Finns had upped their requirements to fifty Gladiators and an additional twelve long-range Blenheim bombers, both of which they considered to be invaluable in winter conditions.[45] Halifax intervened personally in an attempt to persuade the Air Secretary, Kingsley Wood, to sanction the release of the Blenheims on the grounds that they were needed to bomb the Murmansk railway and thereby cut the land communications of Soviet forces operating north of Lake Ladoga with the rest of Soviet Russia. The Foreign Secretary stressed that by maintaining Finnish resistance British interests would be enhanced because the Soviets would be compelled to increase their demand for petroleum and other military supplies, which would then reduce the amounts available for supply to Germany. Moreover, the longer the Soviets were mired in the north the less probable was a Soviet advance in the Balkans and the Middle East, where British interests were directly threatened. By aiding the Finns to destroy the Murmansk railway, they would 'save ourselves the trouble of doing it in less favourable conditions later on' should Anglo-Soviet hostilities materialise; a possibility which, Halifax believed, could not be overlooked.[46]

Prior to Halifax's appeal, the Air Ministry announced that it was prepared to release a further ten Gladiators, as a free gift.[47] Unfortunately, none of the Gladiators would be available to fly to Finland until the end of December and, despite Halifax's appeal, the Ministry continued to vacillate over releasing a further twelve Blenheims; they were more resolute in refusing point-blank a Finnish request to supply Hurricanes. But, to the delight of their French allies, who were just as tardy in responding to Finnish appeals,[48] the Air Ministry eventually agreed to release the first twelve Blenheims, though twenty-four had by now been requested. Meanwhile, the South African Government had agreed to release twenty-eight Gauntlet fighters to the Finns, which were close to being obsolete and suitable only for training.[49]

By the end of 1939 and the end of the first month of the Russo-Finnish War the British had gone only part of the way in responding to Finnish appeals for arms and munitions. As yet, no anti-aircraft guns had been released and the Air Ministry had carefully and slowly controlled the release of aircraft. Moreover, the Air Staff were adamant that they could not advise any further assistance to the besieged Finnish Government. Blenheims were required for home defence and also in the Middle East where they were essential if air operations against Baku were to be carried out. The dispatch of the thirty Gladiators, which were now out of production, had reduced the reserves of British fighter strength to a dangerous degree.[50] The Air Staff doubted whether the Finnish Air Force could cope with additional aircraft, at least in the short run, and there were other pressing demands from countries such as Turkey; if the situation developed in Scandinavia they would be confronted with fuller demands from the Norwegians and Swedes.[51] For their part, the Chiefs of Staff recognised that increased provision of war material to Finland called for a choice. It depended on whether Finland had greater priority than security elsewhere, or rather on Britain's capacity to assist Norway and Sweden should plans for the disruption of Swedish exports of iron ore to the Third Reich be activated.[52] It was with these wider considerations in mind that the British authorities formed their responses to the continuing appeals for arms from the Finns during the early months of 1940.

Indeed, at the beginning of January 1940 Brigadier Christopher Ling, a staff officer with previous experience in Finland, was sent by the Chief of the Imperial General Staff, General Sir Edmund Ironside, to discuss with Field Marshal Mannerheim Finnish requirements in order of urgency.[53] Meanwhile, it was certain that the Finns needed aircraft so that seventeen obsolete Lysander fighters were added to the list and the French announced that they were sending thirty Morane-Saulnier 406 fighters to Finland along with 160 field guns.[54] A request to Halifax from the Finnish Minister at London, Georg Gripenberg, for anti-aircraft guns, and anti-tank guns was less successful.[55] At the same time, it was expected that the Finns would pay for all the weapons they had received, with the exception of the ten Gladiators, but that difficulties over payment would not delay deliveries and there was the possibility that credits would be granted on favourable terms. In other words, and despite their strategic and political concerns, the British Government were not prepared to supply the Finns gratis.

Brigadier Ling's mission to Finland confirmed that the Finns' most pressing needs were fighter aircraft and anti-aircraft guns to counter the incessant Soviet bombing raids.[56] Hore-Belisha was emphatic that in view of the unlikelihood of Finnish resistance lasting much beyond the winter months when the Russians would be able to fully exploit their enormous preponderance in manpower, there was no justification for the diversion of war material which could be vital to the British Army in the coming summer or to the defence of Great Britain against air attack.[57] The Air Ministry was slightly more positive and responded in mid-January by releasing a further twelve Blenheim bombers. However, when on 16 January Gripenberg requested the release of sixty Hurricanes – he anticipated that Spitfires were out of the question – Halifax was discouraging and advised the Finnish Government to explore the possibility of meeting their requirements in Italy.[58] When the Foreign Secretary suggested at the War Cabinet the same day that the British Government might obtain some fighters for Finland from the Italians, Kingsley Wood retorted that there was no possibility of obtaining Italian fighters for immediate delivery to Finland.[59] However, by 20 January the War Cabinet, encouraged by Prime Minister Neville Chamberlain, was prepared to consider sending a few Hurricanes to Finland, possibly manned by RAF pilots.[60] In the event, the Air Ministry released twelve Hurricanes – four immediately and eight a month later - and insisted they were to be flown by Finnish pilots who would first need training in the United Kingdom.[61] The Admiralty also agreed to release twenty Skuas and thirteen Rocs for use as fighter dive-bombers.[62] By early February the British had agreed to supply thirty Gladiators, twenty-eight Gauntlets, twenty-four Blenheims, seventeen Lysanders, twelve Hurricanes, twenty Skuas and thirteen Rocs, but of these only the Gladiators had arrived in Finland, along with ten Blenheims.[63] The French by now had agreed to release 176 aircraft, mainly fighters, and the United States forty-four

Brewster fighters, but many of these had still to reach Finland.[64] Indeed, on 5 February 1940, Risto Ryti, the Finnish President and former governor of the Bank of Finland, confirmed that only fifty-two aircraft had arrived so far from all sources since the outbreak of the war with Soviet Russia.[65]

If the Anglo-French Allies needed reminding that Finland warranted a high priority as far as arms exports were concerned, the Allied Military Committee provided it in late January when it stressed that the Allies had three motives for assisting her: the Russo-Finnish war was disrupting Russian transport and harming the Soviet economy so that supplies of raw materials and liquid fuels to Germany were retarded; the Soviet threat to Balkan countries would diminish as long as the Russians suffered reverses in the north; and allied assistance to Finland would strengthen the Scandinavian countries vis-à-vis Germany and would encourage small neutral powers in their resolve to resist the designs of the totalitarian states.[66] The response of the British authorities, however, continued to be limited by the continuing concern for the rearmament and re-equipment of their own armed forces. On 13 February an urgent request from Mannerheim to Ironside for ninety-six field guns was instantly dismissed on the grounds that there was insufficient artillery equipment for the British divisions preparing to go to France and there were absolutely no reserves of equipment.[67]

It took the dire prospect of Finland losing the war before winter was over to shake the resolve of the service departments and the Cabinet. Previously, Chamberlain and his French counterpart, Edouard Daladier, had agreed at a meeting of the Anglo-French Supreme War Council on 5 February that the collapse of Finland would be a terrible disaster for the Allied cause and that everything must be done to avert it. At the time, they had anticipated that the danger of a Finnish collapse would not become acute before the spring and that they could proceed with planning an expedition of five divisions to Scandinavia with the object of assisting the Finns. But a more significant objective was to control the Swedish iron ore fields and deny Swedish ore to Germany, provided Norway and Sweden agreed to the intervention of allied troops through their territory and Finland appealed for assistance.[68] However, as a result of 'very serious' Russian attacks on the Mannerheim Line in mid-February, the British Prime Minister confessed to Daladier that they had been too optimistic and there was now a 'real and imminent possibility of a breakthrough' unless the Finns were immediately supplied with the arms they had requested. In these circumstances, he confirmed that the War Cabinet had taken the decision 'to take some risk for the future in order to meet the risk for the present' and had sanctioned the release of thirty new eighteen-pounder guns to

Finland, and he appealed to the French Prime Minister to send some field guns as well.⁶⁹ It was important for Chamberlain to encourage Finnish resistance because, as he told his sister, Ida, on 17 February, he had a strong feeling that 'the Finnish war may have an important influence on our own fight. Russia must be fairly drained of the things the Germans hoped to get from her'.⁷⁰ However, the prospects of France sending field guns to Finland seemed anything but favourable. According to Ironside, the French Chief of Staff, General Maurice Gamelin, had returned an 'unfavourable reply' to a suggestion that the French could supply field guns. Ironside speculated that the French had sent all available surplus guns to the Balkans and were in process of equipping ten additional divisions and as a result none were available for the Finns.⁷¹ Ironside's pessimistic view was confounded by the decision of the French Government to send immediately thirty-six 75mm field guns to Finland and a number of French artillery experts by air to Helsinki.⁷²

Despite the urgency, British arms deliveries to Finland continued to be delayed so that it was only at the end of February that the additional Blenheims and Hurricanes were ready to be transported.⁷³ Previously, on 19 February, Kingsley Wood had rejected French suggestions that more British bombers should be sent to Finland, disguised with Finnish markings. The Air Secretary was adamant that considerable quantities of aircraft had already been sent despite serious risks in doing so and no further assistance could be given.⁷⁴ By this time, it was clear that the fate of Finland was tied up more than ever with the Anglo-French plans for intervention in Scandinavia, involving a large 'volunteer force' of some 50,000 men, provided Norwegian and Swedish cooperation could be secured, and this was proving immensely difficult owing to their fears of German retaliation. At the same time, the French began to fear that the Finns might accept a compromise peace which safeguarded 'a semblance of [Finnish] independence and integrity', with the result that any prospect of intervention in Scandinavia to deny vital materials to the Third Reich would be lost.⁷⁵

While the British and French continued to plan at the highest level and to prevaricate over arms deliveries, the war raged on in Finland and at the beginning of March the Finns, confirming French fears, dropped their bombshell. They intended to discuss terms for surrender with the Soviets unless they could be assured of immediate and extensive assistance from Britain and France. They demanded the immediate dispatch of 100 bombers with French and British crews and an Anglo-French expeditionary force of 50,000 men to reach Finland during March, and more thereafter. It was anticipated that the force would place itself under the control of the Finnish High Command.⁷⁶ There was, of course, no prospect whatsoever of sending an expeditionary force directly to Finland and the Cabinet decided that the position was the same with regard to sending fresh bombers. Indeed, at a meeting of the War Cabinet on 5 March Churchill and Kingsley Wood both 'deprecated sending further aircraft to Finland, since we should thereby weaken ourselves against Germany. The Finnish war could not be regarded as a profitable diversion, since German forces were not engaged'.[77] Concerned about his domestic position within France, Daladier ignored this vital point and insisted on promising full support for the Finns, including the 50,000 troops agreed previously, with or without Swedish and Norwegian agreement, but the British Government remained unmoved.[78]

Faced with the less than immediate and positive response of the western powers, the Finns began discussions with the Soviets and it seemed likely that the Helsinki Government would justify seeking terms with Moscow on the grounds of the Anglo-French refusal to respond positively to their final appeal for assistance, thereby placing the responsibility for Finland's collapse on the shoulders of the Allies.[79] As the Permanent Under-Secretary at the Foreign Office, Sir Alexander Cadogan, remarked on receiving the Finnish demands on 1 March, it 'looked as if they [the Finns] want a get out'.[80] Chamberlain agreed that the Finns were 'looking for a good excuse for making terms with the Russians'.[81] Confronted with this possibility the War Cabinet were prepared to consider sending, in the event of a breakdown in the Russo-Finnish talks, fifty Blenheim bombers to Finland within fourteen days of the breakdown and to send an expeditionary force, provided Norway and Sweden allowed it to pass through their territory, which they knew was extremely unlikely.[82] This decision was taken in the knowledge that the case for sending the bombers was weak from the military point of view. Indeed, on 7 March the Chiefs of Staff had warned that if the Blenheims were sent to Finland purely with the objective of sustaining Finnish resistance for a limited period of time the military risks of 'denuding the Home Front and lessening the support which we are able to provide for the British Expeditionary Force in France' outweighed the military advantages which were likely to accrue.[83] The following day they issued a wide-ranging memorandum on the 'Military Implications of Hostilities with Russia' in which they advised that 'on the land and in the air we could not strike directly at Russia' and that the risk of inciting war with Russia would be acceptable only 'if it led to a result which might cause the early defeat of Germany', such as 'the capture of the [Swedish] Galivare orefields'.[84]

Chamberlain himself confirmed the weak military case to the War Cabinet on 8 March. At the same time, the political considerations were compelling because, as the Prime Minister recognised, the Government 'should certainly be held up to obloquy if we sent a flat refusal. The French were plainly anxious to do something for Finland on political grounds'.[85] The Finns were perfectly aware of Norwegian and Swedish aversion to allowing the passage of an allied expeditionary force. None the less, as a final move on 10 March, they appealed directly to Chamberlain to make a public statement to the effect that his Government, together with the French, had decided jointly to give Finland 'all help, using all available resources at their disposal', if the Finnish Government asked them for support.[86] Chamberlain and his War Cabinet were willing to issue such a statement and, indeed, in the House of Commons on 11 March 1940, in reply to a question from the Labour Leader, Clement Attlee, the Prime Minister stated that both his Government and the French Government had already informed the Finns that they were prepared 'in response to an appeal from them for further aid, to proceed immediately and jointly to the help of Finland, using all available resources at their disposal'.[87] In the event, the Finns made no such appeal and concluded their peace negotiations with the Soviets on 12 March 1940 on 'rather lenient terms', which included the cession of the Karelian Isthmus to Russia but also the return of the Petsamo region, formerly occupied by Soviet forces during the war, to Finland.[88]

IV

The Finnish defeat naturally produced recrimination and criticism for the British Government. Daladier was convinced that they had at the last moment lost a golden opportunity because of British scrupulousness with regard to Swedish and Norwegian neutrality, with his own Government prepared to be less so to keep the Finns fighting. Indeed, on 11 March the French Minster at Helsinki, Baron Moisson de Vaux Saint Cyr, had been instructed as a 'matter of extreme urgency' to inform the Finnish Government and Mannerheim that the French Government had taken the decision to respond immediately to the Finnish appeal, irrespective of the position of the Norwegian and Swedish governments.[89] With no inkling of the dreadful fate which was soon to overwhelm his country, he argued that if there was going to be no serious fighting anywhere until the following year, by acquiescing in Finland's defeat they had given the Germans a valuable respite in which to utilise Russian resources to their advantage.[90] At the same time, Paul Reynaud, French Finance Minister, soon to succeed Daladier as Prime Minister, complained to Churchill that the loss of Finland 'would be equivalent to the loss of a great campaign'.[91] Yet French actions scarcely justified this criticism. On 12 March, in the Chamber of Deputies, Daladier maintained that his Government had delivered 175 aircraft to Finland, but four days later it was revealed in a secret meeting that this figure only equated with promised, not actual deliveries, since up to that moment only thirty Morane fighters and twelve Potez-63 bombers had left France for Finland.⁹² Chamberlain was particularly irked by what he regarded as Daladier's duplicity in passing 'the buck to the Nation Amie et Alliée [the friendly and allied nation]. This is what the French always do and it is an unpleasing trait.'⁹³ But the French leader was made to pay a heavy political price for his Finnish policy when compelled, on 19 March 1940, to resign as Prime Minister.

Chamberlain sought to counter parliamentary criticism by insisting on 13 March that the Finnish Government had made 'repeated requests for materials, and every one of these requests has been answered'.⁹⁴ He did not add that some had been answered negatively. Later, on 19 March, he refused any suggestion that Britain and France had 'in any way failed in their obligation to do their utmost to assist Finland in her need', and cited two reasons why it was not possible to provide all the weapons demanded by the Finnish Government, namely, the continuing build-up of British forces to counter the expected German attack in the West and the sheer logistical difficulties of transporting weapons to Finland, which was so dependent on Norwegian and Swedish cooperation that was not forthcoming.⁹⁵ The Prime Minister's critics, including those in the Conservative party, were not mollified. The former Secretary of State for War, Hore-Belisha, complained about the lack of air support, claiming that the uniform opinion of all those who had visited the Finnish Front was that powerful reinforcements in the air 'could have broken the Russian onslaught'. Somewhat recklessly, in view of the perilous position of British air defences, he insisted that it would have been 'worth one month's output of aeroplanes from our factories to have saved the situation'. The future Conservative Prime Minister, Harold Macmillan, who had visited Finland during February as part of a government fact-finding mission, was extremely critical of the delays in sending war material and the limits imposed on the number of weapons supplied to Finland:

> Is it generally known that although 148 aeroplanes were ultimately released...only 101 were sent? Is it realised that of these 101 only four left England in December; only 44 in January; and only 27 in February; and the others were made up in March?...Is it generally known that we were unable to send any anti-tank guns at all when the Field Marshal [Mannerheim] asked for 100?... We could only send 25 howitzers out of 150 asked for; only 30 field guns out of 166 asked for, and these were despatched one month after the request.

He also drew attention to the 'little known fact' that apart from two cases, where there was a gift of a number of aeroplanes, in all other cases payment was made in cash or under the Export Credits scheme and he doubted 'whether the general public recognises that with the exception of two cases the whole of this war material was sold to the Finns on an ordinary commercial basis'.[96]

While the parliamentary debate highlighted the limited and inadequate nature of arms provision for the Finns, the Government was concerned to halt supplies and to recover at least some of the arms which had been delivered before the Finnish surrender. Immediate orders were issued to prevent the dispatch of British aircraft to Finland and also of French aircraft in transit through the United Kingdom.[97] However, Halifax, impressed by Gripenberg's plea that the Soviet-Finnish treaty was merely an armed truce and that recovering arms supplied previously would be a terrible blow to Finland which might at any time have to resume its struggle with Soviet Russia, proposed that the Finns should be allowed to keep them. Churchill disagreed, arguing that the Finns, having lost their strategic advantages, would not be able to resume the struggle against Soviet Russia and that, accordingly, it was essential to recover all the war material, especially the aircraft and guns, which had been sent to Finland at 'so great a sacrifice to ourselves'. Chamberlain was inclined to agree, especially with regard to the Hurricanes and Blenheims, but he wished to keep in step with the French on the issue.[98] In the event, the French decided to allow the Finns to retain all war material already delivered or in transit, with the exception of twelve aircraft which were in Scotland at the time of the signing of the Soviet-Finnish treaty, and the British reluctantly concurred, while prohibiting the further provision of arms to Finland as a neutral power even on a commercial basis.[99]

The overriding reason for the inadequacy of British (and French) arms supplies to Finland, both before and during the Russo-Finnish War, lay with the determined resolve of the service departments not to seriously denude their own limited stocks of weapons, which from September 1939 onwards were required above all for the war with Germany. In the debate on 13 March 1940 Chamberlain had made it perfectly clear that the Government and their French allies, faced as they were with 'the possibility of heavy attacks being made upon them at any moment', could not ignore 'their responsibilities to their own people and to the winning of the war against our enemy, not even to save Finland'. Moreover, the Prime Minister revealed that what material was sent was done so only with the approval of the Chiefs of Staff on military grounds and he admitted that 'if we had considered fully all those things which were actually and properly present to the minds of the Chiefs of Staff, we should have sent very much less than we did'.[100] While constantly bearing in mind the political arguments for supporting Finland, above all the need to promote the democratic cause to neutral, and particularly American, opinion, the Cabinet consistently recognised the overwhelming military argument for prioritising arms deliveries in favour of home defence. Despite their belief that with a speedier and more generous dispatch of aircraft to Finland the collapse of the Finnish Army could have been delayed by at least a month, the Foreign Office concurred and accepted that in the context of the war foreign policy was constrained by the country's military capability. As the Deputy Permanent Under-Secretary at the Foreign Office, Sir Orme Sargent, noted:

> It must be remembered that the Foreign Office were looking at the problem from the purely political view, whereas the Air Ministry were ... examining it from the angle of our own production and supplies. The fact that this examination led them to discourage as far as they could the more lavish despatch of aircraft to Finland does not prove any ill-will or inefficiency on the part of the Air Ministry. What it demonstrates is that so long as our aircraft production fails to give us not merely equality with Germany but an available surplus ready for use wherever required, without home defences and the Western Front being depleted thereby, we cannot hope to carry through successfully any policy which in the last resort requires to be reinforced by military action.[101]

Or as Cadogan put it to the Dominions Secretary, Anthony Eden, 'diplomacy is rather hamstrung by being denied the necessary apparatus – military strength. Words don't do anything.'[102] Sargent's and Cadogan's words, however, were prescient. Britain itself would soon be engulfed in a life-and-death struggle.

But, even if the British and their French allies been able and prepared to fully equip Finland's armed forces it would have made no difference to the outcome of the Russo-Finnish War, just as intervention in Scandinavia as envisaged by the supreme War Council on 5 February 1940 was, in Patrick Salmon's words, 'fantasy'.[103] With the ending of the severe winter conditions the Soviets would never have retreated, as Stalin revealed one month after the end of the war. He told members of the Central Committee and his military advisers that had the war lasted longer, or had any neighbour interfered, it was planned to move sixty-two infantry divisions to prepared footholds and leave ten more in reserve, '72 in all, so as to discourage zealous neighbours. Things did not go that far'.[104] Meanwhile, the peace provided a breathing space for the Finns to contemplate retaliation and in June 1941, equipped to the hilt by the Third Reich, they were able to exact revenge on their Soviet enemy.

NOTES

This chapter is based on a paper which the author presented to a session of the Seventeenth Annual Conference of the British International History Group at Peterhouse, Cambridge in September 2005. He would like to thank the British Academy for supporting the research for this chapter.

1. See G. Stone, 'The British Government and the Sale of Arms to the Lesser European Powers, 1936–1939', *Diplomacy and Statecraft*, 14, 3 (2003), pp. 237–70. For German and French arms sales in the 1930s, see C. Leitz, 'Arms as Levers: *Matériel* and Raw Materials in Germany's Trade with Romania in the 1930s', *International History Review*, 19, 2 (1997), pp. 312–32, and 'Arms Exports from the Third Reich, 1933–1939: The Example of Krupp', *Economic History Review*, 51, 1 (1998), pp. 133–54; M. Thomas, 'To Arm an Ally: French Arms Sales to Romania, 1926–1940', *Journal of Strategic Studies*, 19, 2 (1996), pp. 231–59.
2. The National Archives [TNA], CAB 16/136, DPR (DR), 27th meeting, 8 October 1936.
3. Foreign Office memorandum by Sir Robert Vansittart, 29 September 1936, TNA, CAB 16/140, DPR 122.
4. Stone, 'British Government and the Sale of Arms', pp. 238–51.
5. P. Salmon, 'British Security Interests in Scandinavia and the Baltic, 1918–1939', in J. Hiden and A. Loit (eds), *The Baltic in International Relations between the Two World Wars* (Stockholm: Almqvist and Wiksell, 1988), p. 120. See also C. Gerrard, *The Foreign Office and Finland, 1938–1940: Diplomatic Sideshow* (London: Frank Cass, 2005), pp. 15–16.
6. 'Relative Strategical Importance of Countries Requiring Arms from the United Kingdom: Report of the Deputy Chiefs of Staff', 17 July 1939, TNA, CAB 16/219, AD 28 (DCOS, 110).
7. 'War Cabinet Allied Demands Committee: Annex to Note by the Secretary', 7 November 1939 – Report by the Deputy Chiefs of Staff, TNA, CAB 92/18, AD (39) 42.
8. C. Van Dyke, *The Soviet Invasion of Finland, 1939–1940* (London: Frank Cass, 1997), p. 1.
9. Thomas Snow, British Minister at Helsingfors, to Anthony Eden, Secretary of State for Foreign Affairs, 1 June 1937, enclosing the Legation's Annual Report for 1936, TNA, FO 371/21077/N3261. P. Salmon, *Scandinavia and the Great Powers, 1890–1940* (Cambridge: Cambridge University Press, 1997), p. 302.
10. Salmon, *Scandinavia and the Great Powers*, p. 302.
11. Ibid., p. 301.
12. Snow to Lord Halifax, Secretary of State for Foreign Affairs, 28 February 1939, enclosing the Legation's Annual Report for 1938, TNA, FO 371/23648/N1395.
13. Salmon, *Scandinavia and the Great Powers*, p. 302.
14. Snow to Halifax, 5 June 1939. Air Chief-Marshal Sir Cyril Newall to Sir Lancelot Oliphant, Assistant Under-Secretary at the Foreign Office, 7 July 1939, TNA, FO 371/23643/N3147 and N3256. For full details of the proposed Lundqvist mission, see Gerrard, *The Foreign Office and Finland*, pp. 53–55.
15. Oliphant to Newall, 11 July 1939, TNA, FO 371/23643/N3256.
16. J. Nevakivi, *The Appeal that was Never Made: The Allies, Scandinavia and the Finnish Winter War, 1939–1940* (London: Hurst, 1976), pp. 12–13. Van Dyke, *The Soviet Invasion of Finland*, p. 7. While in Finland General Kirke had extensive talks with Mannerheim and inspected Finnish fortifications on the Karelian Isthmus. Finnish-German military contacts increased from 1937 onwards, including Hitler's reception of the commander-in-chief of the Finnish Army, General Österman, during a visit to Germany in March 1938 and the visits to Finland of Halder and the head of German military intelligence (the *Abwehr*), Admiral Wilhelm Canaris, in 1939. See Salmon, *Scandinavia and the Great Powers*, p. 353.
17. P. Salmon, 'Great Britain, the Soviet Union and Finland at the beginning of the Second World War', in J. Hiden and T. Lane (eds), *The Baltic and the Outbreak of the Second World War* (Cambridge: Cambridge University Press, 1992), p. 101. For the secret protocol, see I. Vizulis, *The Molotov–Ribbentrop Pact of 1939* (New York: Praeger, 1990), pp. 16–17.

BRITAIN AND THE PROVISION OF ARMS TO FINLAND, 1936–1940   169

18. 'Soviet Aggression against Finland or Other Scandinavian Countries: Report by the Chiefs of Staff Committee', 31 October 1939, TNA, CAB 66/3, WP (39) 107.
19. 'Assistance to Scandinavian Countries in the event of Russian and/or German Aggression: Report by the Chiefs of Staff Committee', 21 November 1939, TNA, CAB 66/3, WP (39) 133.
20. Laurence Collier, Head of the Northern Department, to the Service Ministries, 25 September 1939, TNA, FO 371/23643/N4712. H. Creedy, War Office, to Sir Alexander Cadogan, Permanent Under-Secretary at the Foreign Office, 6 October 1939, TNA, FO 371/23644/N5027.
21. Lord Chatfield, Minister for Co-ordination of Defence, to Halifax, 1 November 1939, TNA, FO 371/23644/N5934. See also Salmon, 'Great Britain, the Soviet Union and Finland', pp. 110–11.
22. TNA, CAB 65/2, WM 70 (39), 4 November 1939.
23. Snow to Collier, 17 November 1939. Enclosure: 'Italian Policy in Supplying Fighters to Finland', 14 November 1939, TNA, FO 371/23644/N6511.
24. The information on German support for Finland was provided by the Finnish Minister in London, Georg Gripenberg. See TNA, CAB 65/2, WM 70 (39), 4 November 1939.
25. A.O. Chubaryan, H. Shukman et al., *Stalin and the Soviet-Finnish War, 1939–1940* (London: Frank Cass, 2002), pp. 263–64, 267. Stalin made these observations at a four-day meeting of members of the Central Committee of the Communist party and senior military personnel arranged by himself, between 14–17 April 1940, to analyse the Red Army's performance in the Winter War.
26. Ibid., p. xvi. Van Dyke, *The Soviet Invasion of Finland*, p. 27.
27. Halifax to Snow, 4 December 1939, TNA, FO 371/23644/N6967.
28. Sir Orme Sargent, Deputy Permanent Under-Secretary at the Foreign Office, to Halifax, 3 December 1939, TNA, FO 371/23644/N7040.
29. CAB 65/2, WM 101 (39), 2 December 1939. See also Salmon, 'Great Britain, the Soviet Union and Finland', p. 115.
30. TNA, CAB 65/2, WM 103 (39), 4 December 1939.
31. TNA, CAB 65/2, WM 104 (39), 5 December 1939. In the ensuing negotiations with the Gloster Aircraft Company the Government was compelled to intervene because the Finns wished to pay for the aircraft (£85,000) in instalments while the company wanted a lump-sum payment. The Treasury agreed to cover Glosters against loss provided the aircraft were dispatched immediately to Finland, TNA, CAB 65/2, WM 108 (39), 8 December 1939.
32. Gerrard, *The Foreign Office and Finland*, p. 85.
33. Snow to the Foreign Office, 11 December 1939, TNA, FO 371/23645/N7276. CAB 65/2,WM 112 (39), 12 December 1939.
34. State Secretary, Ernst Weizsäcker, to the Germany Embassy in the Soviet Union, 6 December 1939. *Documents on German Foreign Policy, 1918–1945*, series D, vol. VIII (Washington: United States Government Printing Office, 1954), no. 423, p. 494 [hereafter DGFP].
35. Weizsäcker to Blücher, 2 January 1940. Ibid., no. 500, p. 597.
36. Sir Edmund Monson, British Minister at Stockholm, to the Foreign Office, 11 December 1939, TNA, FO 371/23645/N7296.
37. Gerrard, *The Foreign Office and Finland*, p. 113.
38. TNA, CAB 65/2, WM 110 (39), 10 December 1939.
39. TNA, CAB 65/2, WM 116 (39), 15 December 1939.
40. Corbin to the French Foreign Ministry, 11 December 1939. *Documents Diplomatiques Français*, 1939, 3 Septembre–31 Décembre (Brussels: Presses Interuniversitaires Européenes (PIE) – Peter Lang, 2002), n. 1, p. 816 [hereafter DDF].
41. TNA, CAB 65/2, WM 116 (39), 15 December 1939.
42. M. Muggeridge (ed.), *Ciano's Diary, 1939–1943* (London: Heinemann, 1947), diary entry 3 December 1939, p. 182. According to Generals Georg Thomas, head of the War Economy Staff of the OKW (*Oberkommando der Wehrmacht*, Armed Forces High Command) and Hans Jeschonek, Chief of Staff of the Luftwaffe, four weeks prior to the outbreak of the

Russo-Finnish War only two shipments of arms, each consisting of twenty to thirty 20 mm anti-aircraft guns had gone to Finland from Germany. There had been no further shipments of war material to Finland from Germany. *DGFP*, series D, vol. VIII, n. 2, p. 512.
43. See Nevakivi, *The Appeal that was Never Made*, pp. 59–61.
44. 'Assistance for Finland: Memorandum by the Secretary of State for Foreign Affairs', 21 December 1939. TNA, CAB 66/4, WP (39) 170, TNA, CAB 65/4, WM 122 (39), Confidential Annex, 22 December 1939.
45. Monson to the Foreign Office, 15 December 1939, TNA, FO 371/23645/N7520. According to Monson, who had spoken with the Chief of the Finnish Air Force, on 14 December 1939, the Blenheims had been outstandingly successful and the Finnish air force equipped almost entirely with Bristol engines and largely with British aircraft and equipment, had put up a 'really remarkable performance against enormous odds'.
46. Halifax to Kingsley Wood, 22 December 1939, TNA, FO 371/23645/N7675.
47. TNA, CAB 65/4, WM 120 (39), 20 December 1939.
48. See Prime Minister Edouard Daladier to Corbin, 23 December 1939. *DDF*, 1939, no. 427, p. 870. Daladier informed the French Ambassador that the dispatch of thirty Morane fighters would be delayed by between four and six weeks. A few days later, on 28 December the British Ambassador at Paris, Sir Ronald Campbell, reported that while they had not been able to supply bombers to Finland the French authorities were pleased Britain had done so because they attached 'great importance to the Finns having machines with which they can endeavour to cut the railway link to Murmansk'. TNA, FO 371/23646/N7907.
49. 'Assistance to Finland and the Scandinavian Countries: Report by the Chiefs of Staff Committee', 26 December 1939. TNA, CAB 66/4, WP (39) 173, TNA, CAB 65/4, WM 123 (39), 27 December 1939.
50. In the first ten days they were in action, eighteen of the thirty Gladiators were shot down and the remainder were taken out of action over the Karelian Isthmus and relegated to the quieter sectors in the far north. See W.R. Trotter, *The Winter War: The Russo-Finnish War of 1939–1940* (London: Aurum, 2003), p. 190.
51. Appendix B: 'Air Staff Note on supply of immediate assistance to Finland', n.d., TNA, CAB 66/4, WP (39) 173.
52. 'Assistance to Finland and the Scandinavian Countries: Report by the Chiefs of Staff Committee', 26 December 1939, TNA, CAB 66/4, WP (39) 173.
53. '2nd Meeting of the Military Co-ordination Committee', 4 January 1940. TNA, FO 371/24796/N505. The Committee membership included the Service Ministers and their respective senior expert advisers chaired by the Minister for Co-ordination of Defence, Admiral Lord Chatfield.
54. Appendix A: 'List of naval, military and air equipment asked for by Finland and the extent to which supply is being met', n.d. TNA, CAB 66/4, WP (39) 173. 'Anglo-French Liaison: French War Material for Finland: Note by the Secretary', 8 January 1940, TNA, FO 371/24796/N680.
55. Minute by Halifax, 2 January 1940, TNA, FO 371/24796/N520.
56. Minute by Laurence Collier, 13 January 1940. 'General situation and impressions gained by Brigadier Ling after discussions with the [Finnish] Prime Minister, other Ministers and Field Marshal Mannerheim', circulated to the Military Co-ordination Committee of the War Cabinet,13 January 1940, TNA, FO 371/24796/N606 and CAB 65/5,WM 11 (40), 13 January 1940.
57. Memorandum by the Secretary of State for War, 14 January 1940, TNA, FO 371/24797/N685.
58. Halifax to Snow, 16 January 1940, TNA, FO 371/24797/N664. Certainly, the Finns continued to approach Italy for the provision of arms. Ciano noted in his diary a meeting with the Finnish Minister on 27 January 1940 in which the Minister requested additional arms, particularly heavy artillery. The Italian Foreign Minister further noted that even if the Finnish Minister had painted too dark a picture it was certain that 'to hope for an unlimited resistance is a vain illusion'. Muggeridge (ed.), *Ciano's Diary, 1939–1943*, p. 202.
59. TNA, CAB 65/5, WM 15 (40), 16 January 1940.
60. TNA, CAB 65/5, WM 19 (40), 20 January 1940.

61. TNA, CAB 65/5, WM 20 and 21 (40), 22 and 23 January 1940.
62. TNA, CAB 65/5, WM 22 (40), 24 January 1940.
63. TNA, CAB 65/11, WM 39(40), Confidential Annex, 12 February 1940.
64. Snow to the Foreign Office, 26 January 1940. TNA, FO 371/24798/N1098.
65. Snow to Halifax, 10 February 1940. TNA, FO 371/24800/N1866.
66. 'Allied Military Committee: Note regarding intervention in Scandinavia', 22 January 1940. TNA, FO 371/24814/N994. See also 'Allied Assistance to Finland: Report by the Chiefs of Staff Committee', 28 January 1940. TNA, CAB 66/5, WP (40) 36.
67. '40th meeting of the Allied Military Committee', 13 February 1940, TNA, FO 371/24800/N1893. See also meeting of the War Cabinet the same day, TNA, CAB 65/5, WM 40 (40), 13 February 1940.
68. Nevakivi, *The Appeal that was Never Made*, pp. 97–99. Gerrard, *The Foreign Office and Finland*, pp. 135–37. P. Salmon, 'British Strategy and Norway, 1939–1940', in P. Salmon (ed.), *Britain and Norway in the Second World War* (London: HMSO, 1995), p. 9. R.A.C. Parker, 'Britain, France and Scandinavia, 1939–1940', *History*, 61 (1976), pp. 377–78.
69. Chamberlain to Daladier, 15 February 1940, TNA, FO 371/24801/N1990. TNA, CAB 65/5, WM 41 (40), 14 February 1940.
70. Neville Chamberlain to Ida Chamberlain, 17 February 1940. Neville Chamberlain Papers, NC 18/1/1143, University of Birmingham Library.
71. TNA, CAB 65/5, WM 42 (40), 15 February 1940.
72. TNA, CAB 65/5, WM 46 (40), 19 February 1940.
73. Halifax to Kingsley Wood, Secretary of State for Air, 28 February 1940, TNA, FO 371/24802/N2429.
74. TNA, CAB 65/5, WM 46 (40), 19 February 1940.
75. Daladier to Corbin, 27 February 1940. *DDF*, 1940, 1 Janvier–10 Juillet (Brussels: PIE–Peter Lang, 2004), no. 100, p. 215.
76. Halifax to Gordon Vereker, British Minister at Helsinki (formerly Counsellor at the Moscow Embassy until February 1940), 1 March 1940, TNA, FO 371/24803/N2618. See also 'Note de la Direction Politique: Conditions d'une résistance finlandaise', 1 March 1940. *DDF*, 1940, no. 111, pp. 231–32.
77. CAB 65/12, WM 60 (40), Confidential Annex, 5 March 1940.
78. Parker, 'Britain, France and Scandinavia', pp. 380–81.
79. Minute by Orme Sargent, 6 March 1940, TNA, FO 371/24804/N2895.
80. D. Dilks (ed.), *The Diaries of Sir Alexander Cadogan, 1938–1945* (London: Cassell, 1971), diary entry, 1 March 1940, p. 257.
81. Chamberlain to Ida Chamberlain, 2 March 1940. Neville Chamberlain Papers, NC 18/1/1145.
82. Foreign Office to Vereker, Helsingfors, 8 March 1940. TNA, FO 371/24804/N2994.
83. 'Assistance to Finland: report by the Chiefs of Staff Committee', 7 March 1940. TNA, CAB 66/6, WP (40) 86.
84. 'Military Implications of Hostilities with Russia in 1940: Report by the Chiefs of Staff Committee', 8 March 1940, TNA, CAB 66/6, WP (40) 91. See also Gerrard, *The Foreign Office and Finland*, p. 153.
85. TNA, CAB 65/12, WM 63 (40), Confidential Annex, 8 March 1940.
86. Enclosure: 'Copy of a communication handed to the Prime Minister by the Finnish Minister on 10 March 1940'. Halifax to Vereker, 10 March 1940, TNA, FO 371/24805/N3047. See also TNA, CAB 66/6, WP (40) 93.
87. TNA, CAB 65/12, WM 65 (40), Confidential Annex, 11 March 1940. See also Halifax to Vereker, 13 March 1940, TNA, FO 371/24805/N3132. *Parliamentary Debates*, (Commons), 5th series, vol. 358, col. 836.
88. J. Nevakivi, 'Finnish Perceptions of Britain's Role during the War, 1939–1941', in J. Aunesluoma (ed.), *From War to Cold War: Anglo-Finnish Relations in the Twentieth Century* (Helsinki: SKS/Finnish Literature Society, 2005), p. 34.
89. Daladier to Baron Moisson de Vaux Saint Cyr, French Minister at Helsinki, 11 March 1940. *DDF*, 1940, no. 133, p. 278. See also Daladier to Corbin, 9 and 12 March 1940. *DDF*, 1940, nos 131, 135, pp. 274–75, 281.

90. Campbell to the Foreign Office, 11 March 1940, TNA, FO 371/24805/N3061.
91. TNA, CAB 65/12, WM 66 (40), Confidential Annex, 12 March 1940.
92. Nevakivi, *The Appeal that was Never Made*, p. 140.
93. Chamberlain to Ida Chamberlain, 2 March 1940. Neville Chamberlain Papers, NC 18/1/1145.
94. *Parliamentary Debates* (Commons) 5th series, vol. 358, col. 1163. See also Chamberlain to Hilda Chamberlain, 10 March 1940. Neville Chamberlain Papers, NC 18/1/1146.
95. *Parliamentary Debates*, (Commons) 5th series, vol. 358, cols. 1834–35.
96. Ibid., cols. 1891–93.
97. TNA, CAB 65/6, WM 67 (40), 13 March 1940.
98. TNA, CAB 65/6, WM 69 (40), 15 March 1940. See also Nevakivi, *The Appeal that was Never Made*, p. 148.
99. TNA, CAB 65/6, WM 93 (40), 15 April 1940. 'Arms for Finland: Memorandum by the Secretary of State for Foreign Affairs', 9 April 1940, TNA, CAB 66/7, WP (40) 125.
100. *Parliamentary Debates*, (Commons) 5th series, vol. 358, col. 1163 and cols. 1944–45.
101. Minute by Orme Sargent, 21 March 1940, TNA, FO 371/24806/N3529.
102. Dilks (ed.), *Cadogan Diaries*, entry 16 March 1940, p. 263.
103. Salmon, *Scandinavia and the Great Powers*, p. 360.
104. Chubaryan, Shukman *et al.*, *Stalin and the Soviet-Finnish War*, p. 266.

9

Britain and an International Force: The Experience of the League of Nations and the United Nations Military Staff Committee

EDWARD JOHNSON

Introduction: types of force

In August 1948, the members of the United Nations Military Staff Committee indicated to the UN Security Council that they had reached an impasse in their attempts to create, under article 43 of the UN Charter, the basis of an international force for use by the new world organisation to maintain and enforce peace in the post-war world.[1] The Committee, a group of senior military representatives from the five permanent members of the UN, had been unable, over a period of more than two years, to agree on a set of key principles governing the size, organisation, structure and deployment of any forces contributed by member states to the UN, and consequently this element of the UN Charter was never realised. Article 43 of the Charter requires all members 'to undertake to make available to the Security Council on its call and in accordance with a special agreement or agreements, armed forces and facilities' necessary for the maintenance of international peace and security. It was over these 'special agreements' that the Military Staff Committee effectively collapsed in 1948.

In devising the UN Charter some of the founders, within the USA and Britain particularly, were conscious that a persistent criticism of the League of Nations from certain quarters, was that it always lacked its own force with which to sustain and enforce its decisions. As early as July 1942, the American Secretary of State, Cordell Hull, was convinced that any new post-war international body had to be able to maintain peace through the use of force, to redress the weaknesses of the League.[2]

As a key commentary on the creation of the Charter has noted, there were three broad alternatives available to the architects of the UN to provide military forces for the Security Council.[3] The first model and the most idealistic, and seemingly unrealistic, was that of a standing permanent force, one which had superiority over national forces. The second was an arrangement of ad hoc contributions from major powers. This was the essence of the system created under the League Covenant, in which there had been no provision to have a permanent force, rather, article 16 merely gave the League Council the duty 'to recommended' to member states what forces they would make available to 'protect the covenants of the League'. The provision was *recommendatory* and not obligatory as the founders of the League in 1919 were not convinced, as we shall see, of the possibilities and practicalities of a permanent force at the League's disposal. A third alternative was a system of national contingents, agreed by member states in advance, and provided for the service of the UN Security Council. It was this final model representing a mid-point, a balance, between the rather weak, recommendatory, measures of the League and the seemingly politically impractical idea of having a free-standing, permanently established, international force, which found its way into the Charter at San Francisco in 1945. Yet this was itself to founder over the sharp political differences among the major powers about the use and operation of such a force.

The British approach to the idea of a force was mixed. In the inter-war period, there was consistent government skepticism about the provision for a League force. British policy was cautious about the powers such a force might give to the League or assume on the League's behalf and the ideas were additionally suspect as they were part of French diplomatic efforts to ensure their security against Germany. Nonetheless, official British unease existed against repeated demands within Britain for consideration of a permanent international force. In the UN Military Staff Committee discussions beginning in 1946, the British position was somewhat divided. The Chiefs of Staff sustained the skepticism of the inter-war period towards the UN's own force, even the reduced one of article 43, while the Foreign Office showed some interest in the deliberations for at least two reasons: in general terms it did not wish dissension in the Military Staff Committee to signal a breakdown in allied unity while at the same time it hoped to retain American enthusiasm for the UN by demonstrating interest in the force discussions. The Foreign Office was apprehensive that British reluctance towards the UN force might undermine Anglo-US relations. Thus the international force idea was, in both the inter-war period and the UN Military Staff discussions, made part of the diplomacy of the times and in Britain at least met with a fairly mixed reaction.

While the authors of the League Covenant and the UN Charter may have seen the establishment of a permanent force as impractical, and settled instead on contributions of national contingents, there is a long history surrounding the permanent force idea and it can be found as a central part of many early European peace plans. For example, the *Grand Design* of the Duc de Sully, published in 1638, proposed peace in Europe to be maintained by a General Council of sovereigns supported by a multinational army of 300,000 troops and a naval force of 120 ships.[4] The works on peace of Hugo Grotius, William Penn, John Bellars, the Abbé de Saint-Pierre and Rousseau also fit within this tradition of providing for a common army or force to maintain the peace. Many of these seem wildly utopian, couched as idealistic and intellectual reactions to the ravages of periodic war in Europe, and taking little to no account of the political hurdles to be mounted, but in that they find echoes in some of the ideas of the twentieth century. The Abbé de Saint-Pierre's scheme for a collective security of all Europe supported by force of arms led Frederick the Great to note sardonically that it was, 'most practicable: for its success, all that is lacking is the consent of Europe and a few similar trifles'.[5] When, at the end of the Napoleonic wars, the European states had the opportunity to construct a European order, they chose to do so on the basis of enforcement by great power action against threats to the peace under the Congress System: but there was no talk of formalised and organised international armies. While great powers did use their combined military forces in limited interventions to protect their interests and to maintain order in sensitive areas such as in Crete (1897) and in the Boxer rebellion (1900), these were not part of any plan for European or universal peace.

Such peace plans did however proliferate in the nineteenth century, ones which, as Beales notes, increasingly rested on a number of fundamentals. Chief among these were the compulsory arbitration of disputes, the establishment of an international authority, the codification of international law and the move towards disarmament.[6] If states were to resolve their differences through arbitration, then a standing authority would make greater sense, providing an element of permanence and the means of applying international law and dealing with transgressors. On this question there developed a broad division between the pacifists and the internationalists over whether the use of force was necessary by any standing authority. For the former, disarmament would be a result of peace, its natural corollary: with peace what need would there be for arms? However, the internationalists saw disarmament as a precursor of wider peace – that the limitation of arms and eventually their abolition would be steps on the road to peace. In the circumstances, any international authority would still require a set of sanctions and arms, even an international force, to deal with recalcitrants. This was the idea of collective security, one which is a rational appeal, not to a potential belligerent state's better feelings and to its acceptance of a decent method of resolving conflicts than the resort to war, but rather a warning of the violent and dire consequences that will befall any aggressor who seeks war. Collective security's stock-in-trade is, as Inis Claude has pointed out, diplomatic, economic and eventually – all else having failed – military sanctions, as a means of inducing those states who would wage war, to desist.[7] Thus in many of the internationalists' peace plans of the nineteenth century the idea of an international force occupied a prominent place.[8]

From The Hague to the League of Nations

The peace proponents in Europe and further afield witnessed a significant acknowledgement of some of their fundamental goals with the creation of the Court of Arbitration at The Hague Conference of 1899: a putative international authority and an arbitration mechanism in one. This stimulated interest in the idea of an international force. But it was one to which British governments paid merely formal acknowledgement. In the United States in 1910, both Houses of Congress passed a resolution to create a commission to investigate the possibilities of arms limitation and the parallel construction of an international navy to maintain world peace, although the initiative came to naught. The British Foreign Secretary, Sir Edward Grey, was not unsympathetic to the idea, indicating a willingness to exchange views with the Americans,[9] yet that was as far as the issue went in British official circles before the First World War. Within America, the former President, Theodore Roosevelt, the proponent of 'big stick diplomacy' and one generally more interested in the machinery of war than peace, spoke approvingly of the need for a firm structure of collective security to develop the work of The Hague Conference system in his Nobel Peace Prize acceptance speech of 1910. His suggestions were echoed by senior figures within the American navy and by other American public figures including Andrew Carnegie,[10] and were taken up in parts of Europe.[11] However, the decade before 1914 was to be one of arms races and repeated international crises, and ideas of peace and the international force were somewhat muted against the dissonance of war. Yet, the commencement of hostilities in August 1914 and the attendant casualty rates of the western front led to a resurgence of peace plans, many of which included the prospect of an international force.[12] Consequently, when the armistice came in 1918, there was some momentum for its adoption within the post-war settlement and the League of Nations.

However, the Covenant of the League of Nations, drawn up at Versailles in 1919, was merely a partial step in the creation of a system of collective security, one which had significant weaknesses that were ultimately exposed and exploited in the inter-war years. The League itself represented the establishment of an international authority and its Covenant sought to lay down the foundations of a collective security system. Article 10 prohibited aggression and enjoined all member states to respect and preserve 'the territorial integrity and existing political independence of all Members of the League'. Any war or threat of war was, through article 11, a matter of concern to all members of the League and, via article 16, an act against them all. The sanctions – those required in the peace plans of the internationalists – were found in article 16 and prohibited diplomatic, commercial and economic relations with the transgressor. It also recommended that League members indicate 'what effective, military, naval or air force' they would contribute 'to the armed forces to be used to protect' the Covenant. The article did not specify the creation of a League military force, merely that some force or forces should be available for the League. Thus in drafting the Covenant, the aspirations of the pre-war peace planners for an international force foundered on the realisms of the post-war world which they inhabited.

French ideas and British opposition

It was the French Government which was the most vocal and organised in support of a League force during the drafting of the Covenant. Leon Bourgeois, a former Foreign Minister and Prime Minister with an established reputation in the field of peace plans, was appointed to the drafting Commission in February 1919. Bourgeois believed 'that the League should operate like the justice system in any modern democratic state with the power to intervene where there were breaches of the peace and forcibly restore order'.[13] He reflected broader French views which were skeptical of an international authority without teeth and proposed accordingly an international army for the League commanded by an international general staff.[14] The French proposals were not mere idealism: they had a security design to them, being part of French diplomatic and military efforts to contain Germany. The French Government wished to ensure that any German threat to its security could be met by the League and, with that in mind, the creation of an international force to maintain and widen the responsibility for French security made sense. The French proposals generated much heat and debate and Bourgeois and his colleagues ran into unyielding opposition from the British and the Americans.

From the British position, 'there was no question of an international army, navy or air force, but the French, not unnaturally in view of historical and geographical facts ... wanted a body charged with the duty of working out in advance, schemes of cooperation, and proposing definite contingents to be supplied by different Powers'.[15] But the impracticability, even absurdity, was clear to the British mind, if less so to the French one: that plans and strategy require an enemy and 'either you must select a prospective enemy and exclude him from your discussions, which is contrary to the whole spirit of a universal League of Nations, or else all nations will plan against one another': this was hardly a recipe for international harmony.[16] The Legal Adviser to the American delegation on the Commission noted: 'the French proposals for some international force, some staff, or at least some international supervision of national forces were pressed to the end, but they were doomed in advance to be rejected. Neither the British nor ourselves would listen to them and M. Bourgeois pleaded in vain.'[17] The American President, Woodrow Wilson, was convinced that Congress would never ratify any treaty which would put American forces at the disposal of international command and, given the Senate's later rejection of the whole League, he was surely correct.[18] The British for their part were, on the whole, more inclined to trust in security which depended on those traditional mechanisms of power, national forces and particularly the Royal Navy, rather than the League as a substitute. Sir Henry Wilson, the Chief of the Imperial General Staff, thought the very idea of an international force was 'rubbish' and 'futile nonsense'.[19] Thus the French plan was vanquished. Bourgeois was given article 9 of the Covenant, the provision for an advisory, not an executive, military commission, as a concession to his sensitivities, but the international force idea collapsed. André Tardieu, who served on the French delegation congratulated his government for the 'logical and clear solution' of an international force, without which the influence of the League of Nations would be 'necessarily restricted' and condemned the British and Americans as supposed champions of the League idea of collective security for rejecting it.[20] Thus the League was deprived of its own force, and even the possibility of utilising national contingents to enforce its decisions was left as a vague aspiration, not an obligation.

An international force in the diplomacy of the League

The idea of an international force was however resilient, especially with the French, and figured in diplomatic initiatives to shore up the security provisions of the League Covenant after 1919, those which had not been addressed fully at Versailles and which had been compromised with the American defection from the League in 1920 and the consequent gap in enforcement measures. French reservations about their future security were heightened, given the failure to force their vision of the League into the final version of the Covenant, and explained much of French policy towards the League, and towards Germany, in the years after 1919: if the Americans were absent from the League it followed for the French that the League had to double its efforts to provide security. One course led through disarmament. However, the League was to be crippled by the unwillingness of states to agree levels of disarmament without some corresponding measure of security guaranteed by it. The link between security and disarmament had to be forged if states were to gain confidence in the League's ability to deliver peace, and with this in mind, the League Assembly formulated the Draft Treaty of Mutual Assistance in 1923. This aimed to give military support to victims of aggression. It empowered the League Council to identify the aggressor and to specify what economic sanctions and what levels of military force each signatory should provide to deal with future aggression, and to organise military forces, including the appointment of the Commander-in-Chief of combined military operations, to deal with the aggressor. This was clearly a step in 'beefing up' the Covenant and another attempt at the internationalisation of armed forces to ensure collective security. Yet it fell foul of major states refusing to accord the League what would have been significant initiatives in the direction of policy, and the British for one were key to its collapse. They, while in part authors and proponents of the need to link security and disarmament, could not support the many powers that the Draft Treaty vested in the League Council.[21]

Yet the French were inclined to stay the course and with the support of MacDonald's first Labour Government – always likely to be keen on disarmament – created the Geneva Protocol to link arbitration, security and disarmament. Through this, all disputes would be referred to arbitration, removing the opportunity for states to go to war after a time limit, as the Covenant allowed; recalcitrant states would be labelled aggressors against whom sanctions would be imposed and the signatories agreed to move towards disarmament through a later conference – in the event not called until 1932. The issue of international or League forces lay in the section on security and while states were to retain control of their own military forces, the Council was, 'entitled to receive undertakings from States *determining in advance* the military, naval and air forces which they would be able to bring into action immediately to ensure the fulfilment of the obligations in regard to sanctions' under the Covenant and the Protocol.[22] This was in effect a precursor of article 43 of the UN Charter, but was too ambitious for the British in the 1920s. The government, now Conservative after MacDonald's defeat in the October

1924 election, saw the Protocol as going too far in many areas: for example it placed an obligation on the Dominions to intervene in areas in Europe where they had no interest and sought to convert the League from a body where differences were settled by moral force to one of compulsory arbitration supported by coercion.[23] As for the issue of League forces, the sub-committee of the Committee of Imperial Defence was concerned that the offer of information by states, in advance of the military forces they would make available to the League, would force it to create an Intelligence Department which might be the initial step in the direction of a General Staff.[24] This was, once more, a step too far for the British Cabinet which rejected the Protocol,[25] and with it official opposition to a League force remained.

Yet the French, ever persistent, sought to revive elements of the failed Geneva Protocol in another guise through the Geneva Disarmament Conference in February 1932. It provided a new opportunity for the French Government to lead with a comprehensive scheme for disarmament, the main elements of which were: the internationalisation of civil aircraft, the prohibition of all bombing from the air and all bomber aircraft, and an international force as a means of enforcing what the French hoped would be increased security measures by the League.[26] A contemporary British commentator considered the French proposal suspect: that the French were not interested in disarmament at all but were seeking their consistent goal of widening responsibility for the containment of Germany.[27] Recent evidence from the French archives has supported this interpretation that the plan and the idea of mutual assistance through the League was 'unreal'. One of the authors of the French proposals saw it as a diplomatic device, a tactic, made in a forum bent 'on captivating universal public opinion with simple ideas'.[28]

Yet, however simple, the ideas met with determined opposition within the British Government. Maurice Hankey, the Cabinet Secretary, clearly took the French at their word and wrote a specific and trenchant criticism of the proposals for an international force, which he saw as a consistent element in French ideas for the League stretching back to 1919.[29] Hankey raised many of the technical uncertainties surrounding the idea of an international force as well as questioning the political determination within the League Council to use it. The French plan envisaged a force in two parts: a standing force acting as a deterrent to prevent war and another, a 'first contingent of punitive forces to repress war and bring immediate assistance to any State victim of aggression'. As part of the first force, heavy weapons, artillery, bombers and large ships over 10,000 tons would be placed at the disposal of the League. Hankey wondered on which territory it would be based. Which state would want such military materiel on its territory? How would the League resupply and re-order machines? If the deterrent effect of the international force failed, the League would use its punitive force to fight its way to the assistance of a victim. This had possible repercussions for the British who, through the Royal Navy, might be required to supply naval power at the point of any aggression and there was the grave risk that Britain 'may come to be regarded as an international bully; sometimes a mere threat sometimes called to take action, continually thwarting the national aspirations of other states'. There were further problems of command, of a flexible and large General Staff, ready with plans to call the international punitive force to arms at very short notice. And, in addition to major administrative problems, Hankey noted the political difficulty that would encompass the League in deciding who was the aggressor. Could the League Council act quickly and decisively enough with unanimity over definitions of aggression and would sufficient political will be available to apply the force?[30]

In the event the French withdrew their plan in the face of opposition not only from the British but also from the Russians.[31] Litvinov, the Soviet Foreign Minister, felt the proposals would not necessarily deter an aggressor and, in a portent of later Soviet objections during the UN Military Staff Committee discussions in 1946, was concerned that a major power might seek to subvert a League force for its own interests.[32] Determined to establish some greater security for itself, the French government tabled a further memorandum on 14 November 1932. This, the Paul-Boncour/Herriot plan, now dispensed with the standing and punitive international forces as armies, and instead placed the emphasis on air power. Within the wider scheme, the French plan included: the internationalisation of civil aircraft; the prohibition of all bombing from the air and all bomber aircraft, and a proposal for the establishment of specialised air units placed at the disposal of the League. It also suggested 'the establishment of *an organically international air force* to be set up and maintained permanently by the League of Nations', with the aircraft being provided by the different national air forces who, under the plan, would have abolished their own forces.[33]

The British response to the broad French plan was once again negative, and on the specifics of the international air force, the Air Staff were highly skeptical. In a long detailed memorandum[34] they repeated some of the arguments made by Hankey in what might be seen as a classic objection to international forces generally and those of the French plan in particular. There were problems over the recruitment and organisation of the personnel in such a force, with different languages and divergent interests and it was difficult to envisage that 'a body of men would owe a sort of super-national allegiance to the League, sufficient to overcome their ordinary, national susceptibilities'. Disorganisation could therefore be expected at critical times. The issue of command of the force was problematical as it assumed the League itself would issue orders while in reality the force commanders would still be nationals of members states and the Air Staff were 'unable to imagine how a force would operate in war, if important questions regarding its direction could only be decided by a unanimous, or possibly majority, decision from a body composed of innumerable representatives of different countries'. There were also fundamental difficulties over location: would the force be in Europe and if so would non-European states then be disposed to pay for it? And if Europe were its base, which state other than neutral Switzerland, a state 'quite unsuitable for the location of a large air force' would accommodate it? Which state would welcome a permanent, large air force composed of other nationals? Moreover, which states would pay for it and would they feel the outlay delivered the requisite security? Finally, echoing Hankey, the Air Staff had doubts about the supply of aircraft as the force could be a very heterogeneous body, making re-supply complicated in times of peace 'and still more complicated in war'. The British had further concerns that they were being asked to accept the abolition of bombers linked with the internationalisation of civil aviation, which the British saw, along with the international air force, as impractical: they needed bombers to police parts of the Empire.[35]

The Geneva Conference ultimately failed and the reasons were numerous: Hitler's withdrawal from the Conference, British skepticism, Franco-German rivalry using the Conference to define their status in international politics, as well as the general difficulties of trying to tie over fifty states into a comprehensive agreement.[36] The effect was however to remove for all practical purposes the promotion of a standing international force as part of international diplomacy in the inter-war years. Yet as the Geneva Conference was in its death throes, the League was, ironically, able to demonstrate its ability to launch a small, temporary, international force of its own in the Saar plebiscite as an indication of what might be feasible in certain conditions. Yet before the Saar, the League's experience with international forces had been less than propitious.

International forces: the experience of the League

The experience of the League's early years saw it, as Northedge has indicated, 'all dressed up and nowhere to go', largely because the major powers were not inclined to allow it to interfere in their key foreign policy interests. Consequently it had to concentrate on the 'small change of diplomacy'.[37] Its record up to the Manchurian crisis was one of dealing

BRITAIN AND AN INTERNATIONAL FORCE 183

with these peripheral issues. These included the protection of refugees and the management of small, yet potentially troublesome, disputes such as those of the Aaland islands, the Polish–Lithuanian quarrel over Vilna, and the disposition of the Saar territory; the last two disputes were responsible for providing the League with its only experience of creating international forces. Yet outside the authority of the League, a number of small international forces, with limited mandates, were deployed with mixed success in the early 1920s. These were created under the Treaties of Versailles and St Germain to oversee and monitor the conduct of plebiscites in Schleswig (1920), Allenstein and Marienwerder (1920), Klagenfurt (1920) and Upper Silesia (1921). The launching of these operations, some of which contained British forces, would have given the proponents of the international force concept cause for hope. In the Schleswig operation, the Royal Navy contributed the command of the force, and four ships together with a British army battalion were also deployed. British forces saw further service in Allenstein in the form of 800 men of the Royal Irish regiment, and contributed four battalions to the Upper Silesia force in 1921.[38] Clearly the British Government was quite prepared play a role in providing military personnel and equipment for these forces. In doing so Britain and the other contributory states were acting as responsible signatories of the supporting treaties.

Yet these were not League forces: it did not vote for them, organise, deploy or pay for them. When the League was given an opportunity to deploy a force of its own to monitor the plebiscite in Vilna in 1921, the lessons were mixed. The force of 1,800 troops was established and consisted of a combination of British, Belgian, Spanish, French, Danish, Dutch, Norwegian and Swedish contingents under a French Commander, Colonel Chardigny. But the operation was aborted when the plebiscite was cancelled before the force could be deployed and it encountered some of the difficulties which, a generation later, were to be replicated in the experience of UN peacekeeping forces. Thus while the planning and organisation of the force, its logistic support, accommodation and medical services, had been established, it ran into great power opposition from the Russians who maintained that any League troops sent to Vilna would threaten Russian security and constitute an unfriendly act.[39] These threats, even if rather hollow in reality, unnerved many contributing states and after the Swiss government, defending its neutrality, refused transit rights for the force across its territory, the League dropped the plebiscite plan. In spite of some of the welcoming indicators of international cooperation exemplified through the Vilna force experience, and while the British contribution was not insignificant to these operations, within and outside the League, the British Government retained its previously firm position of giving no encouragement to the idea of the League having a more permanent force.[40]

However, the League's other experience of organising an international presence met with more success when, in 1935, it was able to deploy a small force in the Saar to supervise the plebiscite which determined the future of the territory, it having been governed by a League Commission from 1920. The need for the force arose because of the fears that with the plebiscite pending, unrest might be fomented by Nazi propaganda keen to ensure the vote went Germany's way.[41] The British Foreign Office also had concerns for the safety of the League Commission, whose head, Geoffrey Knox, was a British subject, and feared French unilateral intervention: in the circumstances a significant threat to the peace, given that France had an interest in the plebiscite's result.[42] An international force thus appeared more attractive. Towards the end of 1934, MacDonald's government was pressed by the French to contribute a British contingent to serve alongside them in the Saar during the voting.[43] This raised objections in the War Office as did the alternative that the British and the Italians furnish a bilateral force to ensure order.[44] In discussing the approach the Cabinet came to the conclusion that if the League Council were to vote for an international force to be sent to the Saar, it would be difficult not to contribute a British contingent.[45] Supporting unilateral French action was not an option, nor was inaction, and the Cabinet duly agreed to take the initiative and suggest the deployment of an international force,[46] providing it were truly multinational, even specifying the states with whom the British would be willing to serve, rigorously excluding French and German troops, and seeing Soviet participation as unwelcome.[47] In the event, the League Council was able to vote for the force in December 1934 under the British conditions and it was recruited and successfully deployed at the end of December 1934. The force numbered 3,300, with Britain and Italy contributing 1,500 and 1,300 troops respectively, and with smaller contributions from the Netherlands (250) and Sweden (250). The Saar force was a success in that the hurdles of recruitment, organisation, transport, operations, and finance – it was paid for by the Saar Commission, France and Germany – were successfully navigated without conflict and the plebiscite was conducted in peace in January 1935.[48] The force was then able to withdraw, the last troops leaving in February 1935.

The definitive history of the League of Nations claims that the British role over the Saar force was 'perhaps the most popular action' of Sir John Simon's tenure at the Foreign Office.[49] However, his officials were clear that the Saar force provided no lessons for the creation of a permanent international force. In a long memorandum on the experience of mounting the Saar force, they noted that the difficulties which had been regularly identified opposing proposals for a permanent international force were not without foundation:

> National jealousies inevitably complicate the questions of command and of composition; the question of finance is necessarily hard to resolve; the time factor is all-important. These are difficulties of a general or political order, and the difficulties of a technical or military order cannot be left out of account. The obstacles of every kind were successfully surmounted in this case on account of exceptionally favourable conditions: in more adverse circumstances, or in an operation of greater magnitude (when for example, aggression had taken place and the force was required to fight), the obstacles would, indeed, be formidable. The questions of command and composition might then become more acute, as well as the organization of lines of communication, bases and so forth; the time factor might be even more pressing. In short, the machinery which, with some groaning and creaking, was sufficient to launch the Saar force would be totally inadequate for a major operation. [50]

The Saar force had other advantages which might be denied a permanent force: points that were made in a lively, unofficial memorandum by a serving British officer.[51] The force had benefited greatly from: the commander being British; the professional standard of the contingents and the liaison between them; the use of good linguists; the adoption of conciliatory methods and the fact that the period of deployment was very short, thus minimising the possibilities of friction being created within the force and between it and the local population. Finally the force could not have operated as well as it did without the presence of the British 'tommy', who appears to have generated good will and was an admirable ambassador for the British and for the League.

'Designed to captivate and charm': the debate in Britain

The skepticism of the Foreign Office over the Saar was not however fully echoed outside Whitehall, as in 1930s Britain there was a continuing debate about the possibilities of the League having its own international force. It was perhaps understandably a debate couched in what appears excessive idealism when the realities of international politics were all too graphically evident, something of an echo of the eighteenth- and nineteenth-century peace plans. There were specific external factors which stimulated the debate: the Manchurian crisis as a major challenge to the League's authority, and the League's response to it; the Geneva Disarmament Conference of 1932, providing a focal point for the articulation of ideas on peace, disarmament and security; the rise of Hitler and the German withdrawal from the League, all these contributed to a sense of creeping insecurity.

The endorsement of the idea of an international force as a remedy came from a range of bodies and individuals, the most noteworthy, energetic and enthusiastic being David Davies. As Liberal MP for Montgomeryshire from 1906 to 1929 and then as Lord Davies of Llandinam from 1932 he was a key driving force in the debate in Britain. He founded the League of Nations Union in 1918 and campaigned ceaselessly on the League's behalf after 1919 along with other peace notables such as Professor Gilbert Murray, Lord Robert Cecil, Dorothy Layton, and George Barnes, the former leader of the Labour Party. In 1930 he produced, *The Problem of the Twentieth Century*, a massive volume, almost 800 pages long, devoted almost exclusively to the origins and development of the international force idea, which took as its main theme the fact that the League's failure to achieve any measure of disarmament and create security was caused almost exclusively by its lacking any enforcing body. For Davies, the time was ripe for such a force, one with a monopoly of modern weapons: a centralised, specialist international force and what he interestingly termed, an international police force.

The debate in Britain, much of it led by Davies, was clearly stimulated by the Geneva Conference. In 1932, he formed the *New Commonwealth*, a society 'for the promotion of international law and order through the creation of a Tribunal in Equity and an International Police Force', which proceeded to produce a range of papers and memoranda on the technical, but not the political, problems behind the establishment of an international force. As articulated by Davies and his contemporaries, the emphasis was by 1932 upon an international police force with, reflecting the French views, particular interest given over to the use of air power as its defining element. The cause of an international air force was, by the early 1930s, lent support by Basil Liddell Hart, who contemporaries had termed 'the new Clausewitz'.[52] In a lecture to the Royal Institute of International Affairs in November 1932, Liddell Hart identified the technical problems of what might be termed an article 16 force – one of mixed national contingents supplied to the League – as considerable, but deemed many of these could be overcome by the creation of a supra-national force, one 'in the permanent service of the League as a supra-national institution'.[53] Problems of command, training, supply and morale could all be surmounted in the service of an international body. And, as modern war conditions placed a premium on defence, any international force would require a range of weaponry to overcome a committed aggressor. Liddell Hart envisaged heavy artillery but also international air power as being the most effective weapon to inflict a sustained attack against an aggressor. However, he, like many of his contemporaries, chose to sidestep the political difficulties of the enterprise. Having accepted that 'the political path' was not very promising, he recognised 'the initial approach must be political' and then essentially argued over the technical issues, not the political ones, even noting that 'it seemed to him illogical for people in Great Britain to dismiss the idea of a super-State as absurd'.[54]

In Parliament in the following year the idea of an international police force as promoted by Davies and his *New Commonwealth* was raised on a number of occasions. In November in the Commons, the Opposition put down a motion requesting the Government to support a range of initiatives at the Geneva Disarmament Conference, including the creation of an international police force but this was heavily defeated.[55] The Liberal leader, Sir Herbert Samuel, even voted with the Government, arguing that any force would need to recruit troops or airmen and have money voted for it, and few states would pledge either in advance, especially without any American guarantee. He was fearful that the League would be damaged by such initiatives. In a debate on military and civil aviation in the Lords in December, Lord Londonderry, the Secretary of State for Air, presented the Government's firm opposition to the internationalisation of civil and military aviation. The League would need to be transformed into a super-state, something which, contrary to Liddell Hart, he did not see as possible or desirable: the League existed for the pacific settlement of disputes, not the abolition of war by war.[56] Repeating the arguments of the Air Staff from the previous year, Londonderry shelved any idea of an international air force.[57] In the Commons however, in the same month, Geoffrey Mander, the Liberal MP for Wolverhampton East, with the support of Brigadier-General Spears, the Conservative MP for Carlisle, requested the Government to consider the creation of a an international police force under the League for the better maintenance of security.[58] Anthony Eden, Simon's Parliamentary Under-Secretary, replied for the Government noting the premature nature of the motion: that an international force, police or otherwise, could only prosper in a disarmed world as well as laying out the, by then, standard arguments over command, staffing, planning, bases and the need for the definition of an aggressor.[59] While the motion was withdrawn without a vote, it was not before Viscount Cranborne raised the problem in the title of an 'international police force'. It might lead those in support to think there was nothing military involved: it was, echoing Hillaire Belloc, 'designed to captivate and charm, much rather than to raise alarm'.[60]

These sentiments of Cranborne, not a renowned peace supporter, were shared by those such as Helena Swanwick, a former chairman of the Women's International League for Peace[61] and those pacifists who argued against the idea of an international police force, and who even objected to the term which was not passive but relied on the massive use of force. Swanwick in particular, although from a entirely different perspective, was, like the British Government, highly critical of Davies and the *New Commonwealth* in the way that key issues such as recruitment, command, training and arming were passed off as mere details.[62] This however did not dissuade the *New Commonwealth*, which in 1935, after the relative success of the Saar force, released a raft of papers underpinning the idea,[63] often with the endorsement of a strong list of reasonably senior military personnel.[64] By 1937, the *New Commonwealth* had generated its own military research committee and a Parliamentary group.[65] However, the growing tension within Europe, while it may have spurred many to look for idealistic solutions as a saviour of peace, also brought with it increasing realisation of the futility behind the idea of an international force in the diplomatic environment of the inter-war period. Nonetheless, the American and British plans for the United Nations, from 1942, contained some requirement for a force for the new body: one established with rather more foundation than the recommendatory provisions of the League.[66]

The British and the United Nations Military Staff Committee

The British had given specific thought to the idea of the UN having its own force from 1944 onwards and when the Military Staff Committee convened in 1946, the Attlee Government was hopeful of its success. In the planning period, the Post-Hostilities Planning Sub-Committee of the Chiefs of Staff (COS) bore the responsibility for the British position. However, there very quickly developed a division between, on the one hand, the COS, and on the other the Foreign Office over the role of the Military Staff Committee discussions. Both considered the prospect of a permanent UN force to be a non-starter[67] and the military planners restated many of the technical and military difficulties that had been raised in the 1930s.[68] Consequently, the COS were unwilling to support anything more than a general commitment to some form of UN force,[69] but the Foreign Office sounded warnings on the diplomatic importance of cooperation with the Americans, who could be expected to come forward with plans for at least 'the coordination of national forces under some World Council'.[70] The organisation of potential UN forces was seen by the Foreign Office as a part of improved post-war security and cooperation was vital if the USA was to play an effective role in the post-war world. This was not the only motive for the Foreign Office's support for some UN force, in marked contrast to its position during the League. It saw the force as a means of retaining Britain's seat at the top diplomatic table. The British had played more than a walk-on part in the creation of the UN, and maintenance of post-war security by the British through that body would assist in the fulfillment of Britain's world-wide mission.[71] The Foreign Office also saw the discussions in the Military Staff Committee as a means of cementing post-war allied unity and eventually providing a UN force of sorts to deal, not with communist subversion in Europe, but with Axis revivalism.[72] The COS, on the other hand, were faced with a dilemma in not wishing to be hamstrung in defence of Britain's interests by having to abide by a draining commitment to a UN armed force, but not wishing British contributions to be quantitatively or qualitatively inferior to contributions by the other permanent members. Nor did the Chiefs wish any UN force to be used by a major power as a pretext for maintaining unnecessarily large forces.[73] This position was approved by the Defence Cabinet Committee in March 1946 as British policy to be used as the basis for discussions on the principles behind any UN force.[74]

The British were to find however that there were significant, even irreconcilable, differences between their idea of the requirements of the UN force and that of the Soviet Union.[75] For example, in establishing force levels, the Russians proposed equal contributions, thereby allowing them to determine the strength of the eventual force, whereas the British wanted comparable contributions where their shortfall in land forces could be compensated by their offer of strategic bases. And, moreover, comparable contributions prevented the British from having to match the American figures and thereby straining defence resources. The Russians also pressed for any force to remain no longer than three months after the completion of its tasks, perhaps fearing the USA and Britain would gain a foothold in territory under the aegis of UN operations. When it came to the submission of estimates for the size of any UN force, the British however found themselves far closer to the Soviet levels and significantly divorced from the Americans, who envisaged a very large force with emphasis on mobility, and loaded their estimates with significant numbers of troops, submarines and aircraft.[76] The Foreign Office agreed 'to a considerable extent' with the Russian figures and feared the Americans were trying to wreck the exercise by inflated estimates as a way of keeping US forces safe from Congressional cuts.[77] However, the eventual breakdown of the Military Staff Committee deliberations was symptomatic of the role that each power assumed a UN force would play in post-war international politics. For the Americans, the UN was a keystone of policy and the size of the UN force a reflection of that view. The UN needed overwhelming forces to strike quickly and at long range. For the Russians, their emphasis on a small force would ensure limited UN action and initiative in a predominantly western world after 1945. They did not expect any UN force to confront a permanent member of the Security Council and, given the veto, they could be confident in that assumption. For the British there were initially high expectations from the Foreign Office, from Attlee, Bevin, the Foreign Secretary and the Labour Party for the role of the UN, and that its force discussions could be used to retain allied unity or at least not to damage it. Yet when that unity, was seen to be fracturing as the Cold War tensions developed in other parts of the UN and beyond, the article 43 idea was quietly abandoned, but not before some diplomatic mileage was extracted by the Foreign Office indicating that the Russians should take the blame for the failure.[78]

Conclusion

The experience of the League and the UN thus stands as a testament to the political and military requirements on which the concept of an international force is built and the failures of the international community to meet them. As Claude has noted, the first essential in relation to an international force 'is that its power should be so considerable and that of its possible opponents so negligible, that any contest will be virtually won before it has begun; otherwise its function will be that of conducting warfare, no matter how it may be described'.[79] The 'intrinsic disadvantages' are so great: 'its value depends heavily upon its ability to act quickly, so as to forestall threatened aggression and yet its very inability to concentrate on plans for defeating a specific enemy and its complex structure militate against promptness in the effective mobilization of its potential strength'.[80] Its success also assumes some element of partial disarmament by nation states while requiring the acquisition of military preponderance by the international community for whom the League or UN would have been the agents. In neither the experience of the League nor the UN have the political conditions been found to allow that imbalance to be created. The approach of British governments towards a League or UN force has been either actively opposed or, at best, broadly unenthusiastic. When, in the Military Staff Committee discussions, certain elements of the Foreign Office were predisposed towards promoting the idea, it was done not necessarily because it might be seen as militarily vital to post-war security – although that may have played some role – but predominantely because it served the Foreign Office's diplomatic purpose with respect to the other major powers, the USA and the Soviet Union.

NOTES

1. United Nations doc. MS/417, 6 August 1948.
2. C. Hull, *The Memoirs of Cordell Hull*, 2 vols. (London: Hodder and Stoughton, 1948), 2, pp. 1177–78.
3. L. Goodrich, E. Hambro and A.P. Simons, *Charter of the United Nations: Commentary and Documents*, 3rd edn rev. (New York: Columbia University Press, 1969), pp. 317–18.
4. See A.C.F. Beales, *The History of Peace: A Short Account of the Organised Movements for International Peace* (London: G. Bell, 1931), pp. 28–29; and J. Larus, 'The Myth is Born', in J. Larus (ed.), *From Collective Security to Preventive Diplomacy* (New York: John Wiley, 1965), p. 4.
5. In Stefan Possony, 'Peace Enforcement', *Yale Law Journal*, 55, 5 (1946), pp. 916–17.
6. Beales, *The History of Peace*, p. 8.
7. I.L. Claude, *Swords into Plowshares: The Problems and Progress of International Organization*, 3rd edn (London: University of London Press, 1965), p. 228.
8. For a full discussion of the range of ideas including the use of international forces to maintain peace, see Beales, *The History of Peace*, pp. 119–97; David Davies, *The Problem of the Twentieth Century* (London: Ernest Benn, 1930), pp. 58–115; and also Arthur Eyffinger, *The 1899 Hague Peace Conference, 'The Parliament of Man, The Federation of the World'* (The Hague: Kluwer Law International, 1999), pp. 212–15.
9. *Parliamentary Debates* (Commons), 5th series, vol. 21, col. 2215, 23 February 1911.
10. Davies, *The Problem of the Twentieth Century*, pp. 101–7.
11. 'The Historical Appendix', in G. Rosner, *The United Nations Emergency Force* (London: Columbia University Press, 1963), pp. 208–9.
12. These included proposals by the British League of Nations Society, the American League to Enforce Peace, the American League of Free Nations Association, the Fabian Society as well as plans proposed by individuals such as David [later Lord] Davies and Lord Bryce, see ibid., p. 210, and for a fuller discussion, S.J. Hemleben, *Plans for World Peace Through Six Centuries* (Chicago: University of Chicago Press, 1943), pp. 138–48.
13. Margaret Macmillan, *Peacemakers: The Paris Conference of 1919 and its Attempt to End War* (London: John Murray, 2001), p. 101.
14. See André Tardieu, *The Truth About the Treaty* (London: Hodder and Stoughton, 1921), p. 428.
15. See H.W.V. Temperley (ed.), *A History of the Peace Conference of Paris*, vol. VI (London: Oxford University Press, issued under the auspices of the Royal Institute for International Affairs, 1924; reprint edn. 1969), p. 447.
16. Ibid., p. 448.
17. David Hunter Miller, 'The Making of the League of Nations', in E.H. House and C. Seymour (eds), *What Really Happened at Paris: The Story of the Peace Conference 1918–1919* (New York: Charles Scribners, 1921; reprint edn, Westport, CT: Greenwood Press, 1976), p. 414.
18. See Possony, 'Peace Enforcement', p. 928.
19. Quoted in Macmillan, *The Peacemakers*, p. 102.
20. Tardieu, *The Truth About the Treaty*, p. 428.
21. The National Archives, Kew [hereafter TNA], CAB 24/167, CP311(24), 22 May 1924, which identified the objections to the Draft Treaty and CAB 23/48, CC35(24), 30 May 1924, for the Cabinet decision of rejection.
22. See the text of the Protocol on-line at fletcher.tufts.edu/multi/texts/historical/ LEAGUE-PROTOCOL.txt, emphasised by the author; and F.P. Walters, *A History of the League of Nations* (London: Oxford University Press, 1969), p. 273.
23. Committee of Imperial Defence Paper 559B, 'Report of the sub-Committee on the Geneva Protocol', 23 January 1925, TNA, CAB 24/172, CP105(25), 19 February 1925.
24. Ibid.
25. TNA, CAB 23/49, CC14(25), 4 March 1925.
26. Makins' summary of the French position, 4 July 1935, TNA, FO 371/19663/W6155.

27. A.C. Temperley, *The Whispering Gallery of Europe* (London: Collins, 1938), pp. 147, 187.
28. Thomas R. Davies, 'France and the World Disarmament Conference of 1932–34', *Diplomacy and Statecraft*, 15, 4 (December 2004), p. 766.
29. Hankey's 'Notes on the French Disarmament Proposals', 1 March 1932, TNA, AIR 8/132.
30. Ibid.
31. Temperley, *The Whispering Gallery of Europe*, p. 188.
32. See Possony, 'Peace Enforcement', p. 935.
33. See the copy of the 'Memorandum by the French Delegation to the Geneva Disarmament Conference', p. 5; italics in the original, TNA, FO 371/16467/W12577.
34. 'Note by the Air Staff on the French Proposals, dated 5 February 1932' [n.d.], TNA, AIR 8/132.
35. Dick Richardson, 'The Geneva Disarmament Conference, 1932–34', in D. Richardson and G. Stone (eds), *Decisions and Diplomacy: Essays in Twentieth-Century International History* (London: Routledge, 1995), p. 75.
36. For an analysis of the failure of the conference see ibid., and for a broader discussion of why disarmament failed more generally, see M.Vaïsse, 'Security and Disarmament: Problems in the Development of the Disarmament Debates 1919–1934', in R. Ahman, A.M. Birke and M. Howard (eds), *The Quest for Stability: Problems of West European Security 1918–1957* (Oxford: Oxford University Press, 1993), pp. 173–200.
37. F.S. Northedge, *The League of Nations: Its Life and Times, 1920–1946* (Leicester: Leicester University Press, 1986), pp. 71–72.
38. United Nations Archives, New York, United Nations Secretariat working paper 69, 'Precedents Concerning the Creation of International Forces', 17 October, 1947, DAG – 1/2.3 Box 42, file 399.
39. Walters, *A History of the League of Nations*, pp. 141–42.
40. Notes on a Parliamentary Question on forces for the League, 14 March 1921, TNA, FO 371/7057/W2863.
41. Walters, *A History of the League of Nations*, pp. 591–92; and see also Ian Kershaw, *Hitler 1889–1936: Hubris* (London: Allen Lane, 1998), pp. 546–47.
42. TNA, CAB 24/251, CP261(34), 16 November 1934.
43. TNA, CAB 24/251, CP275(34), 27 November 1934.
44. TNA, CAB 23/80, CC(34)43, 28 November 1934.
45. Ibid.
46. See Eden's note, 'The Council and the Saar', 30 November 1934, where he indicates the line of action to be taken in the League Council, TNA, WO 32/3595.
47. TNA, CAB 23/80, CC (34)45, 5 December 1934.
48. For the official report of Major-General J.R.S. Brind, commander-in-chief of the force, see TNA, WO 32/3601.
49. Walters, *A History of the League of Nations*, p. 593.
50. 'Memorandum respecting the Constitution of the International Force for the Saar Territory', 14 May 1935, TNA, FO 371/18815/C4198.
51. Liddell Hart papers, Liddell Hart Centre for Military Archives, King's College, London, LH15/3/276; A.H. Burne, *The International Police Force in the Saar* (New Commonwealth, 1935).
52. Davies's description in the summary of discussion, B.H. Liddell Hart, 'An International Force', *International Affairs*, 12, 2 (March 1933), p. 219.
53. Ibid., p. 209.
54. Ibid., p. 221.
55. *Parliamentary Debates* (Commons), 5th series, vol. 281, cols. 579–702, 13 November 1933.
56. *Parliamentary Debates* (Lords), 5th series, vol. 90, col. 377, 7 December 1933.
57. Ibid., col. 379.
58. *Parliamentary Debates* (Commons), 5th series, vol. 284, cols. 445–502, 13 December 1933.
59. Ibid., cols. 495–501.
60. Ibid., col. 467.
61. Liddell Hart papers, LH15/3/233; Helen Swanwick, *New Wars for Old* (London: Women's International League, 1934).

62. Ibid., p. 25.
63. See the Liddell Hart papers, the following *New Commonwealth Institute memoranda*: LH15/3/332, K.Capper-Johnson, *The Relationship between Disarmament and the Establishment of an International Police Force*, March 1935; LH15/3/334, Rear-Admiral R.N. Lawson, *A Plan for the Organisation of a European Air Service*, March 1935; LH15/3/336, Major-General, Sir Frederick Maurice, *The First Stage of International Policing*, March 1935.
64. See *The Times*, 17 April 1935, in which Major-General Maurice addressed the group in the Commons with the argument that there were no technical aspects of an international police force which could not be overcome. Interestingly, he overlooked the political aspects.
65. Liddell Hart papers, LH15/3/276.
66. 'The Four Power Plan', 9 September 1942, TNA, FO 371/31525/U742.
67. TNA, CAB 81/41, PHP(43)24a Final, 3 February 1944.
68. TNA, CAB 81/42, PHP(44)34 Final, 15 May 1944.
69. TNA, CAB 79/70, COS(44)50th mtg., 17 February 1944.
70. Jebb note attached to PHP(43)24a Final, 3 February 1944, TNA, CAB 81/41.
71. Lord Gladwyn, *The Memoirs of Lord Gladwyn* (London: Weidenfeld and Nicolson, 1972), pp. 116–17.
72. Ward's [head of the UN dept.] minute, 6 February 1946, TNA, FO 371/57064/U1911.
73. TNA, FO 371/57065/U2552, COS(46)60, 27 February 1946.
74. TNA, CAB 131/1, DO(46) 9th, 27 March 1946.
75. United Nations Doc. MS/264, 30 April 1947.
76. TNA, DEFE 11/4, JP(47)107 and approved at COS(47)113rd mtg., 1 September 1947.
77. Hebblethwaite's minute, 31 March 1948, TNA, FO 371/72641/UN631.
78. Tel. 1260, [FO to Washington], 31 January 1948, TNA, FO 115/4365.
79. Claude, *Swords into Plowshares*, p. 236.
80. Ibid.

Index

à Court, Charles, 17, 28
'acceleration crisis' (1909), 37
Admiralty, Finland, provision of arms to, 160; and Foreign Office, 42; on freedom of the seas, 107; and Hague Peace Conference (1899), 11–12, 26; and naval proposals, 95, 96; and Soviet navy, 119, 123
aero engines, 153
AFI Catalogue (film), 139–40
After the Ball (film), 138–9
Agadir crisis (1911), 46–7
AGNA (Anglo-German Naval Agreement) *see* Anglo-German Naval Agreement (1935)
Air Commission, 84, 85
Air Ministry, 153, 156, 157, 159, 160
aircraft production, 153
Alexander I, Emperor, 1, 2
All at Sea (film), 145
All Quiet on the Western Front (film), 6, 129, 130, 132, 134, 142
Allied Military Committee, 161
Ambassadors' Conference (1922), 78, 80
American Film Institute Catalogue, 136
Anglo-French Supreme War Council, 161
Anglo-German Naval Agreement (1935), Chatfield on, 120; and Craigie, 119–20, 123; and cruisers, 114; and earlier proposals, 40; and Russia, 117; signing, 112; and treaty-breaking, 5
Anglo-German relations, 3, 33–52; Agadir crisis (1911), 46–7; data exchanges, 44–5; naval agreement *see* Anglo-German naval agreement (1935); naval race, 33, 41, 47; reciprocity question, 35, 43, 45; and Russia, 115–16; search for agreement, 33–52; talks (pre-1914), 8; 'Two-Power-Standard', 35, 37, 39, 44; 'Two-to-Three-Standard', 44
Anglo-Japanese alliance (1902), 92
Anglo-Soviet naval agreement (1937), 5, 8; and AGNA, 112; limited importance of, 125; signature of, 122
Anglo-Soviet naval arms control negotiations, and AGNA, 112; and British foreign policy, 123; and Germany, 116; importance of agreement, 113; incompatibility of views, 124–5
Anti-Comintern Pact, 117, 121
arbitration, 175; *see also* Hague Conference (1899), Pauncefote, Permanent Court of International Arbitration
Ardagh, Sir John, on Brussels declaration on laws and customs of war, 24; on bullets, 22; characteristics, 16; and Hague Peace Conference (1899), 22, 24, 25; memorandum of, 12–14; on Tübingen University experiments, 21
Arliss, George, 142
armaments, competition, 34; increased spending on, 3–4
Arms and the Film: War and Peace in European Films (Gheorghiu-Cernat), 134, 136
arms control negotiations (Richardson's criteria), absence from Coolidge Conference, 105–6; belief in disarmament, 96–7; motivation of parties, 124; outline of factors, 91–2, 112; political leadership, 97; political necessity of reaching agreement, 92, 107; political will, 100; same problem, seen in eyes of other parties, 104; technical side of disarmament, 103–4; *see also* Coolidge Naval Conference (1927)
arms exports, 151, 152; *see also* Finland, provision of arms to
arms races, 33; *see also* naval races
Arsenal (film), 130
Asada, Sadao, 97, 104
Asquith, Herbert Henry, 35, 37, 40
Associated Realist Film Producers, 134
Attlee, Clement, 164

balance of power, 76
Baldwin, Stanley, 97, 98, 102, 106
Balfour, Arthur James, 92, 100–1
Baltic countries, 154; *see also* Finland
Barnes, George, 186
battleship costs, 34
Beales, A.C.F., 175

INDEX

Beatty, Earl, 93, 95, 99, 102
Belayev, General, 57
Bellars, John, 175
'belligerent', meaning, 14
Belloc, Hillaire, 187
Berkeley, Busby, 129–30
Bethmann Hollweg, Theobald von, on Anglo-German naval agreement, 39, 40, 42, 43, 44; on data exchanges, 45; and *Novelle*, 38; and RMA, 47
Big Parade, The (film), 129, 134
bilateral agreements, 112–13
Bingham, Sir Francis, 86
Blackmail (film), 138
Black Cat, The (film), 130
Blake of Scotland Yard (film), 142
Blenheim, battle of (1704), 12
Blenheim bombers, 153, 156, 158, 159, 160, 162, 163
Bliss, General Tasker, 77
Blücher, Wipert von, 157
Boer War, 27–8, 34
Bofors guns (Sweden), 153
Bolshevism, 76
Bourgeois, Léon, 17, 18, 177, 178
Boxer rebellion (1900), 175
Bridgeman, Sir William, 98, 99, 101–2
Britain, Anglo-American rivalry, Coolidge Naval Conference *see* Coolidge Naval Conference (1927); Anglo-French friction, and German disarmament, 81–2, 83–4, 86; Anglo-Japanese alliance (1902), 92; arms companies, 151, 153; bilateral agreements, with France/US, 112; Crusade for Peace 11, 28; financial robustness, 34; Finland, provision of arms to *see* Finland, provision of arms to; and Hague Peace Conference (1899) *see* Hague Conference (1899); London Naval Conference (1930), 106; maritime belligerent rights, British doctrine, 107; 'Merchants of Death' controversy, 133; Navy, alleged superiority of, 8, 36, 37, 100, 102; and UN Military Staff Committee, 188–90; Venezuela, conflict with over British Guiana, 15; *see also* Anglo-German naval agreement (1935); Anglo-German relations; Anglo-Soviet naval agreement (1937); Anglo-Soviet naval arms control negotiations
British Board of Film Censors, 131
British Crusade for Peace, 28; National Convention, 11
British Film Institute catalogue, 131
British Sound Films: The Studio Years 1928–1959, 136
Brusilov offensive (1916), 54, 66
Brussels Conference (1874), 1, 13, 24

195

Brussels Convention (1890), 1
Buchan, John, 143
Buchanan, Andrew, 134
Buchanan, George, 57
Bulldog Drummond at Bay (film), 143

Cadogan, Alexander, 122, 163, 167
Calvacanti, Alberto, 133
Capone, Al, 1
Capra, Frank, 142
Carlton, David, 91, 103, 105
Carnegie, Andrew, 176
Carroll, Madeleine, 140
Castlereagh, Lord Robert Stewart, 2, 3
Cavell, Edith, 130
Cawdor programme, 35
Ceadel, Martin, 134
Cecil, Lord Robert, 96–7, 98, 100, 186
Central Powers, disarmament, 74, 76
Chamberlain, Austen, 99, 103
Chamberlain, Neville, and arms exports, 155, 156, 160, 161, 163–4, 165, 166; and film industry, 144
Charlton, E.F.B., 77
Château de Vincennes, 56
Chatfield, Ernle, 113, 120, 122
Chilston, Viscount, 118, 120, 121
China, Japan's resort to force in, 6; 'Open Door' policy with, 96
Churchill, Winston, 47, 99–100, 101, 158, 163
Ciano, Galeazzo, 158
cinema industry, 6, 129–50; American peace films, 135; anti-war films, 130, 132; British films, 138; cartoons, 141, 145–6; and world peace, 136
Cinematograph Exhibitors' Associations (CEAs), 131
Clemenceau, Georges, 77, 137
Cleveland, President Grover, 15
codification of laws and customs of war, need for, 14
Cold War, 7, 190
collective security, 76; League of Nations policy, 134
Collier, Laurence, 116, 118, 119, 123–4
Colman, Ronald, 142
Cologne bridgehead, evacuation, 85
Comité d'entente des grandes associations internationals, 133
comité d'examen (expert legal committee), 17, 18, 19
Commissions of Control, 77, 78
Committee of Imperial Defence, sub-committee, 180
Constant Gardener, The (thriller), 135
Coolidge, Calvin, 'conversations' concept, 102–3; and Geneva conference (1927),

95, 96; MacDonald contrasted, 106; on parity, 102; on Preparatory Commission, 94; presidential style, 97
Coolidge Naval Conference (1927), 5; achievements of, 108; Anglo-American rivalry at, 91–111; collapse of, 96, 97; limitations of, 8, 97, 106; parity issues, 100–2; *see also* arms control negotiations, Richardson's criteria
Corbin, Charles, 158
Council of Ten, 77
Cousins, E.G., 133
Craigie, Sir Robert, and Anglo-German Naval Agreement, 119–20, 123; Collier, disagreement with, 118; and Germany, 116–17; and Maisky, 117, 121; Wassner, talks with, 114–15
Cranborne, Viscount, 187, 188
Crowe, Eyre, Anglo-German relations, 36, 38, 40, 42, 45, 46; and Germany (post-First World War), 83
Crozier, William, 21
cruisers, Anglo-American rivalry, 104–5; British requirement, 96; classes, 103; fixed number of, 101, 102; limitation of, 93; parity issues, 100; and Russia, 114
Cry of the World, The, 139
Cuban Wars, 13
Curzon, Lord, 85

d'Abernon, Lord, 78, 84
Daladier, Edouard, 161, 163, 164
Darcy, 59
Davies, David, 186, 187, 188
Dawn (film), 130
de Martens, Feodor, 11, 25
de Salis, Count John, 40
Death on the Road (film), 131, 132
Defence Cabinet Committee, 189
Defence Policy Requirements Committee (DPRC), 151
Delcassé, Théophile, 18, 19, 59
Derby, Lord Edward Stanley, 14, 80
Descamps, Édouard, 17
destroyers, 96
Diplomaniacs (film), 139
disarmament, belief in, 96; Germany *see* disarmament, Germany (1918–23); inter-war years, 5, 6; naval, 78; pacifists/internationalists debate, 175; technical side of, 103–4
disarmament, Germany (1918–23), 79; air power, destruction, 78; Anglo-French friction, 81–2, 83–4, 86; and Central Powers, disarmament, 74, 76; infringements and non-compliances, 79; land forces, reduction, 81, 83; military clauses, 74; navy, reduction, 74, 78–80; Spa Conference (1920), 82–3; Versailles Treaty (1919), 73–5, 80
disarmament conference (1932–34) *see* Geneva Disarmament Conference (1932–34)
Disarmament Conference (film), 139
Disney, Walt, 6, 144
doctrine of requirements, 101
Documents Diplomatiques Français, 30, 56, 169
Donat, Robert, 140
Dovzhenko, Aleksandr, 130
DPRC (Defence Policy Requirements Committee), 151
Draft Treaty of Mutual Assistance (1923), 179
dreadnoughts, 34, 37, 38
Dulles, Allen, 98, 108
Duma, 4, 68; Progressive Bloc, 54, 61, 62
Dum-Dum bullet, 20, 21, 22

East Meets West (film), 142
Eastern Front, The (Stone), 54, 55
Ebert–Groener pact (1918), 81
Economic and Social History of the World War, The, 54
Eden, Anthony, Anglo-Soviet naval arms control negotiations, 112, 115, 120, 122, 123; and arms exports, 167; on international police force, 187; Mannerheim, meeting with, 153
'effectifs actuels', 12
Einwohnerwehr, 81, 83, 84
Elvey, Maurice, 137, 138
En Natt (film), 130
Escherich, Dr, 83, 84
Evolution of British Disarmament Policy in the 1920s, The (Richardson), 1
Expert's Opinion (film), 141
Export Credits scheme, 166

Fanning, Richard W., 97, 106
Fashoda crisis, 19
Fatal Hour, The (film), 143
Ferdinand the Bull (Walt Disney film), 6, 144
Feud Was There, A (film), 144
Fiat fighters, 155
film industry *see* cinema industry
Finland, British Legation, 158; as category C country, 153; German Legation, 157; provision of arms to, 151–72; and Second World War, 154; Soviet Russia, war with (1939–40), 7, 152, 155, 159, 161, 166
Fire over England (film), 146
First World War, Germany's defeat, 4; lessons learned from, 107–8; military histories,

55; origins of, and Anglo-German naval race, 33; Russian armament production, French assistance to (1914–17), 53, 57–62, 69
Fisher, Cecil, 3
Fisher, Sir John, on British Navy, 8; and 'Dreadnought revolution', 34; and Hague Peace Conference (1899), 16–17, 19, 22, 23, 28; on rules of war, 23–4; temperament, 28; on weapon restrictions, 23
Flottenpolitik, 36
Foch, Marshal, 75, 83; Versailles Military and Naval Council, 84
Fokker Company (Netherlands), 153
Fontainebleau Conference/memorandum (1919), 75–6
Foreign Office, and Admiralty, 42; and arms exports, 151, 152, 154; and freedom of the seas, 107; and German disarmament, 85; and Military Staff Committee, 189; and Saar plebiscite, 185; and Soviet navy, 119; and UN forces, 188–9
Four Just Men, The (film), 145
FPI (film), 139
France, Anglo-French friction, and German disarmament, 81–2, 83–4, 86; bilateral agreements with, 112; economic relations with Russia (1915–16), 63; Franco-Prussian War (1870–71), 14; Franco-Russian combination, Britain's naval race with, 33, 34; Franco-Soviet Pact (1935) *see* Franco-Soviet Pact (1935); and Germany (post-First World War), 77; naval construction schemes, 34; Russian armament production, assistance to (1914–17), 53, 57–62, 69; SFIO (French Socialist Party), 56
Franco-Soviet Pact (1935), Craigie on, 116; German use of, to block naval negotiations, 115; objections to, 121; ratification, 114; Ribbentrop on, 120; signature of, 113
Frankenstein (film), 130
Frederick the Great, 175
freedom of the seas, 107

Gamelin, General Maurice, 162
Gance, Abel, 129, 134
Gauntlets, 159, 160
Geddes, Sir Eric, 75
General Navy Board (US), 93, 96
Geneva Convention (1864), 1, 24; extension to naval warfare, 28; principles, 26
Geneva Convention (1927), British Empire delegation, 104; failure of negotiations at, 107; naval races, 97; and Washington Conference, 106

Geneva Disarmament Conference (1932–34), 5, 180, 185–6, 187
Geneva Protocol, 179, 180
Germany, disarmament of, 73–90; *Einwohnerwehr*, 81, 83, 84; First World War, defeat in, 4; and Hague Peace Conference (1899), 18–19, 36; High Seas Battle Fleet, 36; League of Nations, departure from (1933), 5; naval armaments programme, 35; Nazi–Soviet Pact (1939), 152, 154; *Reichswehr*, 81, 82, 83; Russia, threat to, 125; Weimar Republic, 81; Wilhelmstrasse, 19, 38, 41; *Zeitfreiwilligen*, 81; *see also* Anglo-German naval agreement (1935); Anglo-German relations
Gheorghiu-Cernat, Manuela, 134, 136
Gibson, Hugh, 98, 99, 101
Gladiators, 156, 158, 159, 160
Glyn, Elinor, 138
Gold Diggers (musical), 129–30
Goschen, Sir Edward, Anglo-German relations, 38, 40, 41, 42, 44, 47; on data exchanges, 45
Grant, Jonathan A., 66
Great War *see* First World War
Gregg, Robert W., 135–6
Grey, Sir Edward, Anglo-German relations, 37, 38, 39, 40–1, 43, 44, 46; on growth of armaments, 4, 34, 75; and international initiatives, 176; memorandum of, 42; on technical accord, 3
Gripenberg, Georg, 160, 166
Grotius, Hugo, 175
'Groupement Poutiloff', 68
Guchkov, A.I., 60, 63, 66, 67
guerrilla warfare, 13
Guilty Melody (film), 142
gun calibres, dispute over, 114

Hague Conference (1899), 1, 2, 8, 9–32; Anglo-German relations, 18–19, 36; Court of Arbitration, creation, 176; limitations of, 28; proposals for, 9–10
Hague Conference (1907), 1, 2, 35
Haig, Douglas, 77
Haldane, R.B., 35, 37, 47
Halder, General Franz, 154
Halifax, Lord, and arms exports, 154, 155, 156, 158, 159, 160, 166
Handle with Care (film), 140
Hankey, Sir Maurice, 100, 101, 180, 181
Hara, Rear Admiral, 98
Harding, Warren, 92
Harman, Hugh, 146
Hasegawa, T., 62, 63
Hays Code, 131
Heat Wave (film), 141

Hell and the Way Out (League of Nations film), 133
Hell's Cargo (aka *Dangerous Cargo*) (film), 145
High Treason (film), 137, 138
His Lordship (film), 142
History of Arms Control and Disarmament, A (Richardson), 2
Hitchcock, Alfred, 138, 140, 143
Hitler, Adolf, 115, 157, 182, 186
Hoare, 122
Hobson, Valerie, 136, 144
Holiday's End (film), 142–3
Holls, George, 19
Holman, Adrian, 117, 118
Honeymoon Adventure, A (aka *Footsteps in the Night*) (film), 138
Hore-Belisha, Leslie, 156, 160, 165
hospital ships, 24
House of the Spaniard, The (film), 142
Howard, Sir Esme, 107
Howard, Sir Henry, 16, 17, 28
How's Chances? (film), 140
Hughes, Charles Evans, 92, 98, 102, 105
Hull, Cordell, 173
Hurricanes, 156, 159, 160, 162

I am a Fugitive from a Chain Gang (film), 130
I Spy (film), 139
Imperial National Defence Policy (1923 onwards), 93–4
Inter-Allied Commissions of Control, 74
international forces, and League of Nations, 183
International Relations on Film (Gregg), 135–6
internationalists, 175
inter-war years, diplomacy of disarmament, 6; and disarmament notion, 5; film genres, 146; League force, 174
Ironside, Sir Edmund, 159, 161

J'accuse (film), 129, 134
Jaffe, Lorna, 75
James, Sir William, 113
Janin, General, 56
Japan, Anglo-Japanese alliance (1902), 93; China, force in, 6; London Naval Conference (1936), leaving, 112; as potential adversary, 93; Russian, threat to, 125; Russian defeat (1905), 35; and submarines, 94
Jimmy Boy (film), 141
Joffre, General, 56
Jones, Admiral, 98
Jones, D.R., 55
Josser Joins the Navy (film), 139

Journey's End (film), 129

Kameradschaft (film), 130
Kapp, Gustav, 81
Karelian Isthmus, 155, 157, 164
Karloff, Boris, 130
Kedward, Rod, 134–5
Kellogg, Frank, 98, 99, 105
Kellogg–Briand pact, 132
Kennedy, Greg, 112
Kerr, Philip, 75, 82
Kiderlen-Wächter, Alfred von, 38, 45, 47
Kikijuro, Viscount Ishii, 98
King, George, 138
Kipling, Rudyard, 10
Kirke, General Sir Walter, 154
Kitchener mission, 64
Knox, Geoffrey, 184
Kobayashi, Vice-Admiral, 98, 104
Korda, Alexander, 131
Kuramatsu, Tadashi, 91, 108

La grande illusion (film), 130, 142
Lady Vanishes, The (film), 143
Laemmle, Carl, 129
Laguiche, General, 56, 58, 61
Lammasch, Heinrich, 18
Lane, Lupino, 138
Langlois, Commandant, 56, 59, 61
Lansdowne, Lord, 27
Last Barricade, The (film), 136
Last Hour, The (film), 138
Lawrence, T.E., 131
Layton, Dorothy, 186
Le Creusot, 63, 68
League Council, 174, 179, 180, 181, 184
League of Nations, American exclusion from (1920), 178; and Brussels Convention (1890), 1; collective security policy, 134; Covenant, 76, 174, 175, 177, 179; errors of, 7; experience of, 182–5; and film industry, 136, 138–9; films made by, 133, 146–7; Germany's departure from (1933), 5; international force, 178–82; and international forces, 183; Non-Partisan Association, 133; Preparatory Commission, 5, 94; Soviet Russia expelled from (1939), 158
League of Nations Union, 131, 186
Leningrad, Kirov plant, 70; and Russo-Finnish War (1939–40), 155
Lest We Forget (League of Nations film), 133
Liddell Hart, Basil, 186–7
Lightning Conductor (film), 143
Ling, Brigadier Christopher, 159, 160
Litvinov, Maxim, 115, 120, 181
Lloyd George, David, and film industry,

137; and Germany (post-First World War), 75, 76, 77, 81, 82, 83; and Paris Peace Conference, 79; philosophy, 76
Locarno negotiations, 87
London Conference (1920), 81
London Naval Conference (1930), 106–7, 108
London Naval Conference (1936), Japan, leaving of, 112
Long, Admiral, 98
Lost Horizon (Capra), 142
Lotinga, Ernie, 139
Loucheur, Louis, 65
Low, Sidney, 10
Lubitsch, Ernst, 132
Luck of the Navy (aka *North Sea Patrol*) (film), 143
Lundqvist, Jarl, 153–4, 155
Lysander fighters, 160

MacDonald, Ramsay, 106–7, 109; electoral defeat (1924), 179–80; first Labour Government, 179
Macgregor, Evan, 11–12
Macmillan, Harold, 130, 165
Mahan, Captain Alfred, 22, 24, 26
Maisky, Ivan, 113, 116, 122; and Craigie, 117, 121
Makato, Saito, 98
Mander, Geoffrey, 187
Manikovski, General, 61, 67, 68; memoirs, 66
Mankiewicz, Joseph L., 139
Mannerheim, Carl Gustav, 153, 159–60, 161
Mannerheim Line, 157, 161
Man I Killed, The (film), 132
Man Who Knew Too Much, The (film)), 140
Many Tanks Mr Atkins (film), 143
March of Time, The (newsreel), 136, 139, 147
maritime belligerent rights, British doctrine, 107
Mark IV bullet, 20, 21
Masterman, E.A., 77, 78
McKean, R.B., 62–3
McKenna, Reginald, 38, 44
McKersher, Brian, 96; on belligerent rights, 108; on cruisers, 94; on Geneva negotiations (1927), 107; on politics of naval arms limitation, 91, 92, 94–5; on Winston Churchill, 99–100
McNeile, Herman C., 140
Meet Maxwell Archer (aka *Maxwell Archer Detective*) (film), 144
Men of Yesterday (film), 141
Message from Geneva (film), 133
Messerschmitt fighters, 154

Metternich, Count Paul von Wolff-, 43, 46, 47
Midnight (film), 138
Midnight Menace (aka *Bombs over London*) (film), 143
Milestone, Lewis, 6, 129, 130, 132, 134, 142
Military Commission, 77, 85
Military Effectiveness (Millett and Murray), 55
Military Staff Committee (UN), 173, 174, 181, 190; and Britain, 188–90
Millerand, Alexandre, 81, 82, 83
Millett, A.R., 55
Monroe Doctrine, 96
Montagu, Ivor, 130, 142
Montreux settlement, 116
Morane-Saulnier fighters, 160, 165
Morgan, J.H., 82, 86–7
Motion Picture Problems: The Cinema and the League of Nations (Seabury), 132
Mr Satan (film), 144
Mr Stringfellow Says 'No' (film), 143
Münster, Count Georg zu, 18, 19
Muraviev, Count Michael Nikolaevich, and Brussels Conference (1874), 13; Hague Conference proposals, 9–10, 11, 14, 18, 19, 20, 23
Murder in the Air (film), 145
Murmansk railway, 158, 159
Murray, Gilbert, 186
Murray, Williamson, 55
Mussolini, Benito, 155
Mutual and Balanced Force Reductions (MBFR), 2, 8
mutual assistance pacts, Baltic countries, 154

Napoleonic wars, 1, 13, 175
National Convention of British Crusade for Peace, 11
National Council of Public Morals, Report of Commission, 135
Naval Commission, 77
naval construction schemes, 34
Naval Defence Act (1889), 34
naval races, and Admiralty, 95; Anglo-German relations, 33, 41, 47; British assumption of avoidance necessity, 124; Franco-Russian combination, 34; post-First World War, 92
Navy Board (US), 102
Navy Estimates, 40, 43
Nazi–Soviet Pact (1939), 152, 154
Neighbours (film), 141, 146
Netherlands, and Boer cause, 10
New Commonwealth society, 186, 187, 188
Nicholas, Grand Duke, 58

Nicholas II, Emperor, 9, 54
Nicolson, Sir Arthur, 45, 46
Nieter, Hans, 140
Nigra, Count Constantino, 18
No Lady (film), 138
Nolde, Baron, 69
Nollet, Charles, 77, 85
Northedge, F.S., 182
Novelle (1908), 36, 37, 38, 42

Old Mother Riley in Paris/*Old Mother Riley Joins Up*/*Old Mother Riley MP* (films), 144, 145
Oliphant, Sir Lancelot, 118, 119
Olivier, Laurence, 144
Olney, Richard: arbitration treaty (UK and US), 15–16
Once in a New Moon (film), 140
Open Door policy, United States/China, 96
Orgesch, 83
Orlov, V.M., 117, 118, 121

Pabst, G.W., 129, 130, 134
pacifists, 175
Paléologue, Maurice, 58–9, 69; telegram to Paris, 65–6
Pares, Sir Bernard, 54
Paris declaration (1856), 1
Paris Peace Conference (1919), 79
parity issues, Coolidge Naval Conference (1927), 100–2; mathematical vs maritime parity, 101
Passenger to London (film), 143
Pau, General, 59
Paul-Boncour/Herriot plan, 181
Pauncefote, Sir Julian, and Anglo-American arbitration agreement, proposal for, 15; on Germany, 19; and Hague Peace Conference (1899), 16, 17, 18, 19, 23, 28; as leader of British delegation to Hague, 16; on permanent tribunal of international arbitration, 17, 18
Peace and Plenty (film), 130, 142
Peace Ballot (1935), 134
Peace Conference (film), 141
Peace on Earth (film), 146
Peace Pledge Union, 134
Peaceful Neighbours (film), 145–6
Pemberton-Billing, Noel, 137–8
Peninsular Wars, 13
Penn, William, 175
People of Britain (Peace of Britain), 131, 132
Permanent Court of International Arbitration, proposals for, 2, 17–18, 19
Petrograd, Putilov munitions factory *see* Putilov arms works, St Petersburg
Phillips, T.S.V., 113, 114, 115, 121, 122
Poelzig, Hjalmar, 130

Poland, and arms exports, 152; partition of, 154
police force, international, 187
political leadership, and arms control criteria, 97
political will, and arms control criteria, 100
Polivanov, A.A., 63, 66
Potez-63 bombers, 165
Pound, Sir Dudley, 107
Powell, Michael, 136
Powell, Sandy, 145
Problem of the Twentieth Century, The (Davies), 186
Putilov, A.I., 65, 66; Russo-Asiatic Bank, 67
Putilov arms works, St Petersburg, 4, 59, 60; industrial action, 56, 62, 63–4, 66, 69, 70; planned merger with Hughes firm, Ukraine, 69; sequestration of company, 56, 61, 62, 65, 67
Putilov group, 62
Pyot, Colonel, 59, 60, 61

Q Planes (aka *Clouds over Europe*) (film), 144
Quinlan, David, 136, 138, 140, 143, 145; rating of films by, 139, 144

Ralston, Esther, 138
Rathbone, Basil, 139
Reagan, Ronald, 145
Red Army, 153
Reichsmarineamt (RMA), 36, 45, 47
Reichswehr, 81, 82, 83
Renoir, Jean, 130, 142
Return of Bulldog Drummond, The (film), 140
Revolutionary Wars, 13
Reynaud, Paul, 164
Ribbentrop, Joachim von, 115, 120
Richardson, Dick, 1–2, 5, 6; arms control negotiations criteria (Coolidge Naval Conference) *see* arms control negotiations, Richardson's criteria
Richardson, Ralph, 144
Riddell, Lord, 75
Right to Live, The (film), 139
Road Back, The (film), 131, 142
Roaring Twenties, The (film), 130
Rochemont, Louis de, 139
Rocs (dive-bombers), 160
Roosevelt, Theodore, 176
Roskill, Stephen, 80
Rotha, Paul, 131, 132
Ruhr, occupation (1923), 80
Rumsfeld, Donald, 1
Russia/Soviet Union, and Anglo-German naval relations, 115–16; Anglo-Soviet naval agreement *see* Anglo-Soviet naval

INDEX

agreement (1937); armament production, French assistance (1914–17), 53, 57–62, 69; Bolshevism, 76; and cruisers, 114; Duma, 4, 54, 61, 62, 68; economic relations with France (1915–16), 63; finances of, 10; Finland, war with (1939–40), 7, 152, 155, 159, 161, 166; Franco-Russian combination, Britain's naval race with, 33, 34; Germany, threat of, 125; and Japan, 35, 125; League of Nations, expulsion from (1939), 158; Leningrad, 70, 155; naval construction schemes, 34; Nazi–Soviet Pact (1939), 152, 154; Odessa, Pyot's work in, 61; Red Army, 153; Revolution of 1917, 4, 53, 54, 63, 67; Russo-Asiatic Bank, 67, 68; sequestration practice, 62, 63, 65; shell crisis (1915 and 1916), 55, 57, 66; Soviet–Turkish agreement, rumours of, 116; Special Defence Commission, 67, 68; success of rearmament (1914–17), 53; Union of Municipalities, 60; Union of Zemstvos, 60; Viviani–Thomas mission to (1916), 64; voluntary organisations, 60; War Industry Committees *see* War Industries Committees (Russia); War Ministry, Main Artillery Administration, 60; *see also* Putilov arms works (St Petersburg)
Ryti, Risto, 161

Saar plebiscite, 182, 184–5
Saint-Pierre, Abbé de, 175
Saint-Saveur, 59, 69
Salisbury, Lord Robert Cecil, 2–3; convictions of, 9; and Hague Peace Conference (1899), 11, 15–16, 19–20
Salmon, Patrick, 167
Samuel, Sir Herbert, 187
San Remo Conference (1920), 80, 82
Sargent, Sir Orme, 167
Scapa Flow, 79
Schleswig plebiscite, 183
Schneider-Creusot metallurgical firm, 4, 59, 60, 62
Scott, Sir Charles, 10
Seabury, William Marston, 132
Second World War, and Finland, 154
Secret Journey (aka *Among Human Wolves*) (film), 145
Secret Voice, The (film), 141–2
sequestration practice, 61, 63, 65, 66, 67; definition, 62
Service Historique de l'Armée de Terre, 56
SFIO (French Socialist Party), 56
Shearer, W.B., 105
shell crisis (1915 and 1916), 55, 57, 66
Sheppard, Dick, 134
Shull, Michael, 144

Siegelbaum, Lewis A., 60, 61
Sight and Sound, 134
Silent Battle, The (aka *Continental Express*) (film), 144
Silver Greyhound, The (film), 139
Simon, Sir John, 184
Simons, Walter von, 83
Sir Sidney, 137
Skuas (dive-bombers), 160
Snow, Thomas, 157–8
Sons of the Sea (film), 145
South Africa, arms exports, 159
Spa Conference (1920), 82–3
Spanish Civil War, 6, 142
Spencer programme (1893–94), 34
Spies of the Air (film), 144
Spirit of Lafayette, The (film), 136–7
Spitfire fighters, 154, 156
Spy for a Day (film), 145
Spy in Black, The (aka *U-Boat 29*) (film), 136
St Petersburg conference (1868), 1, 22
Stalin, Josef, 155, 156
Stead, William T., 11, 22
Stevenson, David, 55, 75
Stockholm, British Legation sources in, 157
Stone, Norman, 54, 55
Storck, Henri, 130
Story of an Unknown Soldier, The (film), 130
Strachan, Huw, 55
Strange Boarders (film), 144
submarines, 23, 79; and Coolidge Naval Conference, 96; Japan, 94
Sukhomlinov, Vladimir, 63; as shell crisis scapegoat, 66
Sully, Duc de, 175
Swanwick, Helena, 188
Sydney, John, 133
Syriana (thriller), 135

Tardieu, André, 178
Technische Nothilfe, 81
Tel-el-Kebir, battle of (1882), 12
Things to Come (film), 130, 146
39 Steps, The (film), 140
Thomas, Albert, 56, 58, 65, 67; mission to Russia (1916), 64–6
Three Comrades (film), 131
Thunder in the Air (film), 140
Tickell, Crispin, 2
Tirpitz, Admiral Alfred von, 36, 37, 41, 44
Tomosaburo, Baron Kato, 97
Traitor Spy (aka *The Torso Murder Mystery*) (film), 145
Transvaal, 10, 27
Tsarist army (1915–16), 55
Tübingen University experiments, 21

Tukhachevskii, Marshal Mikhail, 153
Two Shall Be Born (film), 137
'Two-Power-Standard', 35, 37, 39

UN *see* United Nations
Uncle Sam of Freedom Ridge (film), 137
Underneath the Arches (film), 142
United Nations, Charter of, 7, 173, 174, 175; Military Staff Committee, 173, 174, 181, 188–90, 190; Security Council, 174
United States, bilateral agreements with, 112; Coolidge Naval Conference (1927), Anglo-American rivalry, 91–111; General Navy Board, 93, 96; and League of Nations, 94, 178; and Monroe Doctrine, 96; Navy Board, 102; on parity, 102; Versailles Treaty (1919), refusal to ratify, 94; Washington Conference (1921–22), 5, 91, 92, 93, 94, 103, 106
Upper Silesia force, 183

van Karnebeek, Jonkheer, 22
Vankov, General, 59, 60
Vansittart, Sir Robert, on Anglo-Soviet naval arms control negotiations, 114, 115, 117–18, 119, 121, 122; memorandum on arms exports, 152
Vaux Saint Cyr, Baron Moisson de, 164
Veidt, Conrad, 136
Venezuela, arbitration claims, 16; conflict with Britain, over British Guiana, 15
Versailles Treaty (1919), 4, 5; and disarmament of Germany, 73–5, 80; and League Covenant, 177; US Congress, refusal to ratify, 94
Vickers tanks, 153, 155
Vidor, King, 129, 134
Vilna plebiscite, 183
Viviani, René, mission to Russia (1916), 64–6
von Holstein, Friedrich, 18
von Müller, Georg, 41
von Schwarzhoff, Colonel Gross, 2, 23
von Seeckt, General, 81

Walls, Tom, 144
War Against War! (newspaper), 11
War Cabinet, and arms exports, 154, 156, 157, 158, 160, 161, 163, 164
War Council, 167

War Industries Committees (Russia), 68; armaments industry, 64; Movement, 60, 62; as patriotic voluntary organisations, 58; political role, 61; reports of activities, 54
War Office, and arms exports, 155; and German disarmament, 81, 84; and Hague Peace Conference (1899), 11, 12, 27; and Saar plebiscite, 184
Warner Brothers, 144, 145, 146
warships, classes of, 96
Washington, G., 98
Washington Conference (1921–22), 5, 103, 106; and Coolidge Naval Conference (1927), 91; success, 92, 93, 94, 97
Wassner, Captain Erwin, 114–15
Watson, Captain Hugh R., 41, 45
Wehrvorlage (1913), 47
Weimar Republic, 81
Weizsäcker, Ernst von, 157
Wemyss, Wester, 79
Westfront 1918 (film), 129, 130, 134
Whale, James, 129, 130
White, Andrew, 26
Whom the Gods Would Destroy (film), 137
Wickham Mystery, The, 138
Widenmann, Captain Wilhelm, 41, 44
Wife of General Ling (film), 143
Wigram, Ralph, 115
Wilcox, Herbert, 130–1
Wilhelm II, Emperor, 36
Wilhelmstrasse, 19, 38, 41
Williams, B.H., 103–4
Wilson, Sir Henry, 178
Wilson, Thomas Woodrow, 1, 137, 178
Wilt, David, 144
Winter War of 1939–40, 7
Wolf's Clothing (film), 142
Wolseley, Lord, 27
Wood, Kingsley, 158, 160, 162, 163
World War I *see* First World War
World War II *see* Second World War
World War and After, The (League of Nations film), 133

Zaharoff, Sir Basil, 133–4
Zeitfreiwilligen, 81
Zemgor (voluntary organisations), 54, 60
zemstvos, 58
Zhdavov, Andrei, 153
Zorn, Philipp, 18, 19

Recently Published by Vallentine Mitchell

Stafford Cripps in Moscow 1940–1942 Diaries and Papers
Gabriel Gorodetsky
University of Tel Aviv

Sir Stafford Cripps, country gentleman, ascetic, vegetarian and a devout Christian with a lucrative career at the bar, cut an incongruous figure in British politics of the 1930s. By the time war broke out, his position among Labour's most radical backbenchers had made him an outcast. It was his fortuitous appointment as ambassador to Moscow in 1940 which secured for him a prominent position in the War Cabinet and later on a key role in Attlee's Labour government. The diary, which he meticulously kept while in Moscow, describes the metamorphosis in his political fortune. As significant is the witness he bears to the dramatic turnabouts of the war: the German–Soviet collaboration following the Ribbentrop–Molotov Pact, the perfidious German invasion of Russia on 22 June 1941, and the emergence of the Grand Alliance. The diary offers candid glimpses of diplomatic life in Moscow, and of the Kremlin on the eve of the war, and reflects the sombre mood in the following months as the Wehrmacht reached the gates of Moscow. On the political front, Cripps' diary reveals the controversy surrounding the forging and nature of the Grand Alliance, which was deliberately glossed over in the memoirs of Winston Churchill. A sharp critic of Churchill's political vision, Cripps foresaw the emergence of a conflict between the Allies which he hoped to avert by devising a common strategy, and by formulating clear and perceptive guidelines for the post-war settlement.

The Cummings Center Series
February 2007, 120 pages
978 0 85303 739 2 cloth £35.00 / $65.00
978 0 85303 740 8 paper £19.95 / $30.00